BTEC Level 2

Health & Social Care

Elizabeth Rasheed,
Alison Hetherington &
Jo Irvine

DYNAMIC
LEARNING

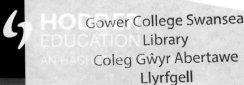

HODDER
EDUCATION
AN HACHETTE

Gower College Swansea
Library
Coleg Gŵyr Abertawe
Llyrfgell

Orders: please contact Bookpoint Ltd, 130 Milton Park, Abingdon, Oxon OX14 4SB. Telephone: (44) 01235 827720. Fax: (44) 01235400454. Lines are open from 9.00–5.00, Monday to Saturday, with a 24 hour message answering service. You can also order through our website www.hoddereducation.co.uk.

British Library Cataloguing in Publication Data
A catalogue record for this title is available from the British Library

ISBN: 9781444111903

First Published 2010
Impression number   10 9 8 7 6 5 4 3
Year   2012

Copyright © 2010 Elizabeth Rasheed, Alison Hetherington and Jo Irvine

Hachette UK's policy is to use papers that are natural, renewable and recyclable products and made from wood grown in sustainable forests. The logging and manufacturing processes are expected to conform to the environmental regulations of the country of origin.

Cover photo © Donna Day / Digital Vision / Getty
Typeset by Fakenham Photosetting, Fakenham, Norfolk
Illustrations by Mike Parsons at Barking Dog Art
Printed in Dubai

Contents

iv   Contents

Walkthrough

Prepare for what you are going to cover in this unit, and what you'll know by the end of it.

Learning outcomes:

By the end of this unit you will learn about:

● different forms of communication

Reinforce concepts with hands-on learning and generate evidence for assignments.

Activity 1

Find out what traditions or customs there are in your family, then compare with the rest of your class. Cultural traditions often happen at important events such as births, marriages and deaths.

Understand how your learning fits into real life and working environments.

Case Study

David is a 65-year-old widowed man. He smokes 15 cigarettes a day. He is a member of a walking club and attends the club's walking and social events. He also reads regularly and has some good, supportive friends.

A handy fact to impress people with and help you evaluate key points.

Did you know...

You can see the census findings for yourself at **www. statistics.gov.uk.**

Key terms

Services – the organisations and people supplying a particular need.

Helps you reinforce and remember key concepts and information.

REMEMBER

Never put a thermometer in a young child's or baby's mouth. They are likely to bite it.

Revise all those new words and what they mean.

The comprehensive guide to what assessors will be looking for in your work.

Assessment and grading criteria

To achieve a pass grade the evidence must show that you are able to:	To achieve a merit grade the evidence must show that, in addition to the pass criteria, you are able to:	To achieve a distinction grade the evidence must show that, in addition to the pass and merit criteria, you are able to:
P1 outline the everyday needs of individuals [IE1, IE2, RL3, SM2, SM3.]	**M2** produce a plan for improving the health and well-being of an individual.	**D1** justify the plan for improving the health and well-being of an individual.

You've just covered a whole unit, so here's a reminder of the key things you've learned!

Summary

Practitioners working in the health and social care sectors need to be expert communicators, which means they need to be good listeners as well as knowing and understanding all the different ways in which people can communicate, including the differences between cultures.

You'll often need to find further information for assignments, so here are some pointers to get you started

Further Reading

Mehrabian, A. (1981). *Silent messages: Implicit communication of emotions and attitudes*. Belmont, CA: Wadsworth

The internet's great for further research. These are pointers to some of the more useful information out there for assignments.

Weblinks

www.bbc.co.uk/skillswise/
www.belbin.com

Author biographies

Elizabeth Rasheed is a qualified nurse and experienced teacher coordinating Health and Social Care including BTEC Health and Social Care at Dudley College. Elizabeth has taught in further education for over 15 years. She has a first degree in Social Sciences, a Post Graduate Certificate in Education and a Master's degree in Education. She is a Fellow of the Institute for Learning. In her spare time, she is an associate lecturer in Health and Social Care for the Open University.

Alison Hetherington was born and educated in Sheffield. A qualified Registered Nurse she worked for several years at the Royal Hallamshire Hospital in Sheffield. In 1985 Alison moved to Cheshire to begin her midwifery career at Leighton Hospital in Crewe, but following a guest speaker role at her local Further Education college continued as a part time lecturer and completed her Certificate in Education qualification. Up until 2000 Alison worked part time in both Midwifery and Lecturing and was then offered a full time post at Halton College in Runcorn teaching on health and social care and childcare courses. In 2004 she returned to Mid Cheshire College as a full time lecturer with the responsibility for coordinating BTEC Health and Social care courses. She also works as an external verifier for a major awarding body. Alison would like to thank her daughters Laura and Sally and her husband John who have always encouraged her next adventure. Alison would like to dedicate this book to her lovely dad, Stephen Fielding (1929–2008).

Jo Irvine has a great deal of experience in both BTEC and the Health and Social Care sector. Originally a Health Care visitor she went on to work as a practitioner and manager in the NHS for many years, and later as a Programme Manager for Skills for Health. Jo went on to manage a portfolio of Health and Social Care qualifications for a major awarding body, before becoming an independent education consultant involved in the development of a range of specifications in this field.

Photo credits

The author and publishers would like to thank the following for permission to reproduce material in this book:

p. 2 (left) © JGI/Blend Images/Corbis; (right) © Christa Renee/Corbis; p. 4 (left) © Ken Welsh / Alamy; (right) © JoeFox / Alamy; p. 5 (top) © JoeFox / Alamy; p. 30 © Voisin/Phanie / Rex Features; p. 35 Courtesy of Marie Curie Cancer Care; p. 38 Courtesy of Mencap 2010; p. 42 Courtesy CPAG; p. 44 © JOHN COLE / SCIENCE PHOTO LIBRARY; p. 67 Courtesy Department of Health © Photos: John Spinks; p. 87 (clockwise from top left) © Andy Drysdale / Rex Features; © Andy Drysdale / Rex Features; © Helen Stone / Photofusion; © Richard Alton / Photofusion; p. 152 © Andrew Drysdale / Rex Features; p. 153 (top) © Monkey Business / Rex Features; (bottom) © 1996 M.Freeman / PhotoLink / PhotoDisc / Getty Images; p. 155 © Image Source / Rex Features; p. 159 © Sipa Press / Rex Features; p. 160 © Jon Santa Cruz / Rex Features; p. 178 (clockwise from left) © STEVE GSCHMEISSNER/SCIENCE PHOTO LIBRARY; © PROF. P. MOTTA/DEPT. OF ANATOMY/UNIVERSITY "LA SAPIENZA", ROME/SCIENCE PHOTO LIBRARY; © CNRI/ SCIENCE PHOTO LIBRARY; © EYE OF SCIENCE / SCIENCE PHOTO LIBRARY p. 205 © PAUL RAPSON/SCIENCE PHOTO LIBRARY; p. 207 (left) © JOSE OTO/SCIENCE PHOTO LIBRARY; (middle) © ADRIENNE HART-DAVIS / SCIENCE PHOTO LIBRARY; (right) © PAUL WHITEHILL/SCIENCE PHOTO LIBRARY; p. 225 (clockwise from left) © Blend Images / Alamy; © Leila Cutler / Alamy; © Imagestate Media; © Nick Kennedy / Alamy; p. 226 (left) © Image Source / Alamy; (middle) © Cultura / Alamy; (right) © UpperCut Images / Alamy; p. 252 © MICHAEL DONNE/SCIENCE PHOTO LIBRARY; p. 253 (top) © Paula Solloway / Photofusion; (middle) © CRISTINA PEDRAZZINI / SCIENCE PHOTO LIBRARY; (bottom) © FAYE NORMAN/ SCIENCE PHOTO LIBRARY; p. 264 (top) © JERRY MASON/SCIENCE PHOTO LIBRARY; (middle) © WILLIAM GAGE/CUSTOM MEDICAL STOCK PHOTO/SCIENCE PHOTO LIBRARY; (bottom) © LARRY MULVEHILL/ SCIENCE PHOTO LIBRARY; p. 316 (top row) (left) © DR P. MARAZZI/SCIENCE PHOTO LIBRARY; (middle)© BIOPHOTO ASSOCIATES/ SCIENCE PHOTO LIBRARY; (right) © US NATIONAL LIBRARY OF MEDICINE/SCIENCE PHOTO LIBRARY; (bottom row) (left) © DR P. MARAZZI/SCIENCE PHOTO LIBRARY; (middle) © Medical-on-Line / Alamy; (right) © PHOTOTAKE Inc. / Alamy

Unit 1
Communication in Health and Social Care

People who work in health and social care need to be able to communicate well so that they can develop positive relationships and share information with others. Communication is the key to good interpersonal skills, which are essential to care work. This means that people who work in health and social care have to be good listeners as well as good at speaking in a way that others can understand. They have to listen to:

- patients in hospitals
- people who use health or social services (service users)
- relatives
- other professionals, such as doctors, social workers, occupational therapists and many others who help to care for people.

This unit aims to enable you to gain the necessary knowledge, understanding and practical skills to communicate effectively within a health and social care environment.

Learning outcomes:

In this unit you will learn about:

- different forms of communication
- barriers to effective communication
- communicating effectively.

1 Know different forms of communication

As a worker in health and social care, you will need to be able to communicate effectively with a wide range of people of different ages and from different backgrounds and cultures. Some of these people may have problems in communicating, so it is important to have an understanding of the different ways of communicating.

What is communication?

Communication is essentially about the way we send and receive messages; for effective communication to take place, there must be mutual understanding. Communication is a skill that we learn very early in life as a way of getting our basic needs met. Next time you see a baby, watch how he or she communicates. Babies learn to communicate very early by crying when they need something. Assuming the baby is only a few weeks old, they will not be able to speak but will use a combination of crying and movement to indicate what they need. For example, babies will pull up their knees if they have tummy ache and vigorously kick and wave their arms as well as cry if their needs are not met.

> **Key term**
>
> Interpersonal skills – the ability to get on with people and form relationships with them.

Are these babies tired? Unhappy? Happy? How do you know? Did you look at their faces? Babies and young children are effective (good) at communicating because their lives depend on it. They communicate not only to indicate their physical needs, such as when they are hungry, tired or uncomfortable, but also to communicate their feelings and emotions, such as when they are happy, frightened or just bored.

What do you think these babies are communicating?

Verbal communication

The babbling and cooing sounds that babies make are early attempts at conversation; they will 'take turns' with an adult who is speaking to them, babbling and listening in turn. This is called pre-language; the baby is practising using the muscles and vocal cords in readiness for forming words. Speech is a complex interaction between muscles and breathing and uses different parts of the face, tongue, lips, teeth and larynx or voice box. We learn our first language by the time we are around three years old and generally improve in that language as we use it to communicate. We even learn to write it and read it so we do not have to make the sounds. Because speech is so complex, there are many things that can affect it, from congenital deformities, such as cleft palate, to the difficulties of coordination caused by a stroke. In extreme cases, emotional trauma can cause loss of speech.

However, although we commonly think of speech – verbal communication – as the main form of communicating, language and the spoken word are not, in fact, the main way we communicate. Most communication does not need words; it is non-verbal.

Non-verbal communication

Non-verbal communication is often called body language, and consists of things like facial expression, touch, eye contact or non-contact and the way we sit, stand and hold our bodies.

> ### Key term
>
> Body language – this term is used to describe how we unconsciously use our faces and bodies when communicating.

Some people are good at reading body language and can tell whether someone is happy or sad by noting how they sit or stand and their facial expression. Experts in body language can even tell when someone is not telling the truth by observing their body language.

Facial expressions tell us what people are thinking even when they do not realise it. Sometimes what we say is contradicted by what our body language is saying; body language does not lie and gives a true reflection of what we are thinking and many people feel this instinctively. For example, a smile can be real or pretend. Real smiles include the eyes. A pretend smile is just the mouth stretched to a smile.

Sometimes a person can seem cold and distant when they may, in fact, be shy. Shy people are often focused on what others may think of them and this makes them nervous. Thinking about how others might feel and trying to put them at ease can help a shy person forget about him or herself. If you are shy, remember that if you smile at someone, they almost always smile back and that will break any tension because it makes people feel relaxed. For example, if you feel nervous next time you go to a placement, try to think of something that usually makes you happy and you will find it easier to smile. Once you smile, people will smile back and you will feel welcomed and more at ease.

Touch or contact can be very comforting, but you must be careful to use touch respectfully and appropriately. For example, a person may be clearly upset and you might feel like giving him or her a comforting hug as you would with a friend or relation. However, you may not know this person well and you may be breaching personal boundaries if you were to do this – in which case, they would be embarrassed and possibly offended. Even if you do know them quite well, they might be a private person and not want to be touched. It is much better to touch an arm or hand briefly, or hold their hand lightly; if they do not like it, they can easily pull away without discomfort or offence.

It is important to ask yourself what the patient wants, not what you want. Sometimes touch can be misunderstood, especially if someone is from a different culture. In some cultures, men and women do not touch, even to shake hands. In some cases, touch is an inevitable part of caring for someone; a service user who needs help with a wash or a steadying hand to help them sit down may appreciate your help. Always ask first what the service user would like you to do and tell them how you will need to touch them before you do so. For example, 'I am just going to put my arm around your waist to help you up from the chair, Mrs Roberts. Is that OK?'

Activity 1   P1   P2

Try this with a partner – think of something you want them to get you when they go shopping next. Now communicate this to them without using any words. Give them two minutes to get the message.

Now ask them what they thought you meant. Did they get it right?

Change places and guess what your partner is asking you to buy for them.

Signs, symbols and pictures

Signs and symbols are very common in public spaces, making sure that as many people as possible have the information they need.

What do these signs mean?

People who cannot read the language can recognise these symbols.

How about these?

Children need to learn these meanings if they are not to get run over by traffic.

Sometimes people use signs to communicate. For example, someone who cannot speak may use a picture board to communicate. You could use a picture board if you go abroad on holiday and do not speak the language. They are sometimes used in care if a service user cannot speak.

Here is an example:

Can you guess which meal this picture board may be used for?

British Sign Language is a method of non-verbal communication that uses movements of the hands, body, face and head, which make up a complete language system. It is the preferred first language of many deaf people and is used by hearing people to communicate with those who are deaf. Other deaf people rely on lip-reading to understand what is being said to them.

Another method of communication that is internationally recognised is Makaton. This method uses signs (pictures) to represent words; the symbols support the written word in the same way that symbols support speech. It helps children and adults who cannot read and write for whatever reason; for example, it has been successfully used in families fostering children whose first language is not English, as gradually the link is made between the sign and the word. It is suitable for use with a wide range of adults and children. People who are good at communication are likely to be good at building relationships, since effective communication has a big influence in getting on with others.

Activity 2

In a group, watch a video or clip of a care situation none of you have seen before with the sound turned off and try to work out what is going on just by the body language. Take it in turns to give your interpretation to the group, then watch the clip again with the sound on and see whose interpretation was the nearest. (The clip can be from a TV programme that is set in a hospital or care home, for example, and does not need to be a real-life situation.)

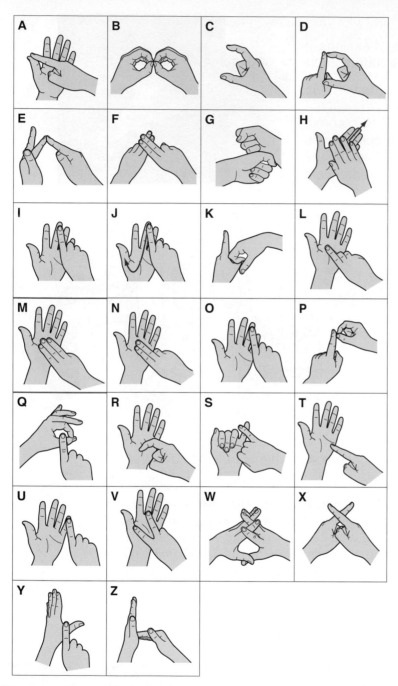

Fingerspelling alphabet

Source: www.british-sign.co.uk

Objects of reference

Objects of reference are any objects that represent other things. Children may have a teddy bear or comfort blanket that represents home and safety. A child will feel more secure if they have their blanket or favourite toy, especially if they are in a strange place, such as hospital. For a child, the smell of these familiar objects is associated with Mum and home.

Older people may have family photographs or ornaments. These objects are reminders of important people and events in their lives and carers must be careful to respect their value to the person they are caring for; an older person may settle better into a care home if they have their own things around them.

A religious person may have a Bible or Koran or other religious text, which means a lot to them. It may signify their cultural identity and sense of who they are.

Objects of reference communicate a lot about a person. A carer must respect such objects as demonstrating important aspects of the person. Sometimes objects of reference bring back memories and carers can learn a lot about service users by listening to their stories. Older people may remember their childhood better than what happened yesterday – for example, a packet of sweets similar to those they had as a child may help them remember stories of their younger days and what it was like to be young. This technique is often used to help minimise memory loss or following brain injury such as stroke; similarly, a person who is suffering from dementia may be helped to communicate by using objects of reference.

Technological aids

Technological aids to communication have developed rapidly, particularly computer-based communication. The internet in particular has changed the way people communicate. For example, many people of all ages use email to keep in contact with friends and family who live far away. Many other people use blogs or Facebook to keep in touch with people. New telephone technology links mobile communications to this worldwide communication network, allowing people to send text messages cheaply around the world and, in some cases, access the internet while away from home.

Computer technology has been of great assistance to people with communication difficulties caused by disability. For instance, a person who is deaf can communicate with friends using email and text messages. People who have visual problems can use computer software to turn their spoken word into written communication. Voice-activated technology can also help people who are physically disabled to maintain some independence; scientist and author Stephen Hawking is a good example of how computer-based technology can support an individual.

If you work with people who have a visual impairment, you may discover they use Braille. Those who are visually impaired or losing their sight may also use talking books – recordings of someone reading the book. Famous people who have helped deaf and blind people communicate include Helen Keller and Louis Braille.

Context

Context refers to the background to the communication and the circumstances in which it takes place. You may need to adapt your preferred method of communication to the context to make sure you are understood and to minimise any potential communication difficulties.

How we communicate will depend on a number of factors, such as whether we are in a one-to-one situation in which we may be communicating face-to-face with one other person, or whether we are using the telephone or email. Other factors, such as the age of the person we are communicating with and how well we know them, will also affect our approach, in particular, the words and expressions we use. For example, if we are communicating as a member of a group, with our friends, we are likely to use different words, expressions and phrases than if we are talking with colleagues about work.

One of the important issues that can affect communication is the cultural context in which communication happens. Understanding cultural differences helps to promote understanding between people. For example, in Japan, it is good manners to leave a little food on the plate. This means your host has fed you so well that you cannot finish the food. In Britain, leaving food on the plate may be considered bad manners because you are implying that the food is not good. Care workers have to be sensitive to cultural differences. If you are not sure, ask the person you are talking to whether there are any differences you need to be aware of.

This is not just about having a different language – as we have seen, non-verbal communication is equally important. However, people from different cultures have evolved signs and gestures that are specific to their culture and which might mean something entirely different – and possibly be rude or offensive – in another culture! With so many cultural differences, it is amazing that people do manage to bridge the gap and communicate with people from different cultures.

Here are some cultural differences, which can have an effect on communication:

- When greeting someone in France, you may be expected to kiss him or her on each cheek as you clasp hands.
- In India, it may be very bad manners to touch the other person at all. Instead you may be greeted by 'Namaste', meaning 'I bow to you', with the word 'Namaste' always being accompanied by the hands clasped together in the *anjali mudra*.
- In Arabic countries, the greeting is 'As-Salam Alaykum', meaning 'Peace be upon you', which is accompanied by two or three light kisses or brushes to the cheek, but only in same-sex greetings. The correct response is 'Wa Alaykum as Salaam', meaning 'And upon you be peace'.
- In England, someone may shake your hand, nod or raise their hat.
- In Japan, you greet someone with a bow. The person of lower status must bow lower.

- Eye contact in Britain is usually expected when people are talking to each other. In India, it is good manners to keep your eyes lowered in the presence of someone older or someone who is your boss. This can lead to problems because many people raised in an Eastern culture may feel it is rude to look someone in the eyes, while the Western person they are talking to may think they are rude not to make eye contact.

Sometimes we need to communicate in a formal way. For example, we may need to write a letter when applying for a job and we will need to use accepted forms of speech and communication when we go for an interview. It is common to use more formal communication when speaking to strangers or when discussing work issues. If we are talking to friends, however, we are more likely to use abbreviations, slang or colloquialisms – informal expressions. This is the difference between formal and informal communication.

Key terms

Formal communication – that which follows the proper conventional grammatical and cultural rules, usually used in communication with strangers or in an official situation.

Informal communication – the use of familiar terms, such as nicknames, slang and jargon, used with friends and people we know well.

Activity 3

The following are different types of communication:

- greetings
- telephone conversations
- written communications – email, letter, memos, patient/service user records, notes of meetings
- discussions with colleagues you see every day
- conversations with professionals
- meetings
- face-to-face dialogue with service users
- giving instructions or advice.

In pairs, decide which of these are formal communications and which are informal communications. Place them in two lists, saying why you think they are formal or informal and discuss with the rest of the group.

Consider both context and content and see if you can give examples of the different terms and expressions you may use to show that the communication is formal or informal. You could also say which of these types of communication would be confidential.

2 Understand barriers to effective communication

We are able to use many different ways to communicate so it is important to use the correct method for effective communication, bearing in mind the context in which it will be occurring.

Communication is a two-way process, and the key elements needed are as follows:

- sender – the person starting the communication
- message – what the sender wishes to communicate
- medium – the method of communication: verbal, written, signed, electronic, telephone, etc.
- receiver – the person who receives the message and interprets it
- understanding – the message has to be correctly interpreted by the receiver
- feedback – the receiver needs to show the sender that they have received and understood the message.

Communication cycle

We sometimes describe the steps that need to be taken for communication to be effective as the communication cycle. Because communication is such a natural part of everyday life, it can seem strange thinking about communication in such an abstract way at first. However, it is precisely because it is natural and common that it can be taken for granted – how we communicate is something we rarely think too much about but is crucial to building relationships, and these are essential for good practice in care work, so you need to practise communication skills.

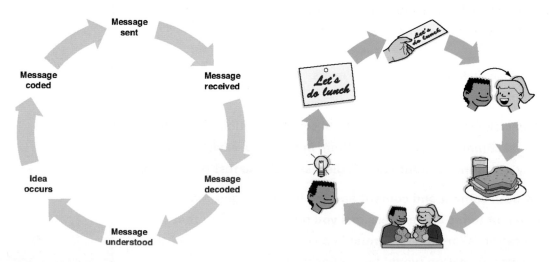

The communication cycle

Activity 4

You decide to tell a friend that you have been to see a good film at the cinema that you think he might enjoy. Using the principles of the communication cycle, write down how you would do this (which method) and how you would know that your communication had been effective.

Activity 4 will help you to reflect on potential barriers to communication in a one-to-one situation.

What affects communication?

Thinking about the communication cycle, you can see that any interruptions to the cycle will cause difficulties with communication – the message will be lost or incomplete.

Sensory difficulties

This refers to people who have difficulty with vision or hearing. If you cannot see very well, you are likely to miss non-verbal signals, such as a smile or a frown, although you may be more sensitive to tone of voice.

Similarly, if you cannot hear very well, you may not be able to tell what someone is saying – for example, in a noisy room or if they are walking away from you, especially if you rely on lip-reading. The term 'sensory deprivation' refers to a person who has no vision, no hearing or neither vision nor hearing.

Language issues

If you do not speak the same language, there can be barriers to communication and you are much more likely to rely on body language. However, as we have seen, there are cultural differences in body language, particularly gestures. Just imagine how difficult it is to ask the doctor about your operation if you do not know the language.

Jargon

Jargon is specialist language. It can be a barrier to communication if the person receiving the message does not understand the jargon. A person might feel scared if they are told they have 'plantar fasciitis'. If the doctor says they have 'heel pain', it sounds a lot less scary because the person understands what the words – heel and pain – actually mean.

Slang

Slang or informal language can be a barrier to communication if the other person does not understand the slang. For example, rhyming slang, such as the original East London slang, replaces ordinary words with others that rhyme with them, so that 'mince pies' means 'eyes' and 'dog and bone' means 'telephone'. This is fine if the other person knows the same slang but it can be utterly confusing if the other person does not recognise the same terms. 'I tripped on the dog and bone lying on the apples and pears' can sound very strange to someone who does not know what the slang words are – it is almost like another language. (Did you guess it means 'I tripped on the telephone lying on the stairs'?) In addition, different generations often have their own slang.

Dialect

Dialect words are specific to a local geographical area. For example, in parts of the Midlands region of the UK, people may use 'y'am' to mean 'you are'. Similarly, in some parts of Yorkshire, people use 'tha' to mean 'you'. This is derived from a time when it was common to use the biblical forms 'thee' and 'thou' during everyday speech, probably because the Bible was commonly used as a teaching aid for reading and writing. So in the Midlands, someone using dialect might say 'Y'am going out?', whereas in Yorkshire they might say 'Tha' going out?'. Someone who comes from the south of England might have difficulty understanding both of these people.

Acronyms

Acronyms are words formed from the initials of other words. EMA, for instance, stands for Education Maintenance Allowance. Perhaps you know what NHS stands for (National Health Service), but how about GP, GSCC or NMC? Acronyms help communication only if everyone knows what they mean, otherwise they actually prevent communication. (GP stands for general practitioner or your local doctor; GSCC stands for General Social Care Council, which registers carers; NMC is the Nursing and Midwifery Council, which registers nurses and midwives.)

Personal barriers

Emotions

Emotions can be barriers to communication. For example, when people are upset or distressed they are often unable to take in what is being said; that is, they have difficulty in decoding or interpreting the message because of fear. A person who has just been told that their parent has cancer may not hear that it is a treatable form of cancer because of the negative associations and implications of the word 'cancer'. It is important to make sure that people in care are able to understand what you are telling them. Sometimes they cannot absorb a lot of information at once and need time to adjust.

Anxiety

Anxiety can pose similar problems for communication in that it prevents a realistic assessment of what is being said because of the emotions the words stir up. This again means the person has difficulty in decoding the message. For example, a person may go for a routine check-up at the doctors, and be told they have high blood pressure and must go to the hospital for an ECG and further tests; they may be so anxious that they do not hear what is being said about the arrangements, dates or other details of the appointment.

Depression

Depression causes feelings of hopelessness and isolation, which can prevent communication. An isolated or depressed person takes a negative view of the world and may not value anything that is said to them. For example, they may misinterpret a smile directed towards them as someone laughing at them, or may not pick up on non-verbal communication. Even when a carer talks to them, they may not hear the message if they are deeply depressed.

Aggression

Aggression of any sort prevents communication because it makes people frightened. When people are frightened, the body responds by releasing a stress hormone called cortisol, which makes the muscles tense, dries the mouth and generally prepares for a 'flight or fight' situation. It is very difficult for a person to focus on communication when they are tensed up ready to act. It is extremely rare for a person to be able to talk their way out of a threatening situation because of this normal physical reaction. Aggression covers both verbal aggression, such as shouting or raised voices, and physical aggression or intimidation, such as towering over the other person, coming physically close or behaving in a threatening manner. In terms of communication, the aggressor communicates only the fact that they are a bully. The victim understands only the fear.

In a care situation, it is never acceptable to be aggressive towards anyone. If bullying or aggressive behaviour is used towards a service user by a carer, it is called abuse. It is absolutely unacceptable and carries serious consequences. Sometimes patients can be aggressive; an aggressive patient is often frightened or confused. It is essential to remain calm and speak softly and soothingly until they have calmed down and you can deal with their fear.

Intellectual difficulties
Mental health

Mental health issues, particularly mental illness, can affect communication, particularly if the person is on medication which may affect their ability to understand the implications of what is said to them. Similarly, someone in the grip of a paranoid episode will be unaware of the real world and not actually hear what is said.

Learning difficulties

People with learning difficulties sometimes have difficulty expressing themselves; for example, they may not be able to process information or remember things well. Others may have coordination (motor skills) problems. Dyslexia is one example of a learning difficulty in which sufferers have trouble reading and writing, although their intelligence is normal or above average. Some people who have Asperger's syndrome or autism may struggle with body language and expression – the social aspects of communication.

Dementia

Dementia literally means 'deprived of mind' and involves gradual deterioration in intellectual capability. As a result, people with dementia also tend to be unaware of the real world, people or places and forget what they have been told. Communicating with people who have dementia takes patience and understanding of the condition as they often cannot remember what has just been said and you will need to repeat things.

Other barriers

Environmental factors

Environmental factors, such as a noisy location or poor lighting, may hamper communication. For example, a person who has problems hearing but usually lip-reads will find this difficult in a darkened room. Have you ever tried to have a mobile phone conversation in the street? How easy was it to have a conversation? Did you ever misunderstand the conversation? What happened?

Misjudgements and misunderstandings

Conversation topics such as jokes can be a source of misunderstanding and tension. Humour differs between people and between cultures, and what might be funny to one person might not necessarily be funny to someone else. Jokes about religion, for example, might not be unusual but can be offensive to a person with strong religious beliefs. In many religions, it is unacceptable to joke about religion or God, and a person with such beliefs may no longer respect a care worker who jokes about what they consider to be serious matters.

Behaviour

Behaviour that is appropriate at home may not be appropriate at work. A family member may benefit from a hug, but a patient may be highly offended. Unwanted or inappropriate contact is unprofessional behaviour for care workers.

Sometimes messages are misinterpreted. For example, nurses in hospital are not allowed to take a verbal prescription from a doctor over the telephone. The doctor must come to the ward and write the prescription, the dose, the route of administration, how much and how often so that there are no mistakes. It is easy to mishear phone conversations and interpret messages wrongly. This may have serious consequences if a medication is given in the wrong dose or by the wrong administration route. There have been cases in which drugs, which are safe to be injected into muscle, have killed or permanently harmed a person because they were injected into other areas of the body by mistake.

Activity 5

This exercise is rather like the game of Chinese Whispers. Sit your group in a circle and all except one person should put either earplugs (the soft rubbery sort you can get for sleeping that fit in your ears) or cotton wool in their ears. The person who has no earplugs in then takes one person aside and tells them something – for example, 'The train from Manchester will arrive in Euston at half past two.' Ask them to pass the message to each person in turn, and then ask the last person to repeat the message. See what they say! What would have helped the communication to be more effective without removing the ear plugs?

Activity 5 will help you to consider how to overcome barriers to effective group communication and contribute to P4.

How can you help improve communication?

First of all, you will need to try and understand the person's communication difficulties, their language needs and communication preferences. It is good practice and respectful to ask the person how they would like to be addressed (e.g. Mr, Mrs, Dr). It is also worth remembering that naming conventions (the order of names and surnames) are different in different cultures and it is better to talk about first and second or last names rather than Christian names as you may be speaking to a person of Jewish or Buddhist faith.

It is never acceptable to call adult service users by 'pet' names, such as 'lovie', 'duckie' or 'gran' as this is both patronising and offensive, as well as being potentially inaccurate – the person may never have had children or grandchildren, or may not have been able to have children. It is much better to start with a more formal approach, which can be gradually relaxed as your relationship develops, than risk insulting someone in the first place.

There are a number of things you can do to minimise some of the specific communication difficulties discussed above. These suggestions are outlined in Table 1.1. You will, of course, need to make your own judgements about which methods to use with a particular person and in a specific context.

Table 1.01 Overcoming communication difficulties

Communication issue	Suggested actions
Poor sight or blindness	• Ask what the person is able to see, e.g. light/dark/shapes. • Make sure they are wearing the correct glasses. • If they have some sight, make sure there is plenty of light and that you are facing the person. • Make sure they have any required aids or equipment, e.g. magnifying glass, especially if you need them to read or write anything down. • If they are blind, speak to them as you approach so they know you are there. • Use language to describe the surroundings and assist them to explore things using touch – they may wish to touch your face. • If escorting a blind person, give a running commentary on where you are going and your progress.
Hearing difficulties	• As with sight-impaired people, you must first make sure any hearing aids or appliances are being worn and are adjusted to the correct level. • Make sure you are face-to-face and at the same level. Try not to have your back to the light as your face will be in shadow. • Make sure it is as quiet as possible. • Do not shout but speak normally, slowly and clearly, giving time for lip-reading. Use gestures. • Use pictures or write messages on a pad or chalkboard. • Learn Makaton or how to sign. • Use an interpreter who can sign.
Language issues	• Use pictures and symbols, including programmes such as Makaton, to illustrate your words. • Make sure you use an interpreter, especially for conversations with medical content, but be wary of getting children to interpret for their parents. Parents may not wish their children to have full knowledge of illness or personal issues. • Be on guard about making assumptions – stereotypical thoughts and phrases often start with 'they all ...'. • Do not use jargon, acronyms or slang and be careful to speak as clearly as possible in plain English, using short sentences.
Emotions	• Learn to become aware of the signs that show someone is becoming upset or angry. • Learn how to recognise anxiety and depression.

	• Remain calm and speak kindly and reassuringly, without being patronising. This will help the person to maintain self-control. • Learn about managing challenging behaviour. • Carefully choose the time and place in which to have difficult conversations. • Be careful not to make jokes initially. Once the person is calmer it may be possible to use gentle humour to reduce the tension, depending on the person and the situation. • Remember, you may have to repeat the information again at a later time.
Intellectual difficulties	• Learn about the most common types of intellectual difficulties in your work area, e.g. if you mostly work with older people, you may need more understanding about dementia or about communicating with someone who is confused and disorientated. • Share your knowledge of what works with other staff members. • Be very patient, repeating things if necessary, using straightforward language and re-wording if necessary. • Use symbols and pictures if the person has learning difficulties. • Remember that people with intellectual difficulties may have normal or above-average intelligence in certain areas and they are not stupid. • Encourage people with intellectual difficulties to join support groups.
Environmental factors	• Choose the time and place for communication carefully, e.g. do not discuss personal issues loudly in the presence of others; this is disrespectful – think how you would feel. • Make sure there is plenty of light, preferably natural daylight and that it is fairly quiet so that you can be clearly seen and heard.
Preventing misunderstanding	• Learn about different cultures and their ways, especially gestures and body language. • Always check for understanding (see active listening, p.19). • Be aware of gender differences in different cultures. • Do not make assumptions. • Try different ways to get your message across and encourage the person you are communicating with to do the same. • Be especially clear when on the phone or using electronic communication (texts and email) as the absence of facial and body language can be a barrier to understanding.

Misunderstandings can be funny and many comedians rely on this as part of their act, particularly the old comedians of the silent movie era, such as Charlie Chaplin, Laurel and Hardy and the Keystone Cops. The actors and comedians in these movies also used exaggerated body language and facial expression in place of dialogue and are well worth watching if you can get hold of them. Try to work out just why these are funny.

Activity 6

M2

Think about a time when you were involved in a misunderstanding. What form of communication were you using? How well did you know the person you were communicating with? What were the actual or potential consequences of the misunderstanding? How could the misunderstanding have been avoided?

Make a note of the situation that occurred, including answers to the above questions. Take it in turns with others in your group to share your experiences and discuss similarities and what you could have done to prevent the misunderstanding arising.

3 Be able to communicate effectively

Communication is a skill that requires practice. Effective communication is when the message you send to the other person is received, accurately interpreted and understood and responded to appropriately. Facial expressions, the tone of voice you use, the type and level of eye contact, the gestures you make, and the way you stand or sit are all part of communicating. Sometimes we are not fully aware of how we appear to other people – for example, the expression we have on our face.

To communicate effectively, we need to be aware of these hidden messages we are giving out unconsciously because our words may not match our actions. For example, if we are communicating with someone who has strong body odour we may not be able to disguise our distaste. Even though we might be observing social conventions by pleasantly asking how they are, our noses might unconsciously be wrinkling or we may turn our faces away slightly. This is especially true when we are talking about our feelings; it has been suggested that body language provides up to 55 per cent of meaning when discussing feelings and emotions.

It is a useful exercise to observe other people communicating. Be observant when you are in social situations and you will learn a lot about how people communicate. Next time you are on a bus, for example, watch people and make a note of how they are communicating. What methods are they using? Can you guess what they are talking about? You must be careful not to stare or pay too much attention though, in case you are accused of eavesdropping!

There are a number of skills and techniques you can practise to enhance and improve your communication skills. In particular, good listening is a key communication skill. What do we mean by good listening? One way of thinking about it is to consider that, as we have two ears but only one mouth, we should listen twice as much as we speak! In other words, you need to develop the skill of active listening, which is much harder than it seems.

Active listening

Active listening is about being involved, really listening and asking questions. If someone is leaning away from the other person, gazing around or looking bored, they are not listening. Active listeners check out what they have heard. They may ask a question to clarify a point or may nod encouragement to the speaker. The key features involved in active listening are outlined below.

> ### Key term
>
> Active listening – being involved, really listening and asking questions.

Paying attention

Show you are paying attention to what the other person is saying by looking at them and making occasional eye contact, but be careful – too much eye contact is intense and can be intimidating. Make sure there are no distractions, such as TV, radio, telephones or other people.

Watching your body language

Sit opposite the other person or slightly to one side in a relaxed manner; lean forward slightly and cock your head a little to one side. Do not cross your arms as this can be seen as angry or defensive. Observe the body language of the person you are communicating with; sometimes it helps to copy the way they are sitting (mirroring). Smile!

Showing you are listening

You can do this by nodding and using words of encouragement, such as 'I see', 'Uh-huh' and 'Go on'. Make sure you do not interrupt.

Checking your understanding

Because we do not always hear exactly what was said (we often mentally finish other people's sentences), it is important to check that what you *think* you heard was actually what the other person said or meant. You can do this with a technique called 'paraphrasing'. For example, 'It sounds like what you are saying is …' and repeating what you think they said back to them in a slightly different way. You can also summarise what they have said. For example, 'You seem to be saying you are concerned that you won't be able to collect your pension when the post office closes.'

Being careful not to pre-judge

Do not interrupt. It wastes time and reduces your ability to understand, as you have not received the entire message. Resist the temptation to be preparing your answer or response and do not butt in with counter-arguments before the other person has finished speaking. Take your time and consider what has been said.

Active listening can only take place where there is mutual respect, honesty and understanding; it is a key part of building relationships. You need to be tolerant of the other person's point of view – even if you disagree – and treat the other person as you would want them to treat you.

In a care situation, you must only offer your opinions if you are asked for them and be considerate of the other person's feelings.

Activity 7

In a group of three, practise active listening. One person needs to tell the other person something, such as what they did over the weekend, including their feelings. The other person is to practise the active listening techniques as described above. The third person is to act as observer. Once you have finished, ask the observer what they observed and then swap places. When all have had a turn at each role, discuss your experiences. You may find that active listening is much harder than it seems!

Speech patterns

To communicate effectively, you also need to pay careful attention to the way you speak. Tone of voice can convey different feelings; it is possible to say the same words in a different tone of voice, perhaps with a slight emphasis on some words rather than others, and yet convey a different meaning. For example, if you say, 'She's looking *very* smart tonight', with the emphasis on the word 'very', it implies admiration. However, if you say, '*She's* looking very smart tonight', it implies resentment or jealousy. It is not a compliment!

Similarly, when speaking, you may have to modify the pace of speech, especially if the person is hard of hearing, or has a language other than English as a first language, or if you are speaking to a child. In most cases, you will speak more slowly to ensure they can understand you – they all have different barriers to communication. The likelihood of being understood is improved if you also make sure you are close to the person (e.g. kneel down so your face is level when communicating with a small child).

Questioning techniques

Open questions

Open questions are a good technique for drawing out more information from people during a conversation. They are a way of preventing one-word answers and are therefore useful for helping to develop relationships. By using open questions, you can begin to understand people's opinions, feelings and views of the things that affect them. Open questions often – but not always – start with why/what/who/how, etc. To ask someone their opinion, knowledge or feelings using open questions, you can start with words like 'Tell me about …' or 'Can you describe …'.

Examples of open questions:
'What did you do over the weekend?'
'How was the party?'
'Tell me what you wore.'
'Who was there?'
'What happened next?'

Any of the questions shown in the box can start a line of conversation – for example, about who was at the party and what happened. On the other hand, a closed question such as, 'Did you go to the party this weekend?' may only get a 'Yes'. Closed questions can rapidly bring a conversation to a halt and are best avoided in the middle of a conversation if the aim is getting to know someone and developing a relationship.

Funnel questions

Funnel questions are another way of obtaining information. This technique involves starting with general questions and asking for more information on each point. It is often used by doctors when trying to establish a diagnosis. For example:

Doctor: 'Can you tell me how you feel?'
Patient: 'I feel sick and I have a pain in my stomach.'
Doctor: 'Whereabouts in your stomach?'
Patient: 'Around here.'
Doctor: 'I see. Can you describe what sort of pain it is?'
Patient: 'It's a dull ache.'
Doctor: 'How long have you had the pain?'
Patient: 'Since this morning.'

The doctor is likely to follow this with a physical examination, simultaneously asking about the severity of the pain until s/he has a more accurate idea of the location of the pain.

It is important to know about other techniques that are not helpful when building relationships For example, *leading questions* are used for seeking agreement and are similar to closed questions. They leave the other person with the feeling they have had little choice in how they answer. Leading questions tend to use techniques such as assumptions:

'You won't want to wear the blue dress today, will you?'

Other methods involve personal appeals:

'I think it's better to have tea in the lounge, don't you?'

Or phrasing questions so that the easiest response is 'Yes':

'Shall we put your chair in the garden?', instead of asking, 'Would you like to sit in the garden?'

Another method involves giving a choice between two options, both of which you would be happy with. For example:

'Would you like your bath before or after tea?'

Strictly speaking the person can refuse but they are more likely to choose.

All of these techniques for effective communication can be used in either one-to-one situations or group work, for formal or informal communication and discussions. It is important to think about the purpose of the communication and the context, together with considering the needs of the person you are going to communicate with.

Remember, if in doubt, ask. You will find that being a good communicator is helpful to everyday situations, not just at work.

Summary

Practitioners working in the health and social care sectors need to be expert communicators, which means they need to be good listeners as well as knowing and understanding all the different ways in which people can communicate, including the differences between cultures.

Communication is a skill we have from birth. However, as we grow older, we put more emphasis on speaking, reading and writing than on any other type of communication, even though we all use body language such as facial expressions and gestures to supplement speech, and it is possible to communicate with others using body language alone. For example, mime artists entertain us by using just body language to tell a story, such as Charlie Chaplin in the silent movies or the actor Rowan Atkinson's character Mr Bean, who is extremely popular in non-English speaking countries, such as India.

Health and social care practitioners also need to be aware of the difficulties and barriers some people face when communicating; these barriers may be temporary, such as following a visit to the dentist, or permanent, such as people who have sight or hearing difficulties. Practitioners need to be able to overcome such barriers in creative and constructive ways, in partnership with the patient and taking account of their wishes. It is helpful to think of the *communication cycle* when considering barriers.

In order to develop your communication skills, you need to practise them at every opportunity. Watching people is very helpful, as is communicating with as many different people as possible, especially in the healthcare setting.

Grading grid

In order to pass this unit, the evidence that the learner presents for assessment needs to demonstrate that they can meet all the learning outcomes for the unit. The assessment criteria for a pass grade describe the level of achievement required to pass this unit.

Assessment and grading criteria		
To achieve a pass grade the evidence must show that the learner is able to:	To achieve a merit grade the evidence must show that, in addition to the pass criteria, the learner is able to:	To achieve a distinction grade the evidence must show that, in addition to the pass and merit criteria, the learner is able to:
P1 identify different forms of communication (see Activities 2 and 3) [IE2, IE4, TW1, SM3]	M1 describe different forms of communication (see Activity 3)	

P2 explain barriers to effective communication within a health and social care environment (see Activities 2 and 3) [IE2, CT1, IE4, SM3]				
P3 take part in an effective one-to-one interaction (see Activities 4 and 7) [IE4, CT5, RL1, TW3, SM3]	**M2** describe the barriers to effective communication in their two interactions (see Activities 5 and 6)		**D1** assess the strengths and weaknesses of their two interactions (see Activities 5 and 7)	
P4 take part in an effective group interaction (see Activities 2, 4 and 5) [CT5, RL1, TW3, SM3]				

The Activities on pp. 11 and 15 will help you to reflect on your everyday communication, however, you may also wish to develop and produce your own role play and set up group discussions, using a health or social care situation or topic to help in meeting the assessment criteria for P3 and P4.

For example:

1. You are a social care worker who is speaking with an older person to try and find out whether they need help with everyday activities. One of your colleagues can act as the older person and may want to develop a 'script' or scenario to act out.
2. As a group, identify 2 or 3 current health or social care issues to discuss in a group. You may need to research the topic, clarify your views and prepare some questions.

Think about trying to use all the effective communication skills you have practised. You could ask your tutor to observe you.

Further Reading

Care and Health Magazine (PSSRU Publications)
Community Care Magazine (Reed Business Information)
Disability Now (Disability Now)
Nursing Times (Emap)

Weblinks

www.ukdpc.net – United Kingdom Disabled People's Council
www.britishsignlanguage.com – basic signs (British sign language)
www.ccwales.org.uk – Care Council for Wales
www.dh.gov.uk – Department of Health
www.makaton.org – the Makaton Charity
www.mencap.org.uk – Mencap (for people with learning disabilities)
www.nhs.uk – National Health Service
www.niscc.info – Northern Ireland Social Care Council
www.rnib.org.uk – Royal National Institute of Blind People
www.rnid.org.uk – Royal National Institute for Deaf People
www.skillsforcare.org.uk – Sector Skills Council for Care
www.skillsforhealth.org.uk – Sector Skills Council for Health
www.socialworkandcare.co.uk – social care careers information

Unit 2
Individual Rights within the Health and Social Care Sectors

Workers in health and social care need to understand the variety in British society today. We are all different. We do not all have the same beliefs or attitudes but the principles and values that underpin care apply to all of us. The health care worker has a duty to promote the rights of all individuals.

This unit outlines the factors contributing to diversity in our society and how this impacts on health and social care. We all have the right to be respected, to be treated equally and fairly and not to be discriminated against – these rights underpin care values. You should study this unit as part of preparation for work experience, so that you are aware of diversity and how ethical care can promote equality of opportunity.

The unit draws on all the other units and gives you a chance to put into practice all you learn in Unit 1 Communication in Health and Social Care and in Unit 3 Individual Needs in the Health and Social Care Sectors. Ideas introduced in this unit are developed in more detail in Unit 6 Cultural Diversity in Health and Social Care.

Key terms

Diversity – difference or variety.
Ethics – what is right or wrong.
Equality of opportunity – giving people the same chances.

In this unit you can also work towards Functional Skills ICT and English at Level 2 and towards Personal, Learning and Thinking Skills.

Learning outcomes:

In this unit you will learn about:

● factors that contribute to a diverse and equal society

● principles and values that underpin the support given to individuals.

1 Know factors that contribute to a diverse and equal society

Let's put this title in plain English. We could say: 'Know the things that help towards a varied and level society'. Even then, it is not very clear. We need to explore this in more detail. Read the sections that follow, then look back at the title. You may find you understand it better once you have worked through the sections.

There are many factors (things) that make our society interesting and varied. We will look at just three. Each of us is affected by social factors, by biological factors and by political factors and they all overlap.

Social factors

Social factors relate to groups of people rather than just one person. They include such things as culture, ethnicity, faith, gender, sexuality, age, family structure, social class and geographical location.

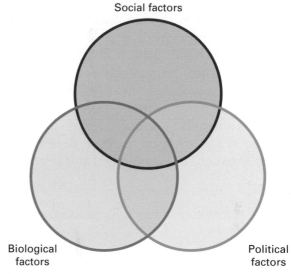

Social, political and biological factors

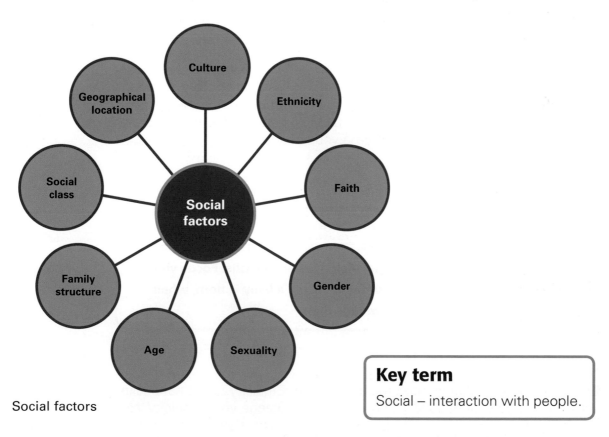

Social factors

Key term

Social – interaction with people.

We will consider the social factors separately, but it is important to realise that in real life a social group may be affected by many or all of these factors.

 Case Study

Tom worked in the steelworks but was made redundant in his fifties. He lives in a flat on a run-down council estate where some of the shops are boarded up. He lost touch with his grown-up children when they moved to Australia. He is affected by social factors – his age makes it unlikely he will get another job. His family structure is common for many families in Western culture where people move for work. His social class determines where he lives.

Tom is affected by social factors just as much as Imran, an 18-year-old Pakistani student living in an extended family in Bradford. Imran's choices are governed by his age, his family structure, his ethnicity and his culture.

Social factors touch us all. Try to keep this in mind as we examine some of these factors.

Culture

Culture is another way of saying 'traditions' or 'customs'. For example, many people have a custom of putting a tree in the house for a few days each year. Perhaps your family does this at Christmas. This tradition or custom was introduced into England in the 1800s and has continued ever since. It is now part of the culture for many people who live in the UK but is originally part of German culture. Other people have different traditions as part of their culture. For example, in many hot countries, babies' heads are shaved in the first weeks of life. In parts of England it is the culture to give a coin to a new baby the first time you see them.

Activity 1

Find out what traditions or customs there are in your family, then compare with the rest of your class. Cultural traditions often happen at important events such as births, marriages and deaths. Focus your research on what happens in your family when a baby is born, when people get married and when someone dies.

Ethnicity

Ethnicity is a term that is often misunderstood. Ethnicity is not nationality. You can change your nationality, but you cannot change your ethnicity, as it is part of your genes. If you find this confusing, think about this example. A person of African Caribbean origin who goes to live in Spain and takes Spanish nationality is not changing their ethnicity. They are still ethnically African Caribbean. Even when they get their Spanish passport, their ethnicity remains the same.

Ethnicity is not clear cut. Respected academic researchers Omi and Winant (1994), quoted in Fought (2006), found it difficult to define ethnicity: 'The definition of the terms "ethnic group" and "ethnicity" is muddy.'

The UK government census has a question on ethnicity but many people no longer wish to put themselves into a specific ethnic category. Many are ethnically mixed. This is the fastest-growing 'ethnic group'.

> **Did you know...?**
> Barack Obama has mixed ethnicity – his mother was white (American) and his father was black (African).

Faith

Faith is about personal beliefs and does not have to be linked with culture or ethnicity. Someone may be born into a family that has always had certain beliefs, but that person may decide that their faith and beliefs are different, and change their faith. People convert from one religion to another, or change to having no religious faith.

> **Did you know...?**
> The actor Richard Gere was brought up by Methodist parents but became a practising Buddhist.

Gender

Gender refers to the sex someone is born with. Most people are categorised as male or female at birth, according to their anatomy and chromosomes. Females have XX chromosomes and males have XY chromosomes. Intersex people may have characteristics of both sexes.

Sexuality

Sexuality refers to the sex a person perceives they belong to. It refers to how a person expresses themselves as a sexual being. Some girls like to be 'girly', while others prefer to be boyish. Sexuality also refers to a person's choice of sexual partner. Some people are heterosexual, which means they are attracted to someone of the opposite sex. Some people are homosexual, which means they are attracted to someone of the same sex. 'Hetero' comes from the Greek and means 'different'. 'Homo' comes from the Greek and means 'same'.

Age

Age refers to how old a person is in years. People under 16 are not recognised as adult in England. Between the ages of 16 and 18 the law allows some things but not others. People can marry at 16 if they have parental consent. If they do not have parental consent they have to wait until they are 18. You can join the Army at 16 but cannot legally buy cigarettes until you are 18. In Scotland the law is different and the age of becoming an adult is 16.

Family structure

According to the Office for National Statistics (ONS) report Focus on Families (2007), 'a family is defined as a married or cohabiting couple with or without children in the household, or a lone parent and children.' It is important to realise that a household is not the same as a family. According to Focus on Families (2007), a household is 'a person living alone, or a group of people living at the same address who either share one main meal a day or share the living accommodation (or both).' So, for example, a group of students sharing a house are a household, not a family.

The nuclear family of mum, dad and children is still the most common type of family. About seven out of ten families are headed by a married couple. However, cohabiting families, where parents are not married to each other, are the fastest-rising type of family in the UK. Many of those who cohabit have already been married and have children. This means that an increasing number of children are living with step-parents. Lone-parent families are families headed by one parent rather than two. London has the highest proportion of lone parents.

Lone-parent families may not have much money

Activity 2

How might the type of family a person is in affect their choices?

Lone-parent family: Jake and his sister live with their mum since their dad left. Jake doesn't like to ask his mum for new trainers. She works all weekend at a care home just to pay the rent. Jake can't keep up with the latest trends so at school he sometimes feels a bit left out.

Nuclear family: Luke lives with his mum and dad and sister. His dad takes him to football practice every Sunday morning and buys him the kit he needs.

Cohabiting family: Ebony's mum lives with Bob, but they are not married. Ebony likes to visit her own dad at weekend but her mum and Bob want her to do family things with them.

What different choices do Jake, Luke and Ebony have because of their different family structures? Discuss this in pairs then share your ideas with another pair.

Social class

According to the Office for National Statistics (ONS), the UK working population falls into the following social classes shown in the table below.

Table 2.01 Social classes in the UK working population

	%
Higher managerial and professional occupations	10.8
Lower managerial and professional occupations	22.2
Intermediate occupations	10.3
Small employers and own-account workers	7.7
Lower supervisory and technical occupation	9.4
Semi-routine occupations	13.3
Routine occupations	9.8
Long-term unemployed (inc. those who have never worked).	16.5

Source: Socio-economic classification of working-age population, summer 2003: Regional Trends 38

Activity 3

- **Which is the biggest social class?**
- **Which is the smallest social class?**
- **What percentage of the population is in semi-routine or routine occupations or is long-term unemployed? (Add them together.)**
- **Pay usually increases with skill levels. How does a person's social class affect their choices in life? Think of the type of house people live in, the holidays they take, the food they can afford, the education their children can have.**

Geographical location

According to the Office for National Statistics report Focus on People and Migration (December, 2005), 80 per cent of the UK population lives in urban areas, and only 20 per cent live in the countryside. The largest group lives in the Greater London area, the next largest is in the West Midlands and then Greater Manchester. Over a quarter of the population lives in the south east of England.

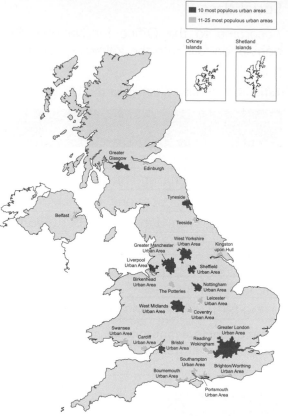

Largest urban populations in the UK

Activity 4

- **Who do you think will have easier access to hospitals and schools – the people who live in the countryside or the people who live in towns?**
- **Why do you think planners need to know where people live?**

As we have seen, social factors relate to groups of people rather than just one person. Factors such as culture, ethnicity, faith, gender, sexuality, age, family structure, social class and geographical location make our society diverse. The problem is that these factors can also make society unequal. Think of Jake in the lone-parent family, or Tom, or Imran. In UK society we believe people should be treated equally, but this is not the case in every society. We try to ensure equality by using laws and policies. This is a big challenge for politicians, who help make the laws.

Political factors

Political factors are factors that relate to the role of government. They are factors that are beyond the control of one individual, but we all as individuals have to abide by the laws of the country we live in. Political factors include the role of legislation, the role of policy, the role of the welfare state, and the delivery of health and social care services.

Did you know...

In London in 2004, there was an average of 4,726 people per square kilometre. The Highland district of Scotland had only eight people per square kilometre.

The role of legislation

Here is an example of a piece of legislation (a law) that was designed to foster equality.

The Racial and Religious Hatred Act 2006 gives protection to groups such as Muslims and Christians by outlawing the use of threatening words or behaviour intended to incite hatred against groups of people defined by their religious beliefs or lack of belief. The values behind the Act were expressed when the Home Office Minister at the time, Vernon Coaker, said:

> 'This Act closes this small but important gap in the law against extremists who stir up hatred in our communities. To be attacked or targeted because of your race or religion is wholly unacceptable. It can have a devastating effect on victims who can find themselves on the receiving end of bigotry and hatred. We are committed to protecting everyone in our society and legislating against this abhorrent behaviour. Our overarching goal is to build a civilised society where we can all achieve our potential free from prejudice.'

Source: www.direct.gov.uk

Another example of the role of legislation can be seen in the Disability Discrimination Act 2005 (DDA), which aims to end the discrimination faced by many people with disabilities. The Act gives rights to employment, education and access to services and facilities. This means that people with disabilities are entitled to an education that meets their needs. They cannot be refused a job if the employer can make a reasonable adaptation to the workplace. All public bodies are required to promote equality of opportunity, so that people with disabilities are treated fairly. One obvious change has been in buses, which now have lower platforms to make it easier for those with mobility problems to get on a bus.

The role of policy

Policy helps shape the laws we have, and is in turn shaped by the laws of the land. Different political parties have different policies. When the Conservatives are in power they will try to bring in Conservative

> **Key term**
>
> Policy – another word for plan.

policies. When Labour is in power they will try to bring in Labour policies. If you study social policy you will learn more about this. Most political parties in the UK agree that people should have equal chances, but they sometimes disagree about how to make this happen.

For now, we will look at how policy in general contributes to a diverse and equal society. In the last section on legislation we saw two examples of laws. Sometimes a law is made because there is a strong policy that everyone agrees about. Most people agree that those with disabilities should be given equal chances. Politicians listened to what the voters thought and brought in the Disability Discrimination Act (DDA). Organisations have to have their own plan or policy saying how they will apply the law in their organisation. The Equality and Human Rights Commission (www.equalityhumanrights.com) provides advice and guidance to make sure the Equality laws are implemented, or put into effect.

In 'Navigating Equality and Diversity' the Department of Health sets out the policy for managers in the National Health Service who employ people. This ensures that they treat people equally when they apply for jobs in the NHS.

The charity Turning Point is the UK's leading social care organisation. Turning Point works with people who face a range of complex needs including substance misuse, mental health problems and learning disabilities. They also have an equality and human rights policy.

The private health company BUPA has a policy that states:

> 'Bupa will not tolerate discrimination in any form, particular in relation to an individual or group's gender, ethnic minority, disability, religion or belief, sexual orientation or age.'

Source: www.bupa.co.uk/careers/people-and-culture

All local government authorities have a duty to publish race, gender and disability equality plans. They have to say what they plan to do to promote equality of opportunity.

Activity 5

Look on your local government website and find their equality plan. How are they going to make equality happen in your area?

Hint: Local government websites are usually the local authority name followed by .gov.uk

The welfare state

The welfare state refers to a system of care brought in after 1945 at the end of the Second World War. William Beveridge designed the welfare state to counteract what he saw as the 'five giants' needed to be tackled in society.

The five giants were:

- want (the need for an adequate income for all)
- disease (the need for health care)
- ignorance (the need for education)
- squalor (the need for adequate housing)
- idleness (the need for employment).

These problems affected the poorest in society. Those who were wealthy did not suffer from these problems. Society was therefore very unequal. If you belonged to a wealthy family, you had health care, education, a good house and an income. If you were poor and you became ill, there was no money to pay a doctor. Many women died in childbirth because they could not afford to pay for health care. Many children died before their fifth birthday because their families could not afford good food, warm clothes and health care when children became ill.

The welfare state meant that government would help people 'from the cradle to the grave'. In other words, the state would provide health care for pregnant women, education for children, help those without work to find jobs and provide housing that people could rent. If someone was ill and unable to work, they would have sickness benefits until they could work again.

All this was to be paid for by national insurance contributions and taxes. The important difference was that when people needed help they could have it free, as they had already paid their contributions. The system was based on the idea that every man would be working, so there would be enough contributions to pay for the welfare state. The welfare state was designed to make people more equal, by giving them the same chances of health, housing, employment and education that wealthy people had.

The delivery of health and social care services

After 1948, services for health and social care were organised by the state. The National Health Service was organised nationally and hospitals were built where they were needed. Some care was delivered in the community by community nurses, dentists and general practitioners.

Social services were organised locally as part of local government so that local needs could be met. An increasing problem for the welfare state and the delivery of services was that the state had not realised that the demands for care would increase. Now people lived healthier lives, they lived longer, and needed more care. The cost of the welfare state became too much, so the government introduced a new law, the NHS and Community Care Act 1990, which brought in the idea that private care and care provided by charities would become an important part of health and care services. This meant that the state was no longer the only provider of health and care services.

In terms of equality and diversity, it meant that people could choose whether to use private services or state services. This was good because it gave choice; however it only gave choice to those who could afford it. Those who could not afford private care were left with state care, or if they could get it, with charitable societies providing care. We now have a mixed economy of care, where people can choose whether to use private, state or charitable services.

Marie Curie logo

An example of charitable care:

Marie Curie Nurses provide free nursing care to cancer patients and those with other terminal illnesses in their own homes: www.mariecurie.org.uk

An example of private care:

Nuffield Health provides private health care in the form of hospitals, fitness centres, treatments and clinics for diagnosis: www.nuffieldhealth.com

Equality
Non-discriminatory practice

'Discriminate' means to 'single out, or prefer one thing or person rather than another'. People do have preferences. They may prefer one person rather than another because they have a lot in common. This is not a problem in someone's personal life. However, it is a problem if health and social care workers discriminate and prefer some patients or service users to others. Can you think why it may be a problem? Here is an example to help you think about the issues.

Case Study

Tom's doctor is a young, newly qualified general practitioner. He thinks Tom is too old to get another job and should adjust to being redundant. He has little sympathy for Tom and tells Tom to snap out of his depression.
The same GP sees Luke's family. Luke received a nasty tackle when playing football. The GP is very sympathetic because he plays football in his spare time. He gives Luke extra time in the surgery and they chat about football.
Tom is not being treated equally. How would you feel if Tom was your relative? Hopefully no GP would do this. Everyone who works in health and social care must take care not to discriminate in their professional work. They must be non-discriminatory in their work.

Discriminatory practice shows itself in many ways. Sometimes people who are not good care workers stereotype others. They may say things like: 'All ... are troublemakers.' You could put any of these words (or other ones) into the gap: teenagers, boys, women, men, old people and foreigners. You have probably heard people say such things. This is stereotyping. It means the person speaking does not see people as individuals but lumps them together as part of a group – often a group they do not like. Sometime people do stereotype in a favorable way, for example, they may say, 'All ... are lovely.' Again you could put a number of different words into the gap. It is still stereotyping because it does not see people as individuals.

Did you know...?

'Anti' means against or opposite. 'Non' means without. Sometimes you will see the words 'anti-discriminatory practice' and sometimes you will see 'non-discriminatory practice'. They both mean that we should not discriminate.

If a care worker stereotypes a group favourably, they may give them preferential treatment. If a care worker stereotypes a group negatively, the group may get poorer treatment. Next time you hear someone stereotyping others, try to work out how it would affect care practice if it was a carer saying this.

'Labelling' is a bit like stereotyping. If you label someone, you put them in a category, or a group. Sometimes people get labelled as being 'clever' or 'stupid'. The issue with labels is that if the person being labelled accepts the label, they begin to live up to it, or down to it. It then may become a self-fulfilling prophecy. If it is a good label, this is not a problem. If someone labels you as 'clever' or 'intelligent' then you will be more confident in your abilities.

If a label is negative or unpleasant, it is a problem. If Tom is labelled as a miserable old man, people may start to avoid him. He would then get more isolated and feel even more depressed and may become really miserable. If Jake can't get fashionable trainers, unkind people may label him as a 'loser'. If people start to avoid him because they don't want to be seen with someone who is unpopular, Jake may end up with few friends. If this happens, Jake will get lonelier and begin to believe he really is a loser, so he won't try to make new friends. People would then think he is unfriendly and won't bother with him. His self-confidence could hit rock bottom. Jake has to be a strong person to ignore the label 'loser' but if he tries to ignore the unkind label he will make friends with people who like him for himself, not for how fashionable he is.

'Prejudice' means pre-judging. It can be positive or negative. If you go to hospital for the first time and meet a nurse who is kind and friendly you might then be prejudiced in favour of nurses. When you meet another nurse you expect them to be friendly because your first encounter with a nurse was positive. If you visit a doctor's surgery for the first time and the receptionist is rude, you might think all receptionists are like that and become prejudiced against doctor's receptionists.

Stereotyping often leads to prejudice and may result in discrimination. Labelling also leads to discrimination. When there is discrimination in care practice there is no equality.

Biological factors

Biological factors relate to an individual person's body. Many people are fortunate to have a body that works perfectly. They are sometimes termed 'able bodied'. Others may have bodies that do not work so well. In this section we consider people who may have learning disabilities and/or physical disabilities.

'Learning disabilities' is a general term that covers a lot of conditions. According to Mencap, a leading charity for people with learning disabilities:

'A learning disability can be caused by something that happens during pregnancy, during birth or in early childhood.'

Mencap logo

Some facts about learning disabilities:

- The development of the brain is affected.
- It is a life-long condition.
- It impacts on daily life – people with learning disabilities may need help with dressing, washing, toileting.
- It is not mental illness or dyslexia.
- Sometimes people with learning disabilities may also have physical disabilities.
- Children with a learning disability are often socially excluded and 8 out of 10 children with a learning disability are bullied.
- 1 in 2 families with a disabled child live in poverty.

Source: www.mencap.org.uk

People with learning disabilities may need extra help to take an equal part in society.

Activity 6

Find out what support people with learning disabilities may need and what Mencap provides. Make a poster of your findings.

'Physical disabilities' is another general term that covers a lot of things.

According to the World Health Organisation:

'"Disabilities" is an umbrella term, covering impairments, activity limitations, and participation restrictions. An impairment is a problem in body function or structure; an activity limitation is a difficulty encountered by an individual in executing a task or action; while a participation restriction is a problem experienced by an individual in involvement in life situations. Thus disability is a complex phenomenon, reflecting an interaction between features of a person's body and features of the society in which he or she lives.'

Source: www.who.int/topics/disabilities/en/

Physical disabilities include:

- hearing impairment – from partial deafness to total deafness
- missing limbs, hands or feet
- visual impairment – from partial sight loss to total blindness.

Perhaps you can list other physical disabilities.

A child with a hearing impairment may appear slow to learn, but if the hearing disability can be treated, perhaps by use of a hearing aid, the child will learn at the same rate as any other child.

Care for people with physical disabilities is aimed at helping them to get the right support so that they can lead a normal life.

Activity 5   **P1**

Think about the factors that contribute to equality. Make a list and then produce a poster or a leaflet to identify factors that contribute to the equality of individuals in society. You may like to use examples to help explain your work.

If you do this you may have work towards P1 Identify factors that contribute to the equality of individuals in society, and towards Personal Learning and Thinking Skills IE2, IE4, CT2, RL3, RL4, SM2, SM3, EP5.

2 Understand principles and values which underpin the support of individuals

Ethical considerations

'Ethical considerations' means 'considering or thinking about what is right or fair'. In the UK we aim to give health and social care that is fair and equally available to all. These are just some of the ways we do this:

- through social justice
- by using a person-centred approach
- by maintaining a right to life

- adherence to codes of practice and policies
- the expectations of individuals receiving the service
- honesty
- empathy.

Right to life

The term 'right to life' is a right protected under the Human Rights Act, passed in England and Wales in 1998. This Act is based on the European Convention on Human Rights. Article two of the conventions states that:

> 'Everyone's right to life shall be protected by law. No one shall be deprived of his life intentionally save in the execution of a sentence of a court following his conviction of a crime for which this penalty is provided by law.'

Source: www.opsi.gov.uk/acts/acts1998

Read the following case studies to see how this law affects health and social care and what it has to do with supporting individuals.

> **Key term**
>
> 'Right' – an entitlement that someone ought to have.

 ### Case Study

After collapsing at her home in the USA, Terri Schiavo remained in a persistent vegetative state (PVS) for several years in a nursing home. Brain scans showed very little brain tissue and an electroencephalogram (EEG) showed no brain activity. She was on a life-support machine. Her husband, who was her legal guardian, argued that she would not want to live in such a condition, and she should be allowed to die. Her parents opposed this, saying she had the right to life. The case went through the courts and eventually it was decided to remove her feeding tube. Terri died, aged 41, in March 2005 in a hospice.

Where ethical issues are involved, health and care workers must know what legal rights a person has in order to support them and if necessary, speak on their behalf.

Case Study

Jean-Dominique Bauby was editor of the French fashion magazine 'Elle' when he suffered a massive stroke that left him unable to move except for the ability to blink his left eye-lid. From being an active person he was now totally dependent on others, surviving by means of a life-support machine. He found that he could communicate by blinking. To do this, a transcriber would recite the alphabet and he would blink when he wanted a particular letter. In this way he managed to dictate a book telling what it is like to be 'locked in' in his condition. He died in 1997, two days after the book was published. A film based on the book of the same name, *The Diving Bell and the Butterfly*, was released in 2007.

Some people might have argued that Bauby's life was not worth living, but he himself certainly had a purpose for living. Fortunately, the law protects the right to life for all.

Another area where this is an issue is the right to life of an unborn child. Some people argue that the mother has the right to do as she wishes with her own body, and that these override the rights of the unborn child. Others argue that the unborn child has a right to life that overrides the mother's right to choose. This is a controversial area.

Liberty, also called the National Council for Civil Liberties, is an organisation that exists to 'promote the values of individual human dignity, equal treatment and fairness as the foundations of a democratic society.'

Activity 6

Look at the Liberty website, at www.liberty-human-rights.org.uk. What rights does Liberty say that individuals have? Make a list. This may help you later in your work for assessment.

Social justice

Social justice refers to laws that promote equality and human rights. It usually implies some kind of sharing of advantages to make a fairer society.

For example, Jake's mum works hard just to pay the rent. Under social justice, she might be able to claim extra benefits to provide Jake and his siblings with a chance to socialise.

According to Child Poverty Action Group, the leading charity campaigning for the abolition of child poverty in the UK and for a better deal for low-income families and children, 'Poverty isolates people, reducing their ability to engage in social and community life. In a study comparing the poorest and

Ethical considerations

richest fifth of households, poorer children had fewer opportunities for activities and entertaining friends.'

Source: www.cpag.org.uk

The person-centred approach to care

This means that we put the person at the centre of everything we do. Person-centred care is standard two of the National Service Framework (NSF) for older people but it is important to remember that person-centred care applies to all, not just to older people.

Standard two of the NSF for older people states:

'The aim of this standard is to ensure that older people are treated as individuals and that they receive appropriate and timely packages of care which meet their needs as individuals, regardless of health and social services boundaries.'

Source: www.dh.gov.uk

In the case of Tom, who has been made redundant and is in his fifties and depressed, his GP might refer him to a social worker. The social worker might assess his needs and find that he would benefit from counselling, and from attending a course designed to help him find a job. Eventually he might no longer need antidepressant medication. By

Key term

Social justice – laws that treat people equally.

CHILD POVERTY ACTION GROUP

Child Poverty Action Group logo

putting the person at the centre of care we can help them more effectively.

Many years ago, the health care approach in the UK was to put the service at centre. This was service-led care. If the service did not exist, the person did not get it. If someone was very ill and dying from a painful illness, they were often kept in hospital and given injections every four hours to manage the pain. Sometimes they needed more injections than were prescribed, and had to wait in pain until the time for their next injection. This was obviously not good. Some people felt very strongly that care for the dying could be much better and they started the hospice movement in 1967 with St Christopher's Hospice.

People who were dying had the choice to go to a hospice where they were at the centre of care and pain relief was given according to individual need. Marie Curie Cancer Care and the Sue Ryder Foundation also developed specialised care for dying people and their families, with an aim to care for a person's physical, spiritual and psychological well-being. This person-centred care spread to the rest of health and social care. Now we try to meet the needs of each person as far as we can with the resources we have.

> ## Key terms
>
> Person-centred approach – puts the person at the centre of care. This is the opposite of a service-led approach which puts the needs of the service first.

Expectations of individuals receiving health and social care services

The expectations of individuals receiving health and social care services have changed. Once, people were happy to accept whatever the doctor, nurse or social worker recommended for them, but now expectations are different. In the twenty-first century the government expects people to know about their own health and take some responsibility for their own health.

On the NHS website, in the section Choice in the NHS, it states that: 'Modern medicine is more a partnership between doctor and patient than ever before.'

Source: www.nhs.uk/choiceintheNHS/Yourchoices

The NHS constitution sets out what rights patients have. They include the right to 'accept or refuse treatment that is offered and not to be given any physical treatment or examination unless you have given valid consent.' (Adapted from the NHS Constitution, January 2009.)

The government encourages people to have realistic expectations of health and care services, but at the same time, encourages people to be responsible for their own health, by staying healthy.

> ### Did you know... ?
>
> Patients have the right to choose their GP, choose their hospital if they need to be referred for treatment, and they are also expected to make informed decisions about their own treatment.

Social care is slightly different. The Northern Ireland Social Care Council document 'Statement of Expectations – of people using services and their carers' was part of a review of the UK Joint Health and Social Care Review of the National Occupational Standards and Awards in Care. (www.niscc.info/content/uploads/downloads/workforce_dev/NOS_health_social/Statement_expectations.pdf)

They found that service users and carers expected that:

> 'Ideal care workers go out of their way for you, try to understand what it's like for the service user and carer; they are happy and interested in their work and knowledgeable about their jobs and sources of help. As people they are friendly, diplomatic, interested, patient and responsible. They are good communicators who listen and don't try to follow their own agenda.'

The section on Children and Young People emphasised that:

> 'Ideal care workers are people you can trust, who listen to you and explain things, get involved in your life, are there for you and stand up for you. They help you with your homework and talk to you.'

Honesty and empathy

Honesty (truthfulness) is expected of everyone who works in health and social care.

Empathy (understanding) is essential for all those who work in this area. Empathy is not the same as sympathy. Sympathy is feeling sorry for someone. Empathy is trying to understand how they feel.

Activity 11

Make a list of the qualities you think people need to work in health or social care. Decide which of them are essential and which are desirable but not vital.

Codes of practice and policies

Codes of practice are rules to work by. Most professions have a code, including social care workers, nurses and midwives.

The code for nurses and midwives says that they must:

- make the care of people your first concern, treating them as individuals and respecting their dignity
- work with others to protect and promote the health and wellbeing of those in your care, their families and carers, and the wider community

- provide a high standard of practice and care at all times
- be open and honest, act with integrity and uphold the reputation of your profession

Source: www.nmc-uk.org

The idea of beneficence is embedded in this code.

Social care workers have a code which states that they must:

- protect the rights and promote the interests of service users and carers
- strive to establish and maintain the trust and confidence of service users and carers
- promote the independence of service users while protecting them as far as possible from danger or harm
- respect the rights of service users whilst seeking to ensure that their behaviour does not harm themselves or other people
- uphold public trust and confidence in social care services; and
- be accountable for the quality of their work and take responsibility for maintaining and improving their knowledge and skills.

Source: www.gscc.org.uk

Again, the idea of beneficence is embedded in the code.

Activity 8

Can you see any other similarities between the two codes? Can you see any differences?

Policies are guidelines that are often developed from laws. We have already mentioned policies that exist to promote equality. Organisations are also required to have a health and safety policy, to ensure people are in a safe environment. In 2006, new legislation was passed to make public buildings smoke-free. In order to comply with this, some organisations wrote a smoke-free policy to show how the law would be applied in their area. The policy balances the rights of those who wish to smoke with the rights of others to have a smoke-free environment. It says where people may safely smoke and where they may not smoke. A policy such as this helps everyone maintain their rights and keep to the law.

Activity 9

Research your local hospital on the internet and see if you can find any policies that underpin equality.

Individual rights

Individuals have rights. This is a key principle that underpins all work in health and social care. You will find more detail about this in Unit 6 Cultural Diversity in Health and Social Care.

We all have the right to be:

- respected
- treated equally and not discriminated against
- treated as an individual
- treated in a dignified way
- allowed privacy
- safeguarded from danger and harm
- allowed access to information about ourselves
- able to communicate using our preferred methods of communication and language
- supported in a way that meets our needs and takes account of our choices.

The right to be respected is written in codes of conduct and in policies, but what does it really mean? Many of these ideas are linked together. If someone is treated with dignity, they are treated as an individual, in a dignified way. They are listened to and where possible their wishes are met.

The Social Care Institute for Excellence publishes research on a variety of social care topics. SCIE Guide 15: Dignity in Care summarises research in this area and finds that dignity includes respect, privacy, self-esteem, self-worth, identity and a sense of self, plus autonomy (freedom of choice).

- Respect, shown to you as a human being and as an individual, by others, and demonstrated by courtesy, good communication and taking time.
- Privacy, in terms of personal space; modesty and privacy in personal care; and confidentiality of treatment and personal information.
- Self-esteem, self-worth, identity and a sense of self, promoted by all the elements of dignity, but also by 'all the little things' – a clean and respectable appearance, pleasant environments – and by choice, and being listened to.
- Autonomy, including freedom to act and freedom to decide, based on clear, comprehensive information and opportunities to participate.

Source: www.scie.org.uk/publications/guides/guide15/overview/means.asp

The national occupational standards for social work published in 2004 by www.topss.org.uk say that social workers should learn values and ethics that include respect for and the promotion of each person as an individual.

Case Study

Maggie lives at Sunnyside, a care home. She is eighty years old, partially sighted and deaf. She used to be a teacher. She has no family and rarely gets visitors. The cook prides herself on feeding the residents well and every day she prepares a full dinner of meat, vegetables and potatoes with a pudding to follow. Sally, her care worker, knows that Maggie likes small meals. For her evening meal Maggie says she prefers a poached egg on toast. Sally asks the cook to prepare this for Maggie. This is an example of showing respect for Maggie. She is valued as an individual and given autonomy to decide what she would like to eat.

Activity 10

P2

- Make a list of local services for health and a list of local services for social care in your area. You can find information about social care on your local government website and information about health services on the NHS website. If you don't have access to the internet, use local telephone directories (e.g. Yellow Pages) but be aware that websites are usually more up to date.
- Choose a service from health, such as a local health centre, and a service from social care such as a centre for homeless people. You may have to look at services in the nearest large city for this.
- Find out if your chosen services have a document that sets out the rights of users. If they have such a document, find out what rights are set out.
- Look at the section on rights in this unit and make notes. A spidergram is a useful way to make notes.
- If you managed to get a list of user's rights from the service, add in any other rights they mention that are not listed in this unit.

Produce a short report that discusses the rights of the people who use:

a your local health centre

b a centre for homeless people in the nearest city.

Remember, a discussion is more than just a list. You will need to discuss each right.

This activity will help you towards P2: Explain the individual rights of people who use services and towards personal learning and thinking skills IE2, CT2, RL3, RL4, SM2, SM3 and EP5.

Worker responsibilities

People who work in health and in social care have a special responsibility to the people they care for. The phrase 'provision of active support' means that the care worker encourages and supports the service user or patient to make choices. One way the care worker does this is to enable people who use services to communicate their needs, views and preferences. You will find more about this in Unit 1 Communication in Health and Social Care and in Unit 6 Cultural Diversity in Health and Social Care.

The care worker Sally enabled Maggie to communicate her preference for what she would like to eat. Sally is a good care worker. She treats all the residents with the same respect.

 Case Study

Sunita is also a resident at Sunnyside. When Sunita first came to Sunnyside, she found she couldn't eat the boiled vegetables provided for her vegetarian diet, and she lost her appetite. She lost weight, which as she was already frail was a real problem. She didn't want to be a nuisance, but Sally saw the problem and talked with Sunita and listened to why she was not eating. Then Sally and the manager listened to Sunita's family's proposal for a solution. It was decided that if the food was freshly cooked there was little risk to Sunita's health, so it was agreed that Sunita's daughter would bring her lunch round every day.

Sunita's case is just one example of the use of communication to support diversity, inclusion and promote equality of opportunity. The next case study provides two more examples.

 Case Study

Amir is diabetic and has to go into hospital to have his insulin dose regulated. He speaks little English and has never learned to read and write it. The nurse gives him a leaflet in Urdu, which he can read to explain his treatment. She then arranges for a translator to visit him to give him the chance to ask any questions. She uses verbal communication, non-verbal and written communication.

Sam has learning difficulties and lives in sheltered housing. He does not get on too well with one of the people in the house. His social worker is about to do a regular review of his care package and realises that Sam is not happy. The social worker arranges for an advocate to come with Sam to the review, so that Sam's views can be put forward. Again, verbal communication and non-verbal communication are used, but this time no written material is given as it will not meet Sam's needs. Having someone to listen to him and to put forward his views is the most effective form of communication here.

Confidentiality

Confidentiality means 'ensuring that information is accessible only to those authorised to have access'. This is the definition used by the International Organization for Standardization. Confidentiality is governed by common law, by Article 8 of the European Convention on Human Rights, and in the UK law by the Human Rights Act 1998. It is also governed by the Data Protection Act 1998. Ethical and professional guidelines also tell care workers what their duties are around confidentiality. Look back at the codes of conduct for nurses and midwives, and the code for social workers. What do they say about confidentiality?

Care workers have a legal duty to keep personal information private. Sally can talk to Maggie about her preferences, and Sally would write this in the care plan, but Sally can't then go and tell all the other residents about Maggie. As a care worker, Sally has a duty to maintain confidentiality. It is the same with Sunita's case. Sally can talk to the relatives if Sunita agrees, but if Sunita doesn't want her daughter to know she is not eating, Sally can't discuss this with the daughter. However, Sally can talk to the manager about Sunita's poor appetite, in fact she must report it, as it is an important aspect of care.

Disclosure

In 2005 the Royal College of Nursing published guidance on Confidentiality for Occupational Health Nurses. The guidance also gives examples of when confidentiality may be broken, and personal information disclosed. These are based on the guidelines for physicians.

> **Key term**
>
> Disclosure – another way of saying 'telling someone'.

The guidance states that there are seven situations when confidential information may be disclosed. They are:

1 with the consent of the client
2 if disclosure is clearly in the patient's interest but it is not possible or is undesirable to seek consent
3 if it is required by law
4 if it is unequivocally in the public interest
5 if it is necessary to safeguard national security or to prevent a serious crime
6 if it will prevent a serious risk to public health
7 in certain circumstances for the purposes of medical research.

Source: www.rcn.org.uk

In 1997, the Caldicott report found weaknesses in handling patient data. As a result, senior people in the NHS and Social services have been appointed as Caldicott Guardians. They have special responsibility to ensure data is kept confidential.

Case Study

Margaret Haywood, a nurse at the Royal Sussex County Hospital, raised concerns about poor quality care, neglect and abuse of patients. Nothing was done, so she agreed to take part in secret filming for the BBC programme *Panorama* in 2005 to expose the situation. Afterwards, the patients and relatives involved gave permission for the programme to be screened. The issue was brought to public attention, but Margaret was struck off the nursing register by the Nursing and Midwifery Council for breaching confidentiality. The Royal College of Nursing raised a petition and the punishment was reduced to a one-year caution. Margaret was a 'whistleblower', which means someone who raises concerns about wrong-doing in an organisation they work in.

Read more about the case on the following websites:

- *Nursing Times*: www.nursingtimes.net/forums-blogs-ideas-debate/nursing-blogs/a-win-for-the-whistleblowers-and-how-to-look-odd-naked/5007366.article
- The social work journal *Community Care*: www.communitycare.co.uk/blogs/social-care-experts-blog/2009/04/margaret-haywood-committed-pro.html.
- Whose interests is the writer concerned about – the patients', the organisation's or the whistleblower's?
- The NMC website states: 'This was an extremely difficult and complex case in which the NMC panel had to balance Ms Haywood's duty to protect patient confidentiality with her duty to raise concerns about poor standards of care.' Source: www.nmc-uk.org Whose interests are the NMC concerned about – the patients', the organisation's or the whistleblower's?
- Royal College of Nursing: www.rcn.org.uk/newsevents/news/article/uk/margaret_haywood__court_case_settled.
- Whose interests are the RCN concerned about – the patients', the organisation's or the whistleblower's?

In November 2009, Margaret Haywood was awarded the Nursing Standard's Patient's Choice Award for standing up for the rights of patients.

This case shows how difficult it is sometimes to know what is in the patient's best interests. The Nursing and Midwifery Council are preparing further guidelines for Summer 2010 to help nurses faced with such situations.

Dealing with tensions between rights and responsibilities

The case of Margaret Haywood shows some of the tensions between rights and responsibilities. She knew that patients were not receiving their rights, and she had a responsibility as a nurse to do something about it.

Sometimes the tension between rights and responsibilities occurs in different ways. A person who is diabetic and dependent on insulin has a right to choose their own diet, but the nurse looking after them has a duty of care to make sure they are given a healthy diet. The tension is between the rights of the person and the duty imposed on the nurse because of his or her legal duty.

Activity 11

If we look at the case of Amir, the diabetic patient in hospital for stabilising his insulin dose, we can examine the situation in more detail. Amir knows that sugary foods are not good for him, but his family come to visit and bring him some Indian sweets, which contain a lot of sugar.

The nurse sees them on his locker. What should the nurse do? Take them away? Or explain to Amir what the sugar will do to his body and how that will change the requirements for insulin?

The nurse cannot take them away. The patient has a right to eat what he wishes. The nurse can only explain what the consequences of his actions will be, and the nurse should report the incident. The nurse has a duty to explain to him what will happen if he eats the sweets, and as he is not very fluent in English, she will need to make sure that this is translated into Urdu for him.

She must report and record the incident. If Amir eats the sweets and no one knows, his insulin may not be sufficient to cope with the extra sugar in his body and he may fall into a coma. If the nurse does not report the incident she is guilty of neglect. The tension here is between the patient's rights and the responsibility of the nurse.

Another example of the tension between rights and responsibilities may occur when a resident in a nursing home refuses to have a bath. The care staff can advise, and suggest alternatives such as having a shower or a wash all over. If the person does not agree and becomes smelly, the care staff cannot forcibly wash the person. This is assault. At the same time, care workers have a responsibility to maintain the person's health. If the person is of sound mind and refuses, care staff must explain the possible consequences of skin infections. Care staff must record and report this refusal to wash, so that the situation can be monitored. If the person's mental health deteriorates or their physical health deteriorates, the doctor in charge may decide that they need to be admitted to a psychiatric unit for assessment.

These examples show the importance of accurate recording, storage and retrieving information (including electronic methods), filing correctly and securely. The recorded entries show what care has been given and how the person responded. Information must be available to those with a right of access and must be stored in a secure place accessible only to those with the right of access. Records must be filed accurately. If Amir's notes have been misfiled and cannot be found, no one will know he has sweets. If he does eat the sweets and falls into a coma, valuable time may be lost while the doctor tries to find out what is wrong. It might even cost Amir his life.

The Data Protection Act 1998 and the Freedom of Information Act 2005

Both the Data Protection Act 1998 and the Freedom of Information Act 2005 are regulated by the Information Commissioner. (See the Information Commissioner's website at www.ico.gov.uk.)

The requirements of the Data Protection Act 1998

The Data Protection Act 1998 applies to 'personal data' about identifiable living individuals, and covers both personal data held electronically and manual or paper data held in structured files or easily accessible systems. The Data Protection Act gives rights to individuals for whom information is held. It also requires those who record and use personal information to follow the eight principles of good information handling.

Data must be:

- fairly and lawfully processed
- processed for limited purposes
- adequate, relevant and not excessive
- accurate
- not kept for longer than is necessary
- processed in line with the data subject's rights
- secure
- not transferred to countries without adequate protection.

Data may be processed only where the individual has given their consent. The Act gives individuals the right of access to information held about them but forbids releasing that information to anyone else without permission, unless there is a legal requirement to do so.

The requirements of the Freedom of Information Act 2005

Under this Act, everyone has a right to request information held by public sector organisations. It is free, but if the cost is likely to be more than £450 the organisation may ask you to be more specific about the information you need.

Organisations that are covered in the Freedom of Information Act include government departments, local authorities, health trusts, hospitals and doctor's surgeries, schools, colleges and universities, the police and many other public bodies. Requests are usually answered within 20 working days.

Everyone is entitled to see what records are held about them. This process is handled under the Data Protection Act. If you require information about other people, you should first obtain their consent, otherwise you may not be given the information.

The worker's responsibility is to be aware what information is confidential and to ensure accurate records are held securely. A worker needs to be aware what laws govern this area to ensure they comply with them. At times patients and users of services may ask for information to which they are not entitled. Sometimes the person may be entitled to the information, but it is never a worker's role just to hand the information over. The worker should find out what the procedure is at their place of work so they can advise the user or patient of the correct procedure.

Activity 12

Principles and values are very important in health and in social care. Choose one of the services you used in Activity 12 for P2 and find out what principles and values underpin the service.

Write an article for your local newspaper explaining the values and principles for your chosen service.

If you discuss the advantages and difficulties with such values you may cover the merit point. If you then go on to evaluate how the principles and values that underpin care relate to the promotion of individual rights, you may cover the distinction point. For this point, an evaluation is necessary, so you will need to come to a conclusion based on your merit point discussion. An evaluation may be that the principles and values underpinning care can closely relate to promoting individual rights, or you may come to an evaluation that the principles and values underpinning care only partly relate to promoting individual rights because the rights of society for a cost effective service must also be considered. Whatever your evaluation, it should be based on your arguments put forward in the merit point discussion.

If you complete this activity you may have evidence towards:

- P3 Explain the principles and values which underpin the support for individuals who use services (IE2, IE4, CT2, CT4, RL3, RL4, SM2, SM3, EP5)
- M1 Discuss the principles and values which underpin the support for individuals who use services
- D1 Evaluate how the principles and values which underpin health and social care can relate to the promotion of the rights of individuals.

Summary

1 A diverse society includes people from many different backgrounds.
2 An equal society is one where people are given equal chances, even though they are different.
3 Principles are beliefs we hold.
4 Values are the morals we live by.
5 In this society we believe it is important to support individuals.
6 Ethical or moral values that respect individuals guide care workers.
7 Individual rights are factors that support equality, so an individual has a right to be respected and to be treated equally.
8 Workers in health and in social care have a duty to help individuals express their needs.
9 Workers in health and in social care have a duty to make sure there is equality of opportunity.
10 Workers in health and in social care have a legal duty to store and safeguard information.

Assessment and grading criteria		
To achieve a pass grade the evidence must show that the learner is able to:	**To achieve a merit grade the evidence must show that, in addition to the pass criteria, the learner is able to:**	**To achieve a distinction grade the evidence must show that, in addition to the pass and merit criteria, the learner is able to:**
P1 identify factors that contribute to the equality of individuals in society (see Activity 5) [IE2, IE4, CT2, RL3, RL4, SM2, SM3, EP5]		
P2 explain the individual rights of people who use services (see Activity 10) [IE2, CT2, RL3, RL4, SM2, SM3, EP5]		

P3 explain the principles and values which underpin the support for individuals who use services (see Activity 12) [IE2, IE4, CT2, CT4, RL3, RL4, SM2, SM3, EP5]	**M1** discuss the principles and values which underpin support for individuals who use services (see Activity 12)	**D1** assess how the principles and values which underpin health and social care relate to the promotion of rights of individuals (see Activity 12)

Further Reading

McFerran, T. and Martin, E. (ed.), 2008, *A Dictionary of Nursing*, Oxford: Oxford University Press

Focus on Families, Office for National Statistics, 2007 edition, London: Palgrave Macmillan

'Focus on People and Migration', Office for National Statistics, December 2005, www.statistics.gov.uk/focuson/migration

Fought, C., 2006, *Language and Ethnicity Key Topics in Sociolinguistics*, New York: Cambridge University Press

'Socio-economic classification of working-age population', Summer 2003: Regional Trends 38, www.statistics.gov.uk

Weblinks

www.cpag.org.uk
www.direct.gov.uk
www.gscc.org.uk/codes
www.liberty-human-rights.org.uk
www.nhs.uk/choiceintheNHS/Yourchoices
www.nmc-uk.org
www.opsi.gov.uk/acts/acts1998
www.rcn.org.uk

Unit 3
Individual Needs in the Health and Social Care Sectors

This unit allows you to identify, assess and plan for service users' individual needs to help them improve their health and well-being. You will investigate the needs of service users and particular factors that influence delivery of care to individuals throughout the life stages. This unit pays particular attention to how care can be adapted to meet the health and well-being of our service users.

Learning outcomes:

In this unit you will learn about:

● everyday needs of individuals

● factors that influence the health and needs of individuals

● planning to meet the health needs of an individual.

1 Know everyday needs of individuals

Importance of needs

To help us assess our service users' needs, we firstly should understand what a 'need' is.

Sometimes we only discover we have a need when we are lacking in something – for example, when we are cold, lonely or hungry. Once we have realised our need, we can find ways to satisfy it. Some service users may not be able to meet their needs for varying reasons, so within this unit you will learn about methods you can use to identify individual needs, thereby helping you to care appropriately for your service users.

Activity 1

What do we really need to survive? Make a list of everything that is essential to survive within society. Remember that what you would like is not necessarily the same as what you need!

Maslow's hierarchy of needs

In 1943 the psychologist Abraham Maslow developed a 'hierarchy of needs', which he illustrated in a pyramid format with different levels. He considered that individuals have a variety of needs and ranked these in order of importance or priority. There are five levels to his hierarchy and the lower level must be completed before moving up to the next level.

The lowest level of need is physical needs. These are the basic needs that are necessary for survival. Maslow considered these to be the most important of all the needs, which will always take priority over meeting any of the other needs. Physical needs include water, air, food and sleep. Once these needs have been met, an individual can move up to the next level of the hierarchy, which is security needs. Maslow considered these important, but not as much of a priority as physical needs. Security needs are about an individual feeling safe within their own environment, and having a sense of predictability and stability. The next level is love and belonging needs. This can include belonging to social

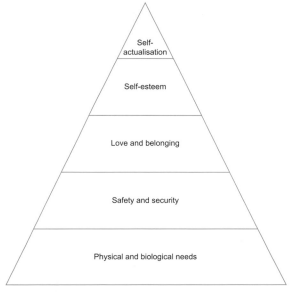

Maslow's hierarchy of needs

groups and having and receiving love. Once these needs have been met, an individual can progress to consider their esteem needs. Self-esteem is about how an individual feels about themselves, their self-worth. This level also includes how others feel about the individual. Therefore, the needs are less about just surviving, as in the physical needs at the lower level of the pyramid, and more about how the individual is doing. The last level, self-actualisation, involves an individual reaching, displaying and using their full potential.

Humans yearn for more than just their basic needs. This model is useful as it provides guidelines when considering the needs of individuals in health and social care.

Activity 2

Using information from a service user in your work setting, write a list of their individual needs according to Maslow's hierarchy. Once you have assessed these needs, take a look at where they are placed within Maslow's hierarchy. How are their needs being met within your setting? Can you suggest anything to change or improve their care?

As health and social care professionals, needs can also be considered in terms of physical, intellectual, emotional, social and spiritual aspects (PIES).

Physical needs relate to the body. These include food, shelter, water, exercise and sleep. It is more than just providing for these needs though; it is about ensuring that food, for example, is adequate and meets an individual's specific needs. This can change according to age or if an individual has specific health and social care needs. For example, babies and young children are fed and cared for physically by parents or responsible adults who make choices for them. As we grow we become involved in our own choices like diet, choice of living accommodation and safety in our environment .Older service users may need help to meet their physical needs, for example, the provision of adequate meals and a safe environment. This could be given by an informal carer like a member of their family or a close friend. Alternatively, this care could be provided formally by outside agencies or nursing or residential homes.

Intellectual needs are about stimulating the brain. This could be through formal education, such as school or college, or other activities, such as crosswords, puzzles or reading a book – anything that involves using the brain. As formal education is compulsory until the age of sixteen, children are in a learning environment each day they attend school. After this some young people choose their next learning environment and may attend a further education college or go into employment. In both instances learning needs are being met whether it is new areas of learning or acquiring new skills.

Emotional needs are about having a sense of well-being and self-esteem. Self-concept is also part of emotional needs. Relationships with others are also included in emotional needs, as well as being able to handle and express your emotions appropriately. One example of this is that it may be seen as acceptable for a two year old to have a tantrum in a shop if they don't get what they want but it would be inappropriate for a sixteen year old to do the same! By this time we have learned to deal with our emotions and act appropriately. Adolescence is seen as a rollercoaster of emotions and this time can be difficult for some teenagers as they face new relationships with friends of the same and opposite sex. Older service users may experience emotions from being new grandparents to the loss of a partner. Their needs can be supported by close friends and family.

Social needs are about having and maintaining supportive relationships, friendships and a place in society. This could be about being part of a family or a group of friends and being accepted within these groups. Children's social needs can be met at playgroups and schools as they begin to learn how to share, play and establish friendships. As adolescents move into new learning environments they will have to make new relationships with a range of people, for example new teachers, peers or work colleagues. As these relationships are established it can give us a sense of belonging and well-being which brings confidence and maturity. If these social needs are not fulfilled then service users can feel isolated and depressed, particularly if they are being exposed to bullying of any form.

Spiritual needs include any personal or specific religious beliefs an individual may have. This may be influenced by cultural upbringing or from values that have been taught in the family. Allowing service users to practice their religious or cultural beliefs in health and social care settings will give them a sense of comfort, belonging and tolerance. If settings do not allow service users to express their spiritual needs they may feel discriminated, undervalued and not accepted in society.

By exploring these needs, we can consider an individual in a holistic way. Needs may be linked – for example, if an individual is accepted and valued in a group of friends (a social need), this will positively impact upon their self-esteem (an emotional need). Conversely, if an individual does not have peer or family support, this can impact upon their emotional needs and self-esteem.

Key term

Holistic care – we should be aware that all parts of the individual are important and we should treat them as a whole; we should not just focus on one area of an individual.

Activity 3

 Case Study

David is a 65-year-old widowed man. He smokes 15 cigarettes a day. He is a member of a walking club and attends the club's walking and social events. He also reads regularly and has some good, supportive friends.

David's daughter, Sharon, is 30 and married with two small children. Her husband works away from home a lot and Dad (David) lives a three-hour drive away. She regularly finds herself exhausted and has little time for herself. Although her children eat a healthy diet, Sharon finds she snacks on chocolate and ready meals. Sharon's friend Stacey works long hours and, as a result, she has little time for herself. She has recently moved into a new area and does not know many people. She eats a healthy diet and exercises on a regular basis. Sharon's friend Usha works long hours and as a result she has little time for herself. She has recently moved into a new area and does not know many people. She eats a healthy vegetarian diet and exercises on a regular basis. She still practices her religious beliefs which she has been brought up with.

1. Identify the physical, intellectual, emotional, social and spiritual needs of each of the individuals in the case study.
2. What are they doing that is good for their health?
3. What are they doing that may harm their health?
4. What would you recommend they do to improve their health?

Needs in relation to life stage

An individual's needs may vary according to the life stage they are in. Some needs are consistent throughout all life stages – for example, the need for an appropriate and nutritious diet and good hygiene. However, the differences can be seen in who meets these needs. Adolescents will need help and support to become independent; adults and older people may need support to maintain this level of independence.

These needs are discussed in Unit 8 when we look at needs throughout the life stages. Have a look at the table on page 245.

P1

Activity 4

Create a poster showing a pictorial form of Maslow's hierarchy of needs and a chart of PIES. This should outline your knowledge of individual needs. Label your chart to show your understanding.

2 Understand factors that influence the health and needs of individuals

There are many different factors that can influence the health and needs of individuals. In some circumstances there may be more than one factor that influences health and individual needs.

Socio-economic factors

Social class

Social class is a way of dividing up the population. In this instance, it is due to occupation and income levels. The way in which social class is determined has changed. Current social class classifications are shown below.

Factors that influence the health and needs of individuals

1 Higher managerial and professional occupations
   1.1 Large employers and higher managerial occupations
   1.2 Higher professional occupations
2 Lower managerial and professional occupations
3 Intermediate occupations
4 Small employers and own account workers
5 Lower supervisory and technical occupations
6 Semi-routine occupations
7 Routine occupations
8 Never worked and long-time unemployed

Source: www.ons.gov.uk/about-statistics/classifications/current/ns-sec/cats-and-classes/ns-sec-classes-and-collapses/index.html

In 1980 the Black report was carried out, which revealed that there were links between social class and health. The report found that the lower the social class, the more likely you were to suffer ill health. This may be because lower social classes are in lower-paid employment so may not have an adequate diet or living conditions, which all affect the health of the family. Those in higher social classes have a higher income and so may be able to afford a wider variety of foods from specialised shops and also may be able to afford membership to gyms or clubs, which will improve their health.

Even recently, links have been found between health and social class. The following graph demonstrates the link between death rates and social class.

The graph shows a link between social class and premature death, with those in lower social classes experiencing more instances of premature death.

Patterns of limiting long-term illness are similar to those of self-reported poor health. Among men, age-standardised rates were five times higher for those who were long-term unemployed or had never worked (43 per cent) than those in the professional and managerial group (9 per cent). The difference for women was slightly smaller, at 36 per cent and 10 per cent respectively

Rate per 1000,000

Age-standardised mortality rate by NS-SEC: men aged 25-64, England and Wales 2001–2003

Source: www.statistics.gov.uk/cci/nugget.asp?id=1899

© Crown copyright material is reproduced with the permission of the Controller of HMSO and the Queen's Printer for Scotland

Source: www.statistics.gov.uk/cci/nugget.asp?id=1007

Employment

Employment can have an impact upon the health and needs of individuals. On the positive side, employment provides a source of income, which impacts upon a person's ability to purchase goods. Employment can also give an individual a sense of value and self-worth, which can increase their self-esteem and well-being. On the negative side, employment can make individuals feel stressed, which can negatively impact upon their health and well-being. Employment could also be in an unsafe environment or in poor conditions, so injury or harm may be more likely. Employment that does not value a person, or undermines them, can negatively impact on that person's self-esteem. Access to employment can vary according to area.

People with impairments or disabilities may suffer from discrimination regarding employment so could be poorly paid, in unsatisfactory jobs or be unemployed and live on state benefits.

Culture

Culture may influence the way an individual acts and behaves. It can also have an impact on the needs of an individual. Because of cultural or religious beliefs, an individual may require special diets or particular care needs.

Diets are discussed in Unit 11 and cultural needs are discussed in Unit 6.

> **Key term**
>
> Culture – this refers to a way of life and does not include just religious beliefs. Service users may be from a travelling culture or vegetarian culture.

Living conditions

Living conditions can affect health depending on where in the world you live. People who live in under-developed countries or countries that have severe weather extremes, political unrest or war zones may suffer serious illness and disease because of a lack of medical care or access to medical help and education.

Living conditions in a western society may affect health if the housing is damp or poorly heated. Cramped or over-crowded conditions will also result in the spread of illnesses.

Poor living conditions may cause stress, depression or low self-esteem.

Income

A good income can have a positive impact, as it means that money is available to buy items for a healthy lifestyle, or to buy luxury goods. Having a low income can be a major source of stress and worry, and can prevent people from buying healthy or essential items, such as food and clothing.

Follow this weblink, which shows you how the wealth of our population is unevenly distributed: www.statistics.gov.uk/cci/nugget.asp?id-2.

Education

A positive experience of education can benefit an individual. It can lead to a sense of achievement and well-being and can increase a person's job prospects in later life. Education may also have some impact on health and well-being – for example, if a member of one family has some knowledge of healthy diets and lifestyles, they can educate their whole family about how to avoid certain illnesses and diseases. Deadlines and exam times can be a source of stress. People may experience bullying, which can negatively impact upon their self-esteem and well-being. Conversely, a lack of education can negatively impact upon someone's achievement. It may also damage their job prospects and financial prospects in later life.

Physical factors
Genetic inheritance

Individuals can inherit conditions from their biological parents. Examples of genetic conditions include cystic fibrosis, sickle-cell anaemia and Down's syndrome.

> ## Key term
>
> Genes – genes are our individual patterns in DNA, which make up our different characteristics, development and appearance.

Cystic fibrosis

Cystic fibrosis is a common, inherited condition and is life-threatening.

The Cystic Fibrosis Trust states the following facts:

- Cystic fibrosis affects over 8,000 people in the UK.
- Over two million people in the UK carry the faulty gene that causes cystic fibrosis – around 1 in 25 of the population.
- If two carriers have a child, the baby has a one in four chance of having cystic fibrosis.
- Each week, five babies are born with cystic fibrosis.
- Each week, three young lives are lost to cystic fibrosis.
- Around half of the CF population can expect to live over 35 years, although improvements in treatments mean a baby born today could expect to live even longer.

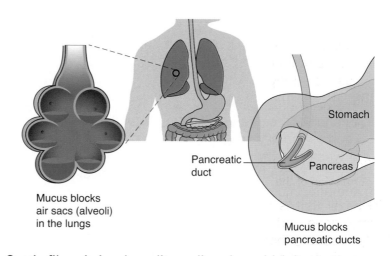

Cystic fibrosis is a hereditary disorder, which impacts primarily on the lungs and digestive system

Cystic fibrosis impacts on the internal organs of the body. Principally, the lungs and digestive system are affected and the result is that they are clogged with thick sticky mucus. As it is the lungs and digestive system that are especially affected, then this makes it hard for the individual with cystic fibrosis to breathe and digest food.

People with cystic fibrosis receive a number of treatments. Physiotherapy helps to clear the lungs. This helps prevent infections. Certain medications assist in clearing the mucus build-up and help prevent infections. Nutrition and enzyme tablets help the body to digest food and exercise benefits an individual's general health, as well as being a form of physiotherapy.

Sickle-cell anaemia

Sickle-cell anaemia is an inherited condition. Sickle-cell anaemia is common among black Caribbean, black African and black British communities. The condition impacts upon the red blood cells in the body. The result is that they sickle (form into a crescent shape). This may result in sickle-cell trait or sickle-cell anaemia.

'If two people who have the sickle-cell trait have a child, there is a chance that the child will inherit a pair of genes that both have the sickle-cell trait.

- 25 per cent chance that the baby will receive a pair of normal haemoglobin genes.
- 50 per cent chance that the baby will receive one normal gene and one mutated gene. In this case, they will not have sickle-cell anaemia, but they will have the sickle-cell trait.
- 25 per cent chance that the baby will receive a pair of mutated genes – they will have sickle-cell anaemia.

If one parent has the sickle-cell trait and the other parent has normal haemoglobin their baby will not get sickle-cell anaemia. But there would be a 50 per cent chance that the baby will receive the sickle-cell trait.'

Source: www.nhs.uk   © Crown copyright material is reproduced with the permission of the Controller of HMSO and the Queen's Printer for Scotland

Sickle-cell trait is a result of inheriting one normal gene and one sickle-cell gene. The body produces both normal and sickle-cell genes. Generally, a person with the sickle-cell trait will have no noticeable symptoms.

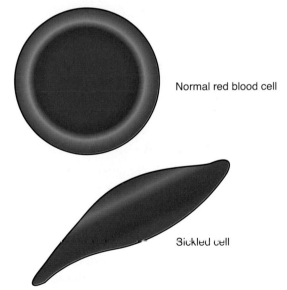

Normal red blood cell

Sickle-cell anaemia leads to a lack of the oxygen-carrying red blood cells. This results in the body not getting all the oxygen required to fully function and can leave the individual feeling tired or breathless.

In addition, one of the first symptoms that may appear is a condition known as 'hand–foot syndrome'. This occurs as a result of the sickle cells blocking the blood vessels in the hands and feet, causing a swelling. An individual may also appear jaundiced, which is an effect of damage to the liver. Sickle-cell anaemia can cause a build-up of dead sickle cells and the liver is not able to break down and deal with these.

Sickled cell

Red blood cells and sickle cells

One of the more serious consequences of sickle-cell anaemia is a sickling crisis. As the red blood cells are sickle-shaped, they can cause blockages and lead to a lack of oxygen. This may require treatment in hospital.

Down's syndrome

Down's syndrome is caused by the genetic make-up of an individual. People with Down's syndrome often have a number of noticeable features. These may include a flat facial profile, a small mouth, which can make the tongue appear slightly larger, and broader hands with shorter fingers. They may have medical conditions, such as heart problems, and sight or hearing problems. They will also have some degree of learning disability. Therefore, having Down's syndrome is likely to impact on that individual's physical, intellectual, emotional and social needs. People with Down's syndrome will need extra support and care throughout their lives.

Activity 5

Research the following genetic conditions: phenylketonuria (PKU), cystic fibrosis, sickle-cell anaemia, Down's syndrome.

- **What are they?**
- **How are they treated?**
- **How might each of these conditions impact upon the health and needs of the individuals affected?**

Disability

Service users who have an impairment may be disabled if adaptations or technical assistance is not provided to allow those service users to be included in everyday living activities. For example, a service user who has a hearing impairment will require hearing loops or aids to enable them to participate in daily living activities.

Sensory impairment

This usually means visual and hearing impairments which can influence service users depending on their age. Younger people may adapt easily to aids or assistance whereas an older person may have difficulty with new technology or accepting that they may have a problem. This may make the service user feel isolated as they may not be able to adapt to new or different surroundings. It is important for carers to recognise the needs of the service user and provide suitable technology, adaption or aids to enable the service user to be included.

Health factors

There are many benefits of physical exercise. These include more energy, reduced stress, stronger bones and muscles, improved sleep and a sense of achievement and enjoyment. Exercise also reduces your chance of developing health problems, such as coronary heart disease, stroke, high blood pressure, obesity or stress. Exercise can benefit mental and physical well-being. Have a look at the information on 'Keeping Your Heart Healthy' and 'Staying Active' on the British Heart Foundation's website at www.bhf.org.uk.

Different ages and gender may also affect a person's health and needs. However, it is important not to stereotype, but to ensure that all people are treated as individuals with individual needs.

> **Key term**
>
> Stereotype – making judgements or assumptions about a person or group of people without knowing the facts about them.

Age

Age impacts on health and needs – for example, the very young will require a lot of adult supervision and care; they will require developmental assessments and an immunisation programme to protect against common childhood illnesses, then education to enable them to become independent. Older service users will require care also to protect them and keep them safe in environments. As we age, we may be more vulnerable to illnesses and disease, so care, health and needs may vary through the life stages.

Gender

Research shows that men are less likely to visit the doctor so are not diagnosed with illness or disease. Research also shows that women have a longer life expectancy than men.

Particular diseases are more prevalent in men – for example, heart disease and bowel cancer. Also, some diseases are said to be genetically inherited and sex linked – for example, Duchenne muscular dystrophy and haemophilia are conditions that only males suffer from.

Women are more susceptible to media influence, and extreme diets may lead to eating disorders such as anorexia or bulimia.

Water and sanitation

A lack of clean water and appropriate sanitation can lead to the spread of water-borne disease, which may result in severe diarrhoea and possible death. Water may also be polluted with toxic or radioactive chemicals. The World Health Organisation (WHO) is responsible for improving access to safe drinking water. Follow this weblink

Health education information about personal hygiene

to discover the work of the WHO in other areas of health and well-being around the world: www.who.int/en.

Pollution

There are many areas of pollution that can impact on our health needs. Pollution may be in the form of air, light, water or noise. These kinds of pollution can have a number of effects on the health and needs of service users. For example, air pollution has been linked to breathing and allergy problems, which may cause or make asthma worse. Noise pollution can impact upon people socially and can be so extreme it can affect sleep patterns and cause anxiety and depression.

Activity 6

Using the internet, look for newspaper articles or news stories on different kinds of pollution and the effects they might have. The BBC News website (www.bbc.co.uk/news) is a good source. What are some of the implications for health listed within these articles? Can you think of any other effects of pollution?

Lifestyle factors

Personal hygiene

Personal hygiene is about cleanliness of the body. Poor or inadequate personal hygiene can impact upon a person's health and their needs. It can have physical consequences and lead to an increased risk of infection and illness. Maintaining a good standard of personal hygiene can prevent the spread of illness and disease.

Furthermore, bacteria and fungus on the skin that are not washed away can lead to acne, body odour or athlete's foot. There may also be social consequences – people may not want to be friends with that person; some people may find it hard to tell someone about poor personal hygiene and may choose to avoid that individual rather than discuss this with them. This in turn can impact upon a person's emotional health and well-being. Personal hygiene of workers in health and social care environments is very important to prevent the spread of infection.

Diet

A diet is the food that a person eats.

A healthy diet is one that is balanced. It should contain foods from all five food groups. The more balanced and nutritious a diet is, then the healthier a person will be.

The five main food groups are as follows:

- Fruit and vegetables – these contain a variety of nutrients such as fibre, vitamins and minerals.
- Bread, cereal and potatoes – these provide energy as they contain carbohydrates and fibre.
- Dairy and milk products, including yoghurt and cheese.
- Meat, fish and alternatives – these provide us with protein, which is essential for growth and repair.
- Fats and foods containing sugars – these should be eaten in small amounts.

Eating too much or too little of a particular food group can have consequences for health. Eating too many fatty foods may lead to obesity. This can lead to an increased risk of heart attacks or heart disease. Eating too much sugar can lead to tooth decay. A lack of certain vitamins and minerals can also lead to health problems. Some examples are shown in the table below.

Table 3.01 Vitamins and minerals

Vitamin/Mineral	Foods	Deficiencies
Vitamin A	Liver, cheese, eggs, oily fish	A weakened immune system; too much can lead to weakened bones
Vitamin B12	Meat, cheese, eggs	Anaemia where not enough oxygen is carried in the blood. Can cause tiredness, fainting and breathlessness
Vitamin C	Orange, broccoli	Deficiency can lead to scurvy
Calcium	Milk, cheese, broccoli, cabbage	Deficiency can lead to bone and tooth decay
Iron	Meat, beans, whole grains, watercress and curly kale	Deficiency can lead to anaemia

The Department of Health also recommends that everyone in the UK should eat at least five portions of fruit and vegetables per day.

There are many benefits of eating a healthy diet. It can help improve concentration and increase energy and it can also prevent diseases such as 'a third of all cancers, diabetes, osteoporosis (thinning bones), heart disease, strokes and tooth decay, as well as many other diet-related conditions'.

Source: www.nhsdirect.nhs.uk/articles/article.aspx?articleId=474&sectionId=34

Exercise

Exercise is beneficial to the body for a number of reasons.

Evidence shows that regular exercise can:

- reduce the risk of getting type 2 diabetes

- reduce the risk of developing coronary heart disease
- reduce high blood pressure
- promote bone density to protect against osteoporosis
- reduce the risk of cancer and prevent bowel cancer
- help to maintain a healthy weight in combination with a balanced diet
- reduce the risk of death or poor health if you are already overweight or obese
- treat depression
- help you to feel better about yourself and reduce stress
- improve sleep.

Source: http://hcd2.bupa.co.uk/fact_sheets/html/exercise.html

Therefore, a lack of exercise can have a negative impact upon an individual. For more information, go to 'Keeping Your Heart Healthy' and 'Staying Active' on the British Heart Foundation's website at www.bhf.org.uk.

There are many benefits of physical exercise. These include more energy, reduced stress, stronger bones and muscles, improved sleep and a sense of achievement and enjoyment. Exercise can also help improve health problems such as coronary heart disease and stroke, high blood pressure, obesity or stress. Exercise can benefit mental and physical wellbeing.

Smoking

Around one in four British adults smoke. According to Cancer Research UK, men are still more likely to smoke than women – 27 per cent of men and 25 per cent of women smoke.

Smoking causes fingers and teeth to become stained, hair, breath and clothes to smell and can cause your skin to dry out. This can affect someone's appearance. If someone continues to smoke, there are many serious effects on the body. The habit can cause cancers, especially of the lung, mouth or throat. It can lead to chronic bronchitis or emphysema and can affect breathing and circulation. The most common conditions caused by smoking are coronary heart disease, lung cancer, bronchitis, emphysema and pneumonia (source: NHS).

Activity 7

Investigate a class discussion. What do you think about the smoking ban which came into effect in England on 1 July 2007? (Scotland, Wales and Northern Ireland already had similar smoking bans in place.) The government hopes it will help smokers to quit and discourage children from taking up the habit. Do you think the smoking ban will work?

Cancer

Smoking is a big risk factor for many types of cancer. Cancer Research UK states that tobacco is the cause of 90 per cent of lung cancers, and 29 per cent of all cancers are linked to smoking (source: www.cancerhelp.org.uk/help/default.asp?page=3823). Smoking can increase your risk of developing cancers in other parts of the body such as the mouth, nose, stomach and larynx (voice box).

Coronary heart disease

Smoking increases the risk of coronary heart disease. The British Heart Foundation found that mortality from coronary heart disease is around 60 per cent higher in smokers than in non-smokers (source: www.heartstats.org/topic.asp?id=876). Smoking can also cause problems such as atherosclerosis, which is a build-up of substances in the arteries. Smokers may be more prone to heart attacks and strokes as smoking can damage the blood vessels of the body. Smoking also damages the airways of the body. This can lead to respiratory conditions such as bronchitis.

Alcohol abuse

Alcohol abuse can affect a person's health and well-being. As different types of drinks have different amounts of alcohol, we use a system of units to compare the amount of alcohol within them. For example, a small glass of wine is about one unit, whereas a pint of standard-strength beer is about two units. The current Department of Health guidelines state that women should drink no more than two to three units of alcohol per day and men should drink no more than four to five units per day. However, statistics show that many people in the UK do not stick to these guidelines.

Over-consumption of alcohol can have serious implications for a person's health. Statistics from the NHS show that around half of motorists (aged 16–60) killed in road accidents have more alcohol in their system than the legal drink-drive limit. Statistics also show that around 1,000 children under the age of 15 are admitted to hospital each year needing emergency treatment due to alcohol poisoning.

In the short term, drinking too much alcohol can lead to blurred eyesight, slurred speech, loss of balance, nausea and vomiting – this is what is meant by 'being drunk'. Alcohol can also affect your reactions and your judgement, causing heightened emotions or loss of inhibitions. Due to the high sugar content and alcohol being a diuretic (it increases the rate of urination), alcohol causes dehydration and headaches. If someone continues to consume an excessive amount of alcohol there can be many long-term consequences. Alcohol itself is a depressant drug and can affect

> **Key term**
>
> Binge drinking – this term relates to drinking an excessive amount of alcohol in a short amount of time, leading to serious health and social consequences.

people in different ways: some may just 'feel down' but others may suffer severe depression. The Department of Health links 25,000 deaths each year to alcohol. Long-term alcohol abuse can lead to liver disease (cirrhosis), heart failure, brain damage, high blood pressure, as well as various types of cancer. For more information, go to the Alcohol Concern website at www.alcoholconcern.org.uk.

Drugs

There is a wide range of drugs – some are legal and some are illegal. We can all think of legal drugs – for example, paracetamol and ibuprofen can be bought in a shop or pharmacy. Used in small quantities, they should not cause harm. However, using illegal drugs can have serious implications – not only can they affect an individual's health and well-being but their use can lead to prosecution.

Drugs can be divided into different categories: stimulants and depressants. Stimulants increase activity in the brain. Some examples of stimulants are tobacco or ecstasy. Depressants, meanwhile, decrease activity in the brain. Alcohol is in this category. Drugs may also be hallucinogens – these alter the way a person sees or hears things. Hallucinogenic drugs include cannabis, magic mushrooms and LSD. Drugs that have a painkilling effect are known as analgesics – such as heroin. Some drugs, such as cocaine, may have a stimulant effect at first, then cause depression later. For some people, alcohol also has this effect. As you can see, people respond to drugs in different ways.

Follow this weblink to find out further information about drug misuse: www.talktofrank.com.

Stress

Stress can help people to work; however too much stress can cause problems.

People can become stressed for a variety of reasons. These may include personal issues (emotional or financial worries) or work-related issues.

There are a number of consequences of stress, including headaches, tiredness and anxiety in the short term and an increased risk of heart disease, depression or stomach ulcers in the long term.

Individuals who are chronically stressed may show some of the following symptoms:

- periods of irritability or anger
- apathy or depression
- constant anxiety
- irrational behaviour
- loss of appetite
- comfort eating
- lack of concentration
- loss of sex drive
- increased smoking, drinking, or taking recreational drugs.

There can also be physical effects, which may include the following:

- excessive tiredness
- skin problems, such as eczema
- aches and pains resulting from tense muscles, including neck ache, back ache and tension headaches
- increased pain from arthritis and other conditions
- heart palpitations
- feeling sick
- stomach problems
- for women, missed periods.

Working patterns

Health problems associated with working shifts include peptic ulcers, cardiovascular disease, chronic fatigue, excessive sleepiness and difficulty sleeping. Shift workers also tend to be more overweight due to poor eating habits and lack of exercise. They also have a higher divorce rate, have worse rates of substance abuse and depression and are more likely to view their jobs as stressful.

However, some families' income depends on anti-social work. Therefore, the economy of the family is improved, so these working patterns can be seen as having a positive effect on the family.

Sexual practices

Sexual orientation

Sexual orientation refers to the general attraction a person feels towards one sex or another (or both). Most people are familiar with the terms 'hetero-sexual' or 'straight', where people are attracted to the opposite sex. Other people are attracted to people who are the same sex as them (lesbian or gay) or people of both sexes (bisexual).

Recently, a number of legal measures have required people to be treated equally regardless of sexual orientation.

- In 2001, the age of consent was standardised at 16 for all.
- In 2003, the Employment Equality (Sexual Orientation) Regulations made it unlawful to discriminate against a person in employment and training on the grounds of sexual orientation.
- Since November 2004, the Civil Partnership Act has given same-sex partners clear legal rights, similar to those previously only available to married couples.
- Since April 2007, the Equality Act (Sexual Orientation Regulations) 2007 has prohibited discrimination on grounds of sexual orientation in the provision of goods, facilities and services.

Source: http://www.dh.gov.uk/prod_consum_dh/groups/dh_digitalassets/documents/ digitalasset/dh_095635.pdf

Sexually Transmitted Infections

There are many examples of sexually transmitted infections (STIs). Some are listed below (source: www.bupa.co.uk).

Chlamydia

This is the most common STI and is a bacterial infection. Often, women with chlamydia will have no symptoms, or only mild ones. It has been estimated that chlamydia affects up to one in ten women, with 75 per cent showing no symptoms at all. For women, possible symptoms include lower abdominal pain, bleeding between periods or unusual vaginal discharge. For men, symptoms include discharge from the penis or pain on passing urine. Chlamydia is serious, as it can cause long-term pelvic pain or even infertility if it is not treated, but it can be treated quite easily with antibiotics. There are now self-testing kits, which can be bought for home testing.

> **Key term**
>
> Sexually transmitted infection (STI) – infections that are transmitted by unprotected sexual activity.

Pubic lice

Pubic lice may live in pubic or other body hair. They lay eggs that stick to the hairs and this can cause itching and inflammation. This can be treated with lotions and special shampoos.

Gonorrhoea

This is also a bacterial infection. For women, symptoms may include an increase in vaginal discharge and pain on passing urine. Men may have a discharge. Again, there may not be any symptoms. If it is not treated, gonorrhoea can lead to pelvic inflammatory disease, infections, inflammations and infertility in both men and women. It can be treated with antibiotics.

HIV and AIDS

AIDS (Acquired Immune Deficiency Syndrome) is a disease of the immune system that is caused by HIV (Human Immunodeficiency Syndrome). HIV can attack the immune system, meaning that a person cannot fight off infections. This causes the immune system to become weaker. It is infectious and can be passed on through unprotected sex.

There is currently no cure for AIDS, although drugs can be taken which slow down the progress of the disease. AIDS is diagnosed through a blood test. For more information, go to the website of the Terrence Higgins Trust (www.tht.org.uk), an HIV and AIDS charity.

There are many different forms of contraception available, although only condoms can protect against STIs. As we have seen, STIs can have a range of short- and long-term consequences. The most important thing to remember is that early detection is the key to successful treatment.

Social and community networks

Living within a community that provides access to support and care will give service users a sense of wellbeing and comfort. How accessible a service is can affect the health and needs of individuals. This accessibility can be for a number of reasons. It could be to do with the services within the local area, or that barriers exist which stop individuals from accessing a service. These barriers could be financial, social or cultural, or from individual preferences.

Health factors

A number of health factors may also impact upon the health and needs of an individual.

Look at the flow charts below which show a range of health factors which could influence the health and wellbeing of individuals:

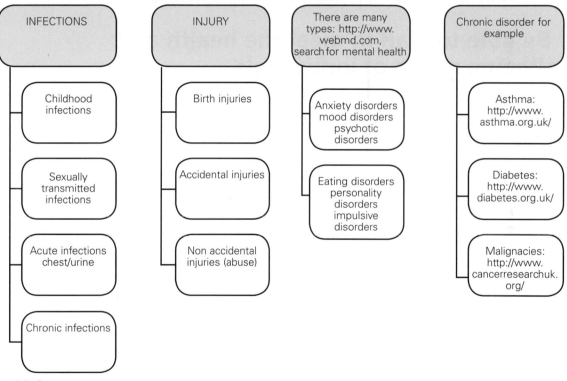

Health factors

Activity 8

Using the headings below create and information booklet with pictures and diagrams that explains factors which affect the everyday needs of individuals.

Divide your booklet into 4 sections.

Use some examples from a range of the following factors:

- Socio-economic factors
- Physical factors
- Lifestyle factors
- Health factors.

3 Be able to plan to meet the health and wellbeing needs of individuals

When assessing the health and well-being of individuals, it is essential to consider all of their needs. These could be physical, intellectual, emotional, or social or spiritual. Sometimes these needs link together and one can impact upon another. For example, if an individual is very isolated within a community, these can affect their emotional needs.

Individuals may have specific health and care needs. These include personal care and, therefore, assistance with washing, dressing, toileting for example may be required. Health and care needs also include mobility needs such as assistance in getting around using mobility aids. Some individuals may have additional learning needs or

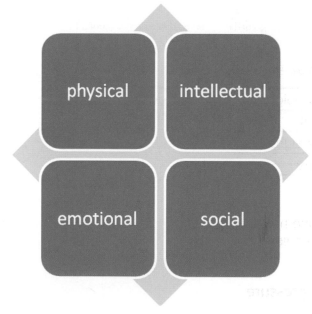

Needs

have medical or surgical interventions which may impact on their specific needs. Service users may require medication or specific care packages.

Needs

Needs are discussed earlier in the unit and can be separated into physical, intellectual, emotional and social aspects (see diagram, p. 76 and table, p. 78).

Assessment of general health and wellbeing

Asking questions such as in a questionnaire is a good source of information for practitioners. Questions could be open or closed and different information may be gained from both types.

Personal history of the individual should be considered and inform future care planning. This could include anything that has been tried in the past and was unsuccessful. It could also include family history. Personal information, such as marital status, living arrangements and support networks, will all be important when planning for individual needs.

Health and care practitioners can take a number of physical and psychological measurements that can give an indication of an individual's health and well-being.

Body mass index

Body mass index or BMI measures the body fat of an individual. It is taken using the height and weight of an individual, which are calculated to give a score. The calculation is weight (kg) divided by height (m^2). This score can then be assessed using the following table.

Table 3.02 Body mass index

Underweight	Below 18.5
Normal	18.5–24.9
Overweight	25.0–29.9
Obesity	30.0 and above

However, the body mass index calculation does have some limitations. If someone has a high level of muscle, then it may lead to a higher reading, which could indicate that an individual is overweight when this is not the case.

Blood pressure

Blood pressure is usually monitored in the upper arm. It measures the force that blood exerts on the walls of the blood vessels. An example of a blood pressure reading is 120/80 mm/Hg. Two figures are given. These are systolic pressure, which is the first and higher reading. This is the pressure in the vessels when the heart is beating. The second and lower reading is

Needs	Health needs from chronic conditions
Physical	Service users who suffer with conditions such as asthma, diabetes or emphysema may have difficulties with mobility so it is important to provide them with the correct medication and any aids or adaptation in their environments they may require to help with their mobility. This may require work with other care agencies so adaptations at home can be made, for example, rails, ramps or stair lifts. Some service users may require a carer on a regular basis for help with personal care and housework. Some chronic conditions require special diets to control the condition for example diabetes or Crohn's disease. Safety and security should be considered in individuals environments to avoid accidents. Warmth of the environment is important, particularly in the very young or older service users. If physical health is being compromised by harmful activities then service users may require additional support and education from other agencies to give up smoking, for example, or to reduce alcohol intake.
Intellectual	As service users are from a range of ages and it is always important to provide intellectual stimulation. For example, if a younger person suffers a chronic condition they may miss some education while they are in hospital so it may be necessary for home tutoring or special tutoring to be provided while they are still in hospital. Older service users should also be offered activities which encourage them to keep their minds active. These may be group or individual activities. It is important to find out what hobbies and interests service users have so that appropriate activities can be provided (this is discussed in Unit 9)
Emotional	Service users who suffer chronic illnesses may feel isolated, lonely or depressed. It is the job of a carer to recognise these signs and encourage service users to learn to adapt to their condition and give them support. Carers can refer service users to relevant support groups who can provide counseling which give service users coping strategies and provide support from others who may have the same condition. Parents may need support to encourage their children to adapt to their condition and to acquire knowledge and awareness about new research and medication.
Social	We should encourage our service users to have positive social contacts so they can help to change habits if necessary. One example of this is that if a service user needs to give up smoking advice can be given to the whole family to encourage a positive attitude towards health. Some service users may need social contact if they are isolated so support groups, lunch clubs or visiting services may be necessary. Younger service users should always be encouraged to see the positive benefits of social activities (discussed in Unit 9). Support groups can play an important role as young service users may feel they are the only one with a chronic condition and may not feel accepted by their peer groups.

the diastolic reading and is the heart at rest. High blood pressure or hypertension can lead to heart conditions or stroke.

Pulse rates

The pulse rate is the rate at which your heart beats and is measured in beats per minute. Pulse rates are taken where an artery crosses a bone. A good example of this is in the wrist. A baseline pulse rate measurement is taken when the person is at rest, often as soon as they have woken up. This is because your pulse rate can vary, especially during and after exercise. A higher or lower pulse rate can indicate different conditions. A high pulse rate, for example, could be due to exercise or could be because a person is anxious or ill. A low pulse rate is often due to high fitness levels but can also be because someone has a condition such as hypothermia.

Peak flow

Peak flow measures the rate of expiration of breathing. The measurements are higher if a person is well and will lower if airways are constricted. A lower reading may be displayed if an individual is asthmatic or has lung problems. The normal value can depend on age, gender and weight of an individual. Results can be monitored or plotted on a graph.

All these measurements can be used to inform and monitor assessments. They provide a baseline from which to begin planning for an individual.

Activity 9

Choose one of the following and produce an action plan. Remember to include possible sources of help and advice.

- Billy eats an unhealthy diet and drinks 30 units of alcohol a week.
- Julie has few friends and smokes 10 cigarettes a day.
- David has poor personal hygiene and does little exercise.

Planning

Once you have established the needs of your service users it is important to plan their care.

Developing a plan to meet the needs of an individual may lead to short-, medium- and long-term goals being identified.

These may be linked and the medium-term and long-term goals may be built upon the short-term goals. All goals should be achievable and realistic. Achieving a goal can increase an individual's self-esteem and feeling of self-worth and, therefore, it should not be unachievable. Goals should also have a time frame and dates for review so the plan can be altered if necessary.

Once an assessment has taken place and the plan has been designed, then it will be implemented. This involves putting the decisions made into place; this should be monitored to ensure that any problems or issues are addressed. They should then be reviewed to address any new needs or to cease anything that is not needed. This also ensures that anything that is in place that is not effective can be altered to meet the needs of the individual.

See Unit 8 for more information on the care planning cycle.

Principles of planning to meet individual needs

Care planning should be holistic. This means that all needs should be considered and not just one type of need, e.g. physical in isolation. By doing this, it can lead to an improvement in health and wellbeing. The personal circumstances and wishes of an individual should be considered. The strengths that an individual could have may also be built upon and should also be considered and not just areas that need to be supported.

Summary

By the end of this unit, you should understand why it is necessary to identify the needs of individuals who will be in your care.

You will understand the need for assessing and planning for individual needs and be aware of the need to plan for different ages, stages and abilities.

This unit will have given you an understanding of the factors that may affect individuals and, therefore, affect how you plan care for them. You will also be aware of how to improve various aspects of a service user's health and well-being or know where to access help for your service user.

As a care provider, you should always focus on your service user and remember that your care is holistic in its approach and non-judgemental in its delivery.

Grading grid

In order to pass this unit, the evidence that the learner presents for assessment needs to demonstrate that they can meet all the learning outcomes for the unit. The assessment criteria for a pass grade describe the level of achievement required to pass this unit.

P3   P4   M1   D1

Activity 10

P3 With permission, you should carry out an assessment on a chosen individual's health and wellbeing. This could be a friend, family member or could be based on a character from a television programme.

You may need to formulate a questionnaire to gather initial information about your individual's needs. You should cover physical, intellectual, emotional and social needs. This could be written in the form of a short case study followed by their needs.

P4 requires you to produce a plan to improve the health and wellbeing of your chosen individual.

The plan should include short-term and long-term targets for your chosen individual; they should be realistic and achievable. You could do this in a table format.

M1 in a piece of writing explain how the plan meets the needs of your chosen individual.

For example, if your case study needs to give up smoking explain why you have put in short-term and long-term goals, the person's long-term goal may be to give up smoking but that would be impossible straight away so in the short-term they could reduce the amount they smoke or buy fewer cigarettes each week, see their GP for help or start nicotine replacement therapy.

D1 requires written evidence that explains why (justifies) the plan.

Take into account the individual circumstances and preferences; you could explain why the individual has to give up smoking gradually. This could be because all their friends smoke so it will be difficult at first to change habits and not have a cigarette at coffee break as usual.

Assessment and grading criteria

To achieve a pass grade the evidence must show that the learner is able to:	To achieve a merit gradethe evidence must show that, in addition to the pass criteria, the learner is able to:	To achieve a distinction grade the evidence must show that, in addition to the pass and merit criteria, the learner is able to:
P1 outline the everyday needs of individuals (see Activity 4) [IE1, IE2, RL3, SM2, SM3]		
P2 explain factors which affect the everyday needs of individuals (see Activity 8) [IE1, IE2, RL3, SM2, SM3]		
P3 explain how the plan meets the health and wellbeing needs of the individual (see Activity 10) [IE1, CT1, RL3, TW3, SM2, SM3, EP4]		
P4 produce a plan for improving the health and wellbeing of an individual (see Activity 10)	**M1** explain how the plan meets the health and well being needs of the individual (see Activity 10)	**D1** justify how the plan takes into account the individual's circumstances and preferences (see Activity 10)

Further Reading

Pritchard, J. and Kemshall, H., 1995, *Good Practice in Risk Assessment and Risk Management,* London: Jessica Kingsley Publishers
Sprenger, R. A. and Fisher, I., 2007, *The Essentials of Health and Safety: A Guide for Carers*, Doncaster: Highfield Publications

Weblinks

www.patient.co.uk
www.netdoctor.co.uk
www.bbc.co.uk/health
www.nhsdirect.nhs.uk
www.bupa.co.uk

Unit 4
Ensuring Safe Environments in Health and Social Care

Health and social care workers have a duty of care to those they care for and to the public in general. This means they have a responsibility to make sure all precautions have been taken so that no one comes to harm. To make sure they can carry out these responsibilities, they need to know the law concerning health and safety, particularly when at work.

This unit provides an introduction to health and safety issues and the knowledge which is needed to ensure that the environments in which health and social care activities take place are safe, for both those who work in them and people who use health and social care services.

Learning outcomes:

In this unit you will learn about:

● potential hazards in health and social care environments

● the main principles of health and safety legislation applied to health and social care

● understand risk assessment processes related to health or social care.

1 Know potential hazards in health and social care environments

It is important to understand the difference between hazard and risk. A hazard is a danger, something that causes harm. A risk is the likelihood of any harm actually occurring.

Hazards can be avoided, or the possibility of harm reduced, if we understand the level of risk that a particular hazard poses, given the specific circumstances.

For instance, many sporting or outdoor activities are hazardous, but the risks of injury or death are minimised by the rules and precautions put in place to protect people who participate in such activities.

Similarly, crossing the road is a hazardous activity and the risk varies according to circumstances. For example, how much traffic is there? How fast is it travelling? How wide is the road and how long would it take you to cross it? You may take longer if you have small children, you are older or you have a lot of things to carry. Where is the best place to cross? How far can you see?

Activity 1

Think about the following activities and write down three hazards and the risks they pose for people engaging in the activity. Then think of three ways in which the risks you have identified could be minimised. You could do this in pairs or as a quiz.

- **Skateboarding**
- **Cricket**
- **Rock climbing**
- **Surfing**
- **Bungee jumping**
- **Leisure park or fairground rides.**

There are many types of hazards and we each face them every day. Even simple activities, such as making a cup of tea, can be hazardous; for example, if the cupboard storing the cups is directly above the kettle and the kettle is switched on, someone reaching for a cup could be scalded by steam from the kettle. If the kettle is very full and therefore heavy, a person may find it difficult to pour out the boiling water accurately and so on.

In health and social care, hazards can arise from situations in which people need help to carry out normal activities because they are incapacitated in some way. For example, someone who has a fracture of the leg or ankle and has to use crutches to get around will be less able to avoid obstacles, will struggle to get up stairs and will be unable to carry things. In such a situation, self-care poses hazards; how can such a person manage to cook a meal? Or make a hot drink? What assistance will they need to keep clean or to have a bath or shower?

An everyday hazard

Health and social care activities take place in many different settings, which are both public and private space. For example, district nurses and social care workers may provide care for people in their own homes, perhaps following a hospital stay. Other health and social care workers may work in a health centre or care home. People who work in these settings have different responsibilities for the health and safety of the people who work there as well as the people who use the setting.

> ### Key term
>
> Setting – the location in which health and social care activities take place.

Sometimes you will hear references to *environments*; these usually refer to the immediate surroundings or location and they can be either public space, which is open to everyone, or private space, which is usually owned by individuals or private companies and is only accessible to certain people, usually by invitation. It is important to understand that health and social care practitioners have no right of entry into a person's home and can only enter with the individual's permission, the same as a guest.

The external environment means outside spaces, and is about what you can see, such as the physical surroundings, as well as the things that are invisible, such as the air you breathe. It takes in geographical location, such as the county, town or village someone lives in, as well as the type of environment, such as urban or built environment (town or city) or rural environment (village or country town). The external environment can have an effect on health and local authorities have responsibility for much of the external environment in towns and cities, since much of it is public space. It is important to note that external health and care environments also include recreational space, e.g. garden, playground, or an outing and this can be either public (playground) or private (garden).

The internal environment is inside or indoors, often in a particular room or space. Internal health and care environments can be private space, such as an individual's home, a private facility, such as a residential care home, or public space, such as a health centre or clinic.

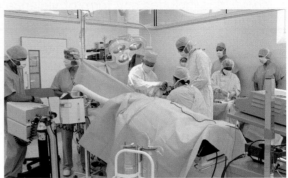

Different environments

External hazards

There are different types of hazards found in the external environment, all of which can have an effect on the physical or mental health of individuals. Broadly, these are as follows:

- *physical*: such as the condition of pavements and roads, the volume of traffic and the adequacy of street lighting
- *biological*: such as the presence of rats, mice or other vermin, wasps and other stinging insects, dogs and farm animals
- *chemical*: examples include herbicides and pesticides used in gardens and allotments, fertilisers used on farms, which can pollute water, traffic fumes and other industrial pollution
- *social*: external social hazards include things like noise pollution and anti-social behaviour.

Clearly, some of these things are more hazardous than others and people's exposure to any of them will depend on where they live; for example, noisy neighbours are not likely to disturb someone living on a farm, but they are likely to be more at risk from pesticides and fertilisers than someone living in an inner-city flat.

Internal hazards

Internal hazards can be considered in the same categories as external hazards, although the actual hazards are slightly different. For example:

- *physical*: includes things like faulty or dangerous appliances and furniture that is broken, unsafe or does not meet fire safety regulations, worn and dangerous carpets or floor coverings, insufficient heating, leaking and draughty accommodation
- *biological*: this might include mice or cockroaches, lice or other vermin or parasites; biological hazards are also caused by poor food hygiene, preparation and cooking and general lack of cleanliness, including the inadequate control of infection
- *chemical*: chemical hazards include cleaning products and other household products, such as air fresheners as well as medicines
- *social*: this includes any form of violence or abuse, including bullying and harassment.

Some biological hazards are specific to certain environments – for example, ionising radiation occurs as either electromagnetic rays (present in X-rays and gamma rays) or particles and can be found in hospital environments, where the technology is used in diagnostic imaging.

Accidents

The most common accident suffered by people of all ages is falls. Many of these occur in the home and they are common across all age groups. However, the risk of falls is greater among children, who may not realise the risk of, for example, climbing onto objects, and older people whose balance and judgement may be impaired by illness or medication. In addition, older people may have weaker muscles due to lack of exercise, making them more likely to lose their balance and fall. Falls are the most common reason for older people being admitted to hospital, most of which occur in the home. It is estimated that 75 per cent of deaths from falls occur in the home environment. Other common accidents include burns and scalds, cuts and bruises and accidental poisoning.

People who use health and care services often move from one environment to another and this can mean that the hazards and risks they face will change, so practitioners need to be aware of this and make an assessment of any precautions that may need to be taken, remembering that hazards might affect workers as well as those receiving care. It is also possible that a person may move from a safe environment (e.g. their home) to a less safe environment – for example, if they were taken on an outing or decided to go out by themselves. At the same time, it is the practitioner's role to keep individuals safe by assessing any risk and taking action, so in some cases it might be necessary for a person to be moved from an unsafe environment to a safer one.

The level of risk posed by hazards will depend on the nature of the hazard and how capable the person is of identifying the hazard and taking appropriate action. For example, older people may be at risk

> **Key term**
>
> Assessment – a judgement or estimate (e.g. of the level of risk).

when crossing the road because, while they can see the traffic and assess how fast it is travelling, they may believe they can walk faster than they actually can and underestimate the time taken to get across to safety. Children may be equally at risk when crossing the road but for different reasons. For example, they may be less able to judge how fast cars are moving due to lack of experience, and run across the road.

Activity 2   P1 M1

Ernest is an 85-year-old man who lives alone. He takes regular medication for high blood pressure and has some arthritis in his hips and knees.

Examine the picture of Ernest's living area above. How many hazards can you spot? What actions could you take to make Ernest's room safer?

Infection control

People receiving health and social care services are at greater risk of acquiring infection, mainly because they are likely to have poor immunity as a result of long-standing ill health or general frailty. They may already have an infection that is being treated. Common infections include urinary infections, especially where there is a catheter in place, and respiratory infections. Both of these can become very serious if not treated.

In settings where people live close together, infection spreads rapidly and can be fatal – for example, in cases where there is vomiting and diarrhoea – so it is crucial that health and care workers know, understand and implement the principles of infection control, including *universal precautions*. Universal precautions prevent contact with body fluids and apply to all staff. Applying universal precautions involves wearing protective clothing and equipment such as barrier gowns, masks, gloves, goggles, etc. to prevent the infection of workers by blood-borne infective agents. Universal precautions must be used when treating any person, as it is not possible to tell who may have an infection.

> **Key term**
>
> Universal precautions – precautions taken to protect staff and patients from contamination and cross infection (e.g. wearing gloves and personal protective clothing).

Care workers can easily transmit infection from one person to another – not just in the care environment, but also from the care environment to their home and into the wider community. This is called *cross infection* and can happen when germs and bacteria present on a person's clothes or hands are passed to another by touching. Another way infection can be spread is by the inadequate cleaning of equipment or surgical instruments or through the air by sneezing – germs and bacteria are present in the nose and mouth and are carried through the air in droplets of moist air. This is why it is important to use a handkerchief or tissue and wash hands after blowing the nose. Most healthy people are able to resist infections as the body's immune system provides an effective defence; however, if the germs or bacteria are overwhelming in number or very virulent, infection may follow even in healthy people. In people who are ill, frail or who have an immature or compromised immune system, the risk of infection is much higher.

> **Key term**
>
> Cross infection – the passing on or transmission of harmful bacteria and viruses (germs) from one person to another.

To prevent infection, there must be constant monitoring of the care environment. This will involve:

- making sure that regular cleaning takes place, including cleaning of soft furnishings, and that deep cleaning of the care environment is undertaken periodically
- ensuring that all furniture and equipment is cleaned thoroughly after use and in between use by different service users – for example, cleaning the bath after every person
- ensuring that people suffering from infection are appropriately cared for (e.g. by ensuring protective clothing is worn and that, if necessary, they are cared for away from others)
- making sure that hand-washing facilities are easily available and hands are washed after every contact with a service user, before handling food and especially after helping with toilet care
- reporting broken or faulty equipment, or people who seem unwell
- staying away from work if you are not well.

Hand washing

Remember the most effective way of preventing infection is regular and thorough hand washing, because germs and bacteria are found on the skin, in folds and creases and under the nails. If hands are not washed regularly, after contact with each person, a care worker can spread germs and bacteria from one person to another.

When to wash hands:

- After direct contact with individuals receiving care and before dealing with the next person.
- Before carrying out any clinical activity, such as dealing with dressings or changing catheters.
- Before preparing, handling, cooking, serving or eating food or helping someone with eating or drinking.
- When hands look dirty or are likely to have come into contact with body fluids – blood, faeces, urine, and pus, for example. This applies even if gloves have been worn.
- After removing surgical or protective gloves.
- Following personal body functions, such as blowing the nose or using the toilet.
- When in doubt – wash!

These guidelines also apply to helping service users, patients and residents wash their hands.

How to wash hands:

- Remove any jewellery to make sure all areas are attended to.
- Rinse hands under warm running water. This loosens germs and dirt.
- Apply soap thoroughly over all surfaces of hands, paying particular attention to the backs of hands and fingers, the thumbs and under the nails as these areas are often missed.
- Rinse hands under warm running water to wash off remaining soap and bacteria.
- Dry hands thoroughly – wet or damp hands attract more germs and bacteria as they thrive in moist, warm conditions. Use paper towels or hot-air dryer. Cloth towels can harbour germs and bacteria so hands can easily be re-contaminated.
- Turn off the tap without touching it if possible – lever taps are best.
- Use hand lotion regularly to prevent chafing and broken skin as this is also a potential reservoir for germs and bacteria.

Waste disposal

Effective disposal of waste is important for helping to protect staff and service users, and for preventing infection and cross infection. Within health and social care settings, there are three main aspects of waste disposal.

- Non-clinical waste: including packaging, paper and general rubbish, which can all be disposed of through normal local authority waste collection and recycling processes.
- Food waste: this needs to be separated into compostable and non-compostable waste and disposed of according to local arrangements.
- Clinical waste: this includes contaminated (used) dressings, hygiene products, needles, catheters and soiled dressings, many of which may have been in contact with body fluids or other potentially infective material. Needles must be disposed of in a special hard plastic container called a *sharps* box, which has a special lid to prevent accidental injury through pricks and scratches. These are called needle-stick injuries and must be reported on an accident form (see RIDDOR below); procedures should also be in place for preventive medical treatment of needle-stick injuries. Other clinical waste must be placed in special bags and collected by an organisation licensed to dispose of it. Clinical waste is usually incinerated.

If waste is not disposed of promptly and safely, it can become a health hazard, attracting flies and vermin in extreme cases.

Safety and security

It is the responsibility of health and social care workers to ensure the safety and security of those they are caring for. However, employers also have a responsibility to keep their workers safe. Where health and care activities take place in hospitals, residential care or nursing homes, clinics and other places open to the public, these are called *regulated settings*. This is because the government approves regulations so there are rules about how such settings should be organised and run, and the authorities inspect them to make sure the rules are being followed. The regulations help organisations to keep both staff and service users safe; for example, the regulations say how many qualified members of staff should be available to look after a given number of children or older people in a particular setting.

In care settings where there are children or vulnerable adults, there may be restricted entry to the setting, including locked doors and entry phones. ('Vulnerable adults' is the term used to describe people who are unable to look after themselves and who may have mental impairment, such as dementia or mental ill health.) Visitors will have their identity checked and must sign the visitor's book, noting the time of their arrival and departure. This is not only to protect service users, but also to ensure that everyone can be accounted for in case of fire, for example. Service users have a right to refuse to see visitors and their wishes must be respected; it is good practice to ask visitors to wait until it is certain that the person is willing to see the visitor and that they are not receiving personal care or treatments at the time. All members of staff should wear an identity badge.

Everyone in health and social care settings contributes to health and safety, including service users, and all have different responsibilities. Employer's responsibilities include the following:

- Ensuring the health, safety and welfare of employees at work as far as is reasonably possible. This includes making sure the law relating to health and safety is upheld and regulations followed – for example, by having agreed policies and procedures in place and monitoring compliance.
- Consulting employees or their safety representatives on aspects of health and safety at work, making sure that employees have appropriate health and safety training – for example, about what to do in case of fire and how to move and handle the people being cared for, and how to use equipment safely.
- Carrying out risk assessments of the workplace and implementing measures that will minimise risk. In a health and care setting, this might mean making sure there are enough staff on duty, for example.
- Reporting injuries, accidents and infectious diseases as required by law.

Employee responsibilities include the following:

- Being responsible for following policies and procedures and taking reasonable care for their own safety and well-being and that of the people in their care.
- Cooperating with their employer – for example, by reporting any health and safety issues or concerns, making sure they take up training opportunities and keep up to date with current policies.
- Using the correct equipment, including personal and protective clothing, and anything provided for their health, safety and welfare.
- Using work items correctly and asking when unsure of the right way to do things.

Responsibilities of service users include the following:

- Cooperating with activities and procedures intended to keep them or those caring for them safe – for example, being prepared to be lifted using equipment.
- Not being aggressive towards staff or other people and letting staff know where they are going and when they will be returning.
- Reporting anything dangerous or hazardous that has not been attended to.
- Following the rules and asking questions if it is not clear why they are being asked to cooperate with a particular course of action.

While it is important for people to have the freedom to carry out their daily lives with the minimum of interference, it is important to remember that some of the people care workers look after are very vulnerable for different reasons. Some older people may be physically frail and not very strong, which can limit physical activity. Others may be physically strong but mentally vulnerable or confused, if they have suffered from mental ill health or dementia, for example. Others may have relatives who do not have the older person's best interests at heart. Children are vulnerable due to their small size and lack of understanding or experience of danger or hazardous situations.

The settings or premises in which care activities take place must be secure; that is, only people who are authorised to be on the premises should be there. This is why staff may be required to wear name badges, for example, and why it is everyone's responsibility to politely ask unfamiliar people why they are there. In people's homes, the care worker does not have any authority to take such action but must discuss this with the service user and remind them, if necessary, why they need to be sure of whom they allow into their homes.

When people are living in residential homes or sheltered housing, they should be free to come and go as they please, in theory. In practice, the fact that they need such support means that they often are unable to go out by themselves. Nevertheless, outings can and should be arranged. It may be possible for several residents to go out together, perhaps with a volunteer or care worker. When planning such an outing, a risk assessment should be carried out and everyone, residents included, needs to be aware of the rules that have been agreed. For example, that they all stay together and come back together, and that travel arrangements are agreed.

Activity 3   P1   M1   D1

Take a walk around your local area and make a note of all the things that could be considered a hazard to someone; think about who might be affected by the hazards (e.g. someone with limited eyesight or in a wheelchair, or a person on crutches). You can take pictures to show what you have found.

Next, do the same thing for an internal environment, preferably a care environment. Do not forget to ask permission first, especially if you want to take photos.

You could turn your findings into a presentation for the class, showing the pictures and stating why the things you have identified are hazards and what could be done to minimise the risk. You could also use your findings as the starting point to put together a health and safety poster.

2 Know the main principles of health and safety legislation applied to health and social care environments

When working in health and social care settings, it is important to be aware of the laws that are in place to protect both workers and those they care for. This includes knowing how the law influences what employers and employees must do to ensure health and safety in the care setting.

Health and Safety at Work Act 1974

This is the main piece of legislation (law) that covers workplace health and safety in the UK. The act makes clear the responsibilities of both employers and employees for safety and security, as well as any members of the public on the work premises (see on page 92). The Health and Safety at Work Act (HASAW) covers working conditions. For example, under the act, employers have responsibility for ensuring the workplace has:

- adequate ventilation: the circulation of fresh air without causing draughts
- an appropriate temperature, usually between 13 and 16 degrees Celsius, unless there are special circumstances (e.g. the work is very physical or the conditions are exceptional, such as working with frozen goods – in such circumstances, the employer has to provide protective clothing and extra breaks)
- facilities for workers to take regular breaks, every four hours
- a safe level of lighting and emergency lighting and power where a sudden loss would be dangerous (e.g. in a hospital where equipment is used to maintain life).

The role of the Health and Safety Executive (HSE)

The Health and Safety Executive (HSE) is responsible for ensuring compliance with the law in relation to safety at work (i.e. the 1974 HASAW Act).

The HSE website states that:

'our job is to prevent death, injury and ill health to those at work and those affected by work activities'.

In order to undertake these duties, the HSE is able to carry out inspections of work premises, investigate complaints about health and safety rules being broken and take action to enforce the rules. This can involve a range of actions, such as serving notice on duty holders.

For example, an improvement notice tells the duty holder such as the employer, what they must do to observe the rules and comply with the HASAW laws, and gives them a date by which they must have completed any action, such as replacing faulty equipment or parts.

A prohibition notice tells the duty holder to stop the activity immediately. This is used in situations where there is immediate and serious danger to workers or others.

In the most serious cases – for example, where there has been loss of life or continued breaches of the law in spite of notice being served – the HSE can prosecute organisations or individuals who are responsible and they can be heavily fined.

Below is an example of a HSE decision.

 ## Case Study – Manual handling at an NHS trust

'An HSE audit of an NHS Trust found poor manual handling practices, including employees transporting large quantities of medical records on inadequate trolleys. The Trust had failed to carry out suitable and sufficient risk assessments.

Outcome:

An Improvement Notice was served on the Trust requiring them to carry out suitable and sufficient risk assessments. The Trust complied with the Notice implementing the controls which involved among other things – redesigning medical records to avoid standing on desks; placing more records on micro fiche to reduce paper amounts and purchasing new trolleys which could be opened at the top and which also limited the weight staff had to push.'

Source: www.hse.gov.uk

The main responsibilities of the HSE can be summarised as follows:

- to provide information, advice and support on different aspects of health and safety to help prevent accidents, injury and ill health caused by work activities and ensure workplaces are safe
- to monitor compliance with the health and safety law and inspect work premises
- to enforce the law and prosecute those who fail to safeguard workers and others in the workplace.

(Source: www.hse.gov.uk)

Health and safety information should be available to all employees and it is the employee's responsibility to make sure they understand the rules designed to protect them. In workplaces with more than five employees, the law states that there must be a Health and Safety Law poster displayed where it can be clearly seen. The poster must provide the names and details of all health and safety representatives in the workplace with responsibilities under the HASAW laws, such as the designated first-aid person.

Activity 4

In pairs, carry out an investigation and research to find out how many fatal injuries there have been to workers according to the most recent figures.

See if you can also find out how many reported injuries there were and how many working days were lost.

Useful sources are the Health and Safety Executive and the Office for National Statistics.

The HASAW Act is the overarching law under which sit a number of important regulations, dealing with specific areas of health and safety. The combination of laws and the regulations covered by a particular law is known as *legislation.* Regulations say how the law should be applied and only by following the regulations properly can the law be obeyed. Some of these regulations are outlined below.

Management of Health and Safety at Work Regulations 1999 (amended 2003)

These regulations state how the HASAW Act must be interpreted as a legal requirement. They have been modified and amended over time to ensure that the UK laws are in line with those of the European Union (EU) Directive. Examples of areas covered by the regulations include the requirement to carry out risk assessment and eliminate risk as far as possible; to ensure that work is adapted so that most individuals can do it; to replace dangerous items used in work processes with less dangerous ones and to develop prevention policies to cover working conditions and the organisation of work.

In addition, the regulations require that a 'competent person' from within the organisation be appointed to be responsible for health and safety. A competent person is someone who has sufficient training and expertise in relation to health and safety to carry out such duties.

The revised regulations now cover the law relating to young people and expectant mothers at work and state that the Fire Precautions (Workplace) Regulations 1997 (amended 2003) are now enforced by health and safety authorities rather than the fire services. See www.hse.gov.uk/index.htm for more information.

Reporting of Injuries, Diseases and Dangerous Occurrences Regulations (RIDDOR) 1995

These regulations are intended to help the regulatory authorities identify where and how risks might arise. Consequently, there is a legal requirement for employers to record and report certain work-related accidents, diseases and dangerous occurrences. Accidents and dangerous occurrences are usually recorded in an accident or incident book. Similarly, some work-related diseases must be reported as they may be caused by exposure to environmental hazard. For example, some cancers, especially of bone or blood, can be caused by exposure to radiation such as from X-rays, and lung diseases can be caused by dust particles from coal or other minerals, mould or spores. Biological hazards from live or dead humans or animals can cause diseases such as anthrax, TB or leptospirosis.

Infectious diseases must be reported to minimise outbreaks or prevent epidemics (e.g. some types of influenza, measles, E-coli and salmonella). A dangerous occurrence is sometimes referred to as a 'near miss' or a 'critical incident' that could have resulted in a reportable injury. Dangerous occurrences must be reported to the local authority immediately and the accident/incident form sent to the Health and Safety Executive within ten days. Reports must be kept for three years. See www.hse.gov.uk/riddor/index.htm for more information.

Manual Handling Operations Regulations 1992 (amended 2002)

The aim of these regulations is to reduce injuries from lifting and handling objects and people. The term 'handling' refers to actions such as pushing, pulling, carrying, raising and lowering, as well as actual lifting. The regulations provide information for employers and employees in relation to things such as safe weights; however, the basis of the regulations is that manual handling should be avoided if at all possible and equipment used in preference. A risk assessment should always be carried out prior to lifting and handling, which means the whole operation must be assessed, including the role of the service user in manual handling and their capabilities. It is important and a statutory requirement (legal requirement) that employees in health and social care must all receive authorised manual handling training; many back and spinal injuries were caused to health workers in the past through inappropriate lifting. Regulations may include the type of clothes and shoes staff must wear to work to avoid injury when carrying out manual handling. Health and social care employers have responsibility for training employees in moving and handling techniques, including the correct and appropriate use of equipment. See www.hse.gov.uk/contact/faqs/manualhandling.htm for more information.

Control of Substances Hazardous to Health (COSHH) 1994 (amended 2002)

These regulations are very important as they cover using, storing and disposing of a range of substances that are potentially hazardous. Substances covered include things such as solvents, glues, and acids, together with cleaning agents and products containing such substances.

Many of these substances will have hazard signs displayed on them. As with other health and safety regulations, employers have a duty to carry out an assessment of the risk posed by hazardous substances and take action to minimise the risk, such as providing protective clothing and ventilation and ensuring people have been properly trained and instructed in the proper use of dangerous substances, including what action to take in case of spillages. See www.hse.gov.uk/COSHH/index.htm for more information.

Regulatory Reform (Fire Safety) Order 2005

This is known as the Fire Safety Order (FSO) and applies to all non-domestic premises in England and Wales, including common areas in blocks of flats or multiple-occupancy accommodation. Under this legislation, an appointed *responsible person* must carry out a fire safety risk assessment and put in place, implement and maintain a fire risk management plan. (The responsible person is likely to be the owner or manager, but in a larger organisation, such as an NHS trust, this is likely to be a particular post within the management structure.) Responsibilities include ensuring there is sufficient fire safety equipment in place (e.g. fire blankets, fire extinguishers) and that this is maintained. In practice, many organisations will have maintenance contracts with equipment suppliers for this. The local fire and rescue authorities are the enforcing authorities for the FSO and are required to audit business premises within their local area. They will provide support and advice on how to improve fire safety arrangements. As with other legislation under the HASAW Act, they can issue enforcement orders and instigate court proceedings for failure to comply. See www.communities.gov.uk/fire/firesafety/firesafetylaw for more information.

Another significant aspect of the HASAW Act is the requirement for employers to undertake a risk assessment of the workplace to employers and others. They are then responsible for putting in place the policies and procedures that ensure health and well-being – for example, making sure that warning signs are in place to identify a potential hazard, such as very hot water in the hand-washing facility. The water is required to be a particular temperature to minimise the risk of contamination (e.g. legionnaires' disease) so a warning sign is necessary so that people using the water can take precautions.

The role of the Health Protection Agency

The Health Protection Agency (HPA) was set up by the government in 2003 to provide advice and information to the general public, health professionals, national and local government. The main role of the HPA is to protect the public from infectious diseases and environmental hazards; for example, they are responsible for identifying and responding to health hazards and emergencies caused by infectious diseases such as influenza outbreaks or E-coli, and environmental hazards from chemicals, poisons or radiation. They work alongside the NHS and liaise closely with other agencies, such as the HSE and the Food Standards Agency (see below).

Activity 5

Carry out an inventory of your workplace, home or training placement. Identify hazardous substances by the signs on the containers and make a list of special precautions you need to take when using them and why

In addition to the HASAW Act, there are other laws that are important for ensuring the safety and security of people receiving health and social care services. One vital aspect concerns food safety, from production and supply, to handling and preparation.

Food safety

The main law relating to food safety is the Food Safety Act 1990 which has, since 1999, been amended to comply with European Union rules; it is important to note that the devolved administrations of the UK (Scotland, Wales and Northern Ireland) have their own country-specific versions of the act. This is the key legislation under which sit a number of important regulations. The main purpose of the Food Safety Act 1990 is to ensure that the food that people buy to eat is fit for human consumption and will do no harm. Although food safety legislation applies to everyone, the act is particularly relevant for food producers and anyone working in the production, storage, distribution and sale of food. It concentrates on fundamental issues and leaves much of the detail to secondary legislation and regulations. The main regulations relevant to health and social care work are concerned with food preparation for public consumption.

Food Hygiene Regulations 2006

These regulations apply to everyone who manages or works in a food business and provides food for the public, whether in a five-star restaurant or a village hall. In particular, anyone who handles food and whose actions could affect its safety must be properly trained in food hygiene so that they can identify the potential hazards relating to food storage, handling and preparation.

The responsibilities for food safety are shared between central and local government and their relevant counterparts in the devolved administrations (see above). The main bodies are the Department for Environment, Food and Rural Affairs (DEFRA), and the Food Standards Agency, created by the government in 2000 to protect the public's health and consumer interests in relation to food. At local government level, local authorities have responsibility for monitoring compliance with the laws concerning food safety. Part of the work of environmental health officers involves ensuring food hygiene regulations are enforced.

Table 4.01 Summary of key laws

Health and safety legislation	Brief description	Example of activities covered by this law
Health and Safety at Work Act 1974	This is the main law covering health and safety in the workplace. Both employers and employees have responsibility for complying with the law.	All activities in the workplace, including activities with service users.
Food Safety Act 1990; Food Hygiene Regulations 2006	Covers all aspects up to and including the production and supply, storage, preparation, cooking and serving of food.	The sourcing and supply of food for residential homes, the preparation, cooking and serving of food to residents. Meals on Wheels.
Manual Handling Operations Regulations 1992	Relates to any activities that involve moving objects or people.	Moving a person from bed to chair, from room to room or bathing.
Control of Substances Hazardous to Health (COSHH) 1994 (amended 2002)	Ensures substances are kept safe. This includes storing, using and disposing of substances. There should be guidelines and a risk assessment in place.	Activities involving flammable substances, such as some cleaning products, chemicals used in medical procedures, glues or paints.
Reporting of Injuries, Diseases and Dangerous Occurrences Regulations (RIDDOR) 1995	Ensures that incidents and accidents are documented, reported and monitored in the accident book.	Any accident, incident or 'near miss' (e.g. needle-stick injuries) needs to be recorded and reported.
Regulatory Reform (Fire Safety) Order (FSO) 2005	Relates to the arrangements for fire safety, including risk assessment.	All staff need to know what to do in case of fire.
Management of Health and Safety at Work Regulations 1999 (amended 2003)	Ensures that employers train staff in aspects of health and safety in the workplace.	Applies to all workplace activities.

3 Understand risk assessment processes related to health or social care

A risk assessment is an investigation into what can harm people in a particular situation or circumstance. The purpose of risk assessment is to help employers and staff decide whether there are sufficient precautions in place to prevent accidents or incidents, taking any additional action necessary to prevent or minimise the risk of harm from hazards that have been identified.

Risk assessments may be carried out in relation to the workplace and work activities, or they may be carried out in relation to the risks associated with personal care activities such as washing, dressing or bathing. When an assessment of someone's need for services is carried out, a person's general ability to undertake self-care and other daily activities such as shopping and cooking is usually part of the assessment.

Depending on the care setting, care workers may be involved in supporting access to leisure or learning for service users, for example, outings. The risks to health and safety must be assessed for everyone likely to be affected by the activity – staff, service users and the general public.

There are five steps in the planning of a risk assessment, as shown in the diagram below.

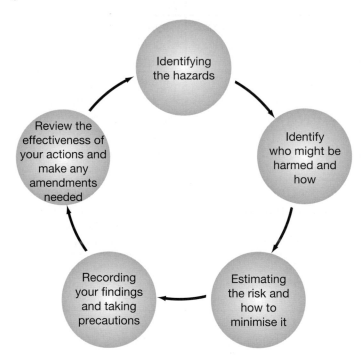

Five steps in planning a risk assessment

Identifying hazards

People identify hazards all the time. Activity 2 was, in effect, a risk assessment of Ernest's living accommodation. It is easier to identify hazards if you can see them, so the most common way of starting a risk assessment is to look closely at the environment you are assessing and, thinking about what usually happens in that particular environment, make a note of what might cause an accident or incident. For example, you might be working in a residential home where many of the residents use walking aids. Some residents may have poor eyesight or impaired hearing. The residents generally move from their rooms to the dining room for breakfast, then into the lounge for daily activities. It would be fairly straightforward to follow one of the residents and see what obstacles they needed to overcome or hazards they encountered during their journey.

It is not as easy to identify hazards that might be encountered in a less predictable environment, such as an outing with several residents, or young children. If an outing is being considered for the first time, it is advisable to have a 'dry run' if possible; drawing up a plan for the activity, thinking about potential hazards, then checking it out for real before considering the precautions to be taken.

Estimating and minimising the risk

It is important to think about who might be harmed and how; in other words, who might be at risk from the hazard? For example, falling on a hard surface while running might harm a child, but an adult may not have the same level of risk, as they are unlikely to be running. Therefore, in this situation, the risk would be higher to the child than the adult.

It is possible to estimate the risk on a scale of 1 to 5, with 5 representing the highest risk. In the example above, the risk to the adult of falling would be 0–1, whereas the risk to the child might be 2–3. If the child was very young and had not been walking long, the risk might be 4–5. If the path was icy and the adult old and frail, the risk would also increase to perhaps 3–4.

It is important to minimise any risk in a proportionate way; for example, it is not helpful to try and stop children running at all. However, in order to minimise the risk, there are several things you could do. For example:

- make sure the child is wearing sturdy shoes
- make sure they walk when on hard surfaces but provide the opportunity to run on grass, for example
- make sure younger children hold your hand until you come to a place where it is safer to run
- make sure you minimise any potential injuries by ensuring they are wearing thick trousers and a jacket to protect knees and elbows.

In health and care environments, you will need to consider the abilities and disadvantages faced by the particular service user group you are caring for, because what might pose a hazard to one group may be less hazardous to another.

For example, a fall indoors may cause a serious injury such as a fracture in an adult, especially an elderly, frail person. This can have a long-term effect on their ability to care for themselves; for example, if they fracture a hip and their mobility becomes permanently impaired or they break a wrist and it fails to regain full rotation. On the other hand, if a toddler falls indoors they are much less likely to sustain serious injury, partly because they have less far to fall, and partly because they can absorb the shock of falling better as their muscles and joints are less stiff. So whereas a small child may be more likely to fall (frequency increased) they are less likely to damage themselves unless they fall onto a hard surface or hit a projection (seriousness reduced).

Example of a risk assessment

You will need to list all the activities and all the hazards for each activity and fill in the review column after the activity. This can then be used to identify the success of the measures and any further precautions that need to be taken. It is impossible to completely eliminate risk, due to unforeseen and unexpected or unusual circumstances, which is why 0–1 is the lowest rating. It is important to show that all reasonable steps have been taken to reduce the risk from expected hazards.

Table 4.02 Example of a risk assessment

A	B	C	D	E	F	G
Activity	Hazard	Hazard rating	Person at risk	Control measures/ precautions	Hazard rating with precautions in place	Review
Making Christmas cards with children aged seven years	Cuts from scissors Poisoning from swallowing glue Inhaling glitter	2 1 3	Children	Use blunt-ended plastic scissors Use non-toxic glue Adult supervision of glitter use	0–1 0–1 0–1	

Activity 6

P1 P3 M1 D1

You are a domiciliary care worker and have been asked to undertake a risk assessment for helping 79-year-old Bill Williams to get ready for bed.

Bill has suffered a stroke and is paralysed on his left-hand side. He has some difficulty forming words and occasionally in swallowing. He sometimes gets depressed. He has a set of flash cards which he keeps with him to help him with communication. Bill uses a wheelchair.

This activity will involve helping him to move from the living room to the bathroom to wash and clean his teeth, then from the bathroom to his bedroom. He will need help to change into his nightwear and help to get into bed.

Following the sequence shown in the diagram on page 102, carry out a risk assessment for this activity with Bill, identifying potential hazards, and saying how you will minimise the risk. You may need to refer to moving and handling regulations.

How will you know that your risk assessment has been successful?

What things might need changing to minimise any risks to Bill or yourself?

How would you make a persuasive case for action to your manager?

You can use the example in Table 4.02 to write up your risk assessment, or access the HSE website for a form.

Summary

As a health and social care practitioner, you have a legal responsibility to keep yourself, the people you are caring for, the colleagues you work with and any members of the public in your work area as safe as possible. In order to do this, you need to understand what the laws say about your duties and responsibilities and how to implement the law, as detailed in the various regulations under the Health and Safety at Work Act 1974 and the other acts relevant to safety and security.

You need to know the sorts of hazards you are likely to come across in your everyday work and the level of risks posed by these hazards. The level of risk relates to the likelihood of someone being harmed by a hazard, and this will vary according to the circumstances and the individual person. You need to understand that the same hazard might be more risky to some people than others. For example, a person who is unsteady on their feet is more likely to trip over a rug than someone who is not.

You need to be aware of hazards that are specific to health and social care environments, such as the risk of infection, and how this can be minimised. You also need to know how to avoid risks to yourself and your colleagues from your everyday work activities, such as moving and handling patients and equipment, or sharps.

In order to minimise these risks, you need to be able to carry out a risk assessment, which is basically evaluating the hazard, the circumstances, the people involved and assessing the level of risk and who is most likely to be at risk. You then need to be able to take appropriate action to minimise the risk, either by removing the hazard or by making people aware of the hazard. It is important to understand that risks cannot be eliminated, only minimised; however, if you can show that you have taken all possible steps to follow the rules and prevent accidents, you will have fulfilled your duty.

Grading grid

In order to pass this unit, the evidence that the learner presents for assessment needs to demonstrate that they can meet all the learning outcomes for the unit. The assessment criteria for a pass grade describe the level of achievement required to pass this unit.

Assessment and grading criteria

To achieve a pass grade the evidence must show that the learner is able to:	To achieve a merit grade the evidence must show that, in addition to the pass criteria, the learner is able to:	To achieve a distinction grade the evidence must show that, in addition to the pass and merit criteria, the learner is able to:
P1 identify potential hazards in health and social care environments (see Activities 2, 3 and 6) [IE3, CT4, RL5, TW1, TW2, SM3, SM5]		
P2 outline the main features of current health and safety legislation as applied to health and social care (see Activities 2 and 3) [IE4, CT4, RL5, TW2, SM5]		
P3 explain risk assessment processes in the context of everyday activities in health or social care (see Activity 6) [IE4, CT4, SM5, EP2]	**M1** carry out a risk assessment of an outdoor space used for everyday activity (see Activities 2, 3 and 6)	**D1** discuss possible ways of reducing risk to users of the indoor space (see Activity 3)

Weblinks

www.hpa.org.uk – Health Protection Agency
www.bohs.org – British Occupational Hygiene Society
www.cqc.org.uk – Care Quality Commission
www.dh.gov.uk – Department of Health
www.food.gov.uk – Food Standards Agency
www.hse.gov.uk – Health and Safety Executive

- When do you want it? Half a day a week, or 9–5, Monday to Friday?
- Where do you want to work? They may have more than one site.

When you apply for a job, an organisation will send you a job specification – a list of skills and experience relating to the job. Often these are listed as essential criteria – the skills and experience you must have – and then desirable criteria – what they would prefer the applicant to have. There may be a person specification as well as a job specification. A person specification lists the qualities that the person in the job role should have, or be prepared to develop. Read any specifications you are sent carefully to see whether the job is what you thought it was. If you decide to apply, use the application method they ask for. If they send you an application form, complete it. If they ask for three copies of your CV, send three copies. If they ask for a letter of application, send that.

Completing application forms

Application forms are sometimes used. If you are asked to complete an application form, make sure you fill in every box required. Leaving gaps gives the impression you can't follow basic instructions, or, even worse, that you don't care. It is a good idea to photocopy the form first and work on the practice copy. Then you can change it if you make any mistakes. Once you have the right information in the right box, transferring it to the best copy is easy.

Letters of application

If you are asked to send a letter of application, include the basic information you would put in a CV but make sure it is tailored for the job you are applying for. You may like making cakes as a hobby but it is not relevant in your application for a job as a paramedic. Your clean driving licence is much more relevant to the job.

Letters of acceptance/decline

Some employers may ask you to write to confirm that you accept or decline the job. It is good manners to do this as soon as possible. If they have offered you a job and you want to accept it, you need to let them know as soon as possible. If you don't want it, you need to let them know so they can offer it to someone else. In either case, do remember to thank them for offering you the job.

Did you know...❓

The BBC website has lots of tips on letter writing. See www.bbc.co.uk/skillswise

Appropriate content and format

Read the two letters shown below – which do you think would be better if applying for a volunteer placement?

Letter 1

Hiya there

Wndrn if u have a job 4 me?

I'm gr8 with old folks and can shout really loud.

I wnt to wrk Mon & Tues 10–3 as I have to pck up kids frm schl.

Txt bck if ok. 0789XXX

Lv

Sal

Letter 2

12 Rose Terrace
Onetown
OX1 XXX
Mobile: 0789XXX
12 October 20XX

Dear Mrs Siddons

I am writing to ask if you would accept me as a volunteer at Sunnyside care home.

I am 16 years old, a student on a health and social care course and I have a clear CRB police check.

I helped my grandmother after she had a stroke and found I really enjoyed helping her to speak again. I am hoping to develop my career working with older people and eventually I would like to apply for nursing.

I am able to attend placement on Monday or Tuesday from 9am to 4pm from the beginning of December through until the end of March. I have permission from my college to attend if you decide to offer me an interview.

I hope to hear from you soon.

Yours sincerely

Sally Jones

The first letter is informal and very casual. The format is fine between friends or in a text message, but is not suitable to impress an employer. The second letter is formal and says who the person is and what they want as well as what they can offer the residents. The second person has taken time to think about the letter and to spell words correctly. She has highlighted her previous experience and what she can offer. The first person seems more interested in her own needs.

Writing a good letter takes practice.

Activity 1

Writing a letter of application to a local health and social care setting

- Make a list of everything you want to include. Look at the advice for CVs if you are not sure.
- Write all your ideas on Post-it notes first, and then put them into the order you want to write them in your letter.
- Draft your letter and check for spelling and grammar.
- Then ask a teacher or someone else to read it. Listen to their suggestions and re-draft your letter. You may need two or three drafts before it is right.

This activity may help you to achieve personal learning and thinking skills IE2, CT4, SM3 and it will link to P1.

Writing a CV

'CV' stands for curriculum vitae. It is a brief summary of your life and is an important document to get right. Research has shown that a CV has about five seconds to make a good first impression, so that employers will want to go on to read it. So, how can you save your CV from going in the bin within the first five seconds?

You need to make sure that your CV:

- is clean and tidy, with no smudges, or food or coffee stains
- is laid out in a style that is clear and easy to read
- has no spelling mistakes.

Did you know...?

'Curriculum vitae' is Latin and means 'the course of one's life'.

Key term

CV – a brief summary of your life.

Tips for a good CV
- Keep it to a maximum of two pages.
- Set the information out so that it is easy to find. Remember, managers are busy people.
- Be truthful.
- Use good-quality A4 paper.

Include the following sections:

1 Name, address and contact details.
2 Skills.
3 Experience – you may not have much yet, but perhaps you have done some babysitting or helped an older person with their garden.

4 Immediate career goals.

5 Career history – have you had a part-time job?

6 Education – what did you achieve at school? Include dates.

7 Interests and hobbies.

8 Any other relevant personal details.

9 References – if you are at school or college your teacher should be the first referee.

Don't attach certificates – take them to the interview.

Attach a covering letter saying how you meet the requirements for this job. When you have finished your CV, read it and re-read it, then ask another person to read it to spot any mistakes.

> **!**
>
> **REMEMBER**
>
> **Never criticise a school or a previous employer. You may need their help for future references.**

Activity 2

Produce a CV to accompany a letter of application to a local health and social care setting.

- Use the guide above to produce your own draft CV, or your tutor may give you a template.
- When you think you have all the information, swap with a friend and let them read yours. See if you can spot any gaps or spelling mistakes.
- If you think it is as good as it can be, use a computer to produce it.

This activity may help you to achieve personal learning and thinking skills IE2, CT4, SM3 and it will link to P1.

Using ICT

Most people use ICT to write formal letters. Here are some advantages and disadvantages of using ICT or writing by hand.

> **Did you know...?**
>
> The University of Kent have a skills map with useful words to describe the skills that employers look for. See www.kent.ac.uk/careers

	ICT	Handwriting
Advantages	You can use the spell check and grammar check. You can move things around and make changes easily. It looks professional. You can keep a copy easily.	Some people prefer to write letters by hand because it seems more personal.
Disadvantages	Poor layout can spoil the effect.	There is no spell check or grammar check. If you make a mistake you may need to start again. You will need to take a photocopy of the letter before you send it.

Interview skills

Sam wants a voluntary placement at Sunnyside residential home. She has applied and been given a date and time for interview. What advice could you give her about:

- verbal and non-verbal communication skills?
- the importance of listening?
- answering questions?
- asking questions?
- personal and social skills?
- punctuality?

Verbal and non-verbal communication skills

When talking about our likes and dislikes, 55 per cent of communication is by body language and 38 per cent is the tone of voice. Only 7 per cent relates to the words we say. (Mehrabian, 1981)

Verbal skills matter. People do judge you by what you say and how you say it. If you don't understand a question, you can say: 'I'm sorry, I didn't quite get that. Can you repeat it please?' Just saying 'What?' (I don't advise it!) doesn't give a good impression of a person.

If you have a strong accent, take care that the person interviewing can understand what you are saying. For example, in parts of the West Midlands, people say 'Y'am', as in 'Y'am going to the shop?' In an interview it is much better to say 'Are you ...?' Don't leave the interviewer to do the work of trying to understand you. They may not bother, if they have other equally good candidates to interview.

Non-verbal communication is even more important. How you relate to others shows in your body language. If you are anxious, your face may be tense and unwelcoming. This can appear to others as anger or disapproval. You may be nervous but they might think you are not interested. If you chew your nails, they will know you are nervous.

Lack of eye contact gives the impression you don't want to be there. You may just be nervous or you may be from a culture where it is rude to make eye contact. Make an effort to look up and make eye contact with the people around you, so you appear confident even if you don't feel it.

Looking away and hesitating when speaking makes you seem unsure of yourself. Physical barriers show someone is feeling threatened. Crossed arms, crossed legs or holding an object in front of you all form protective barriers and show you feel defensive. Try to keep your body language open. Turn to the person you are talking to, keep your arms and legs uncrossed. Your hands should be open and relaxed. This way you will seem confident even if inside you are nervous.

Your body language can give you away. Communication experts can usually tell when people are not telling the truth. What changed? Did you look away when telling a lie? Or touch your ear or nose? Perhaps your hand went to your mouth? These are indicators when we are not sure or are uncomfortable with what we are doing or saying. Try to avoid doing these things.

The importance of listening

Listening is an important part of interview skills. Sometimes when people are nervous they don't hear what is said. If you are nervous, take some slow, deep breaths. If you have not understood, you can ask the interviewer to repeat the question.

Answering questions

Don't feel you have to rush. Take a little time to think about the question you are asked. Experienced interviewers know to ask one question at a time, but not every interviewer is experienced. If they ask you more than one question at once, try to answer each part carefully.

Asking questions

At the end of an interview you are often invited to ask questions. It is always a good idea to prepare one or two questions. This shows you have thought about the organisation and really are interested. It is not usually the best time to ask about salary if you are applying for a paid job. Wait until you are offered the job before discussing pay.

Personal and social skills

People make judgements about us based on our personal and social skills – how we talk and interact with people – so it's important to be aware of how we present ourselves.

Case Study

Sam was running late for her interview and only had five minutes to spare. She arrived at reception and asked the way to the interview room. The receptionist told her to take the first door on the right and follow the corridor to the end. As Sam got to the door a resident approached, walking slowly using a walking frame. Sam knew she did not have much time to spare and for a split second thought of rushing through and letting the door slam on the resident, but she couldn't do it. She held the door open, though it cost her precious minutes. As she hurried down the corridor she worried she might be late.

The interview was delayed for a short while because one of the panel members was late. To Sam's surprise, when the last panel member arrived she saw it was the same person she had held the door for earlier. Sam got the job – no doubt partly because she had demonstrated her consideration for other people.

Social skills matter, especially when you work with people. If you leave rubbish behind when you have a snack, people may think you are lazy and untidy. If you speak rudely, they may think you don't know how to interact with others. If you are quarrelsome and argumentative, they may not want to work with you. If you swear, even if it is just with your friends, people may judge that you don't know how to behave.

Preparation for interview

Phoning the organisation

The first impression the organisation has of you may well be when you speak to them on the phone. It is a good idea to develop a standard way of answering the phone so that it is an automatic response. A polite and friendly tone is more important than what you say. Most people use a polite 'Hello' when answering a call. If it is an official who is ringing, you can then increase the formality of your responses. If it is a friend, you can become less formal. Unfortunately, it is difficult to correct a poor first impression. If you answer the phone using a curt, angry tone, they may think you are unapproachable – not the best way to impress an employer.

If you phone an organisation, prepare what you want to say. Don't assume they have all the time in the world to listen to you. If you phone and speak to a receptionist, always be polite. Explain who you need to speak to and why. The receptionist may be able to redirect your call if the person you need is away. When you are put through to the person you need to speak to, be brief. Say who you are and why you are phoning. At that point they may be able to help you, or tell you who is a better person to answer your questions.

If you are phoning about a job advertisement, say what job it is and where you saw the advertisement. When you phone it is not an opportunity to tell them your life story or to ask for careers advice. They may be in the middle of an important job, but even if they are not, it's not appropriate at this point.

Transport

Use a reliable means of transport for getting to your interview. Make sure you know the bus routes and the bus timetable if you are travelling by bus. If you are driving, where will you park? You may need to check that they have a car park and that you are allowed to use it. Find out how far the car park is from where your interview is to take place. You don't want to get lost on the way from the car park.

Allow plenty of time. The unexpected does happen. There may be road works or a road traffic accident, or you may get a puncture, or the bus may break down. Plan to arrive 20 minutes early so you have time to spare.

Dress code and general appearance

Always look clean and tidy. Even if the dress code is casual it doesn't mean scruffy. Clean your shoes. This is not the time for exposing cleavage or hairy chests! Avoid too much jewellery or make-up. Your appearance should convey the message that you are sensible and reliable, not that you are on a night out. Make sure you make a good first impression and half the battle is over. First impressions really do count.

Punctuality

Punctuality means being on time. It is very important to be on time for an interview because it shows you are interested in the job and that you are reliable. Make sure you know where the interview is and how to get there at that time of day. If you are travelling by bus, do the buses run at that time? How long does it take to get there? Have you allowed for any road works or traffic problems? If you are punctual you will feel more relaxed for the interview.

Conveying interest

Your body language shows whether you are interested. A person who chews gum during an interview is either unaware that it is rude or doesn't care. In either case they are unlikely to get the job.

Employers often classify people into two types – the 'Can do's' and the 'Can't do's'.

'Can do's' say things like:

- I'll give it a try …
- I'll do my best …
- I'll have a go …

'Can't do's' say:

- No way ...
- I'm not doing that ...
- I've always done it that way and I'm not changing ...

Which type of person would you rather work with?

How to show you are interested:

Make eye contact (the best way to do this is to look at the area from the nose to the eyes).

- Smile.
- Lean forward slightly in your seat.
- Look at each person on the interview panel when they are talking.
- Make sure you have turned off your mobile phone.

How to show you are not interested: (Definitely not recommended if you want the job!)

- Look at your watch.
- Answer your mobile phone. (Turn it off before you go in.)
- Ask how long they will take
- Look round the room and ignore the interview panel, or look at your feet.
- Fidget and tap your feet or fingers.

Appropriate questions

Always find out as much as you can about the organisation before the interview.

Good questions to ask at interview include:

- What training do they give to new staff?
- What opportunities are there to develop your career with the organisation?
- What changes do they think may happen to the organisation in the future?
- How do they plan to build on their strengths (if the latest inspection report was good)?

These questions show you want to be involved and are willing to learn new skills to add to those you already have. The last question shows that you are interested in the organisation, have already read the report and know what they do well.

Knowledge of interview procedures

Knowing what to expect reduces your anxiety levels. Arrive at the right place at the right time and tell them you have arrived. You will probably be asked to sit down and may be offered a cup of coffee or tea. It is probably better to thank them but decline the offer of a drink. If you are really nervous, the last thing you want is to be juggling a cup and saucer. A glass of water is a better option if your lips are dry.

You may be waiting with others applying for the same post. If you are, be friendly and smile.

When you are called into the interview room, walk tall and smile, making eye contact with everyone. Formal interviews usually consist of a panel of three interviewers. This is so that when they discuss the candidates later, they don't have an even split of votes but have to decide 2 to 1. One person generally takes the lead and explains what will happen. The usual procedure is for one person to ask questions which you answer, then the next interviewer asks their questions which you answer, and so on. At the end you are usually invited to ask your questions. Interviewers often make notes about how you meet (or do not meet) the criteria for the job.

In a formal interview situation it is not usual to be told there and then whether you have the post – they will usually phone or write to you. If you are applying for a voluntary position you may sometimes be told if you have got it at that point. In an interview for voluntary work, never assume that they have to allow you to work there.

Always thank the interviewers for their time. If you get the post they know they have someone with good manners. If you don't get the post, thank them for their time and ask for feedback so that you know what to improve on next time you have an interview.

Planning

If you want to be successful in interviews and in life you can help yourself a lot by planning properly. If you are taking the trouble to go for an interview, you probably want to get the job, so you will need to prioritise. Which matters more to you? Going out with your mates the night before an interview and risking oversleeping or being fresh for the interview and getting the job?

> **REMEMBER**
>
> **Proper planning prevents poor performance.**

Make a checklist and tick off things as you do them.

- Do you know how to get there?
- Have you a back-up plan if the transport fails?
- Have you got your clothes cleaned and pressed?
- Are your shoes clean?
- Have you planned your questions? (It is fine to write them down and take them with you.)
- Have you practised the things that might make you nervous such as making eye contact, smiling, taking a deep breath before rushing to answer a question?

Roleplay can help a lot, especially if someone records it and plays it back to you.

Activity 3

Roleplay an interview

Do this activity in groups of five. One person is to be interviewed, three will form the interview panel, and the fifth person is the observer. The interview should take no more than ten minutes. Allow another ten minutes to give feedback.

Preparation:

- Decide the type of placement the person is applying for.
- Re-read the sections from 'Interview skills' up to this point.
- Decide what are the key points to focus on in an interview, e.g. body language, eye contact, verbal communication and appearance. Use these key points as a checklist for the observer.
- Write a list of questions for interviewers and decide who will ask which questions. Remember you have ten minutes in total.
- Set up the 'interview panel'. Move chairs and tables to make it more formal. The observer should be seated where they can see everything but where the interviewee will not be distracted by them.

During the interview, the observer should make notes on the checklist. After the interview, take turns to say how it felt. The main feedback should be from the observer and should be written so that the person being interviewed has specific points they can work on.

Feedback should be given in the form of:

- What you were good at.
- What to work on.

Allow about ten minutes to give feedback.

Take turns to be the interviewee. Alternatively, you could video the process so that everyone can observe after the interviews have been recorded, using the checklist.

You may be able to invite employers in to conduct the interviews. They will provide valuable feedback and say whether they would have given the person the job.

If you write up your planning notes, demonstrate your skills and write your reflection on your strengths and weaknesses. This activity may provide evidence towards P2, M1, D1 and PLTS (RL2, RL3, EP2).

2 Be able to complete a period of work experience in a health or social care setting

Your school or college will make sure that all placements have been checked for safety and suitability. You will need to have a Criminal Records Bureau (CRB) check as part of the Vetting and Barring procedure, which makes sure that unsuitable people don't work with children and vulnerable adults. This is now administered by the Independent Safeguarding Authority (ISA). In addition to the CRB, increased safeguards and checks were introduced under the Vetting and Barring scheme to protect vulnerable children and adults. CRB checks will still be needed.

Skills for work experience

There are some skills and ways of behaving that are needed in every job and also apply to work experience.

REMEMBER

When you do work experience you are representing your school or college. If you make a good impression they will be willing to offer more learners the chance to volunteer with them.

Punctuality

This means 'being on time'. Why do you think being on time matters? Imagine what would happen if a carer did not arrive for work on time in the morning. The night staff can't go home until the day staff arrives. They can't leave residents alone without staff. Night staff may have been working from 9pm to 7.30am. How would you feel if you had worked those hours and then your colleague did not arrive on time?

Regular attendance

Have you ever missed a class at school and when you go back you don't quite know what you have missed? When we work with people regular attendance is even more important. If you attend regularly you will soon feel you are part of the team and you will know what is happening.

Case Study

Sarah likes her work placement at Sunnyside care home. She doesn't mind helping serve the meals but she doesn't like having to clean the tables after lunch. She doesn't see why she should do it.

Think of three reasons why Sarah should clean the tables after the meal.

Here are some of my ideas:

- If the tables are not cleaned then the bits of food will attract flies and become smelly.
- The tables need to be ready for the next meal.
- Everyone has to take a turn at all the jobs so there is no reason why Sarah should get to pick and choose only the things she likes.

Timely reporting of incidents and accidents

What do we mean by timely? If Sarah slips on a wet floor and doesn't tell anyone until the following day, that is not timely reporting. Someone else might have slipped on the wet floor and broken a leg. Sarah should have reported it straight away.

Following instructions

The ability to follow instructions is a very important skill.

 Case Study

Jenny volunteers at Sunnyside care home. She has been told that the fire doors must never be propped open. One warm summer morning she notices that the door to the kitchen, which is a fire door, has been propped open with a chair. She closes it. The manager notices and thanks her. Sometime later the fire alarm sounds. The carers know just what to do and everyone is led to safety. The fire brigade arrives and the firemen put out the fire, which was in the kitchen. 'It was good thing the fire door was closed,' said the fire officer. 'If it had been propped open, the fire would have spread and it would have been a very dangerous situation.'

The person who propped open the fire door did not follow instructions. By not following instructions they put everyone at risk.

Case Study

Pat has a placement at the local hospital. She is on the rehabilitation ward and enjoys working with patients to get them mobile again. Most people are recovering slowly but surely. One day she is talking to a patient when she hears a crash. She turns round to see Mr Green on the floor. His walking frame has fallen too. He is very pale and his lips are blue. The nurse in charge hurries over and checks his airway, breathing and pulse then starts CPR. She calls for the senior care assistant to ring for help, and then asks Pat to bring the emergency trolley and draw the screens. Pat does this then the senior care assistant comes back and asks her to move the other patients to the day room at the other end of the ward, as some of them are getting upset.

Because Pat follows instructions, the care Mr Green gets is the best available in the situation. She brings the emergency trolley so the nurse can get any equipment she needs. This frees the senior care assistant to phone for help. Pat moves the other patients away so the nurse and senior care assistant can focus on Mr Green. If she had said no, or not been listening, his care would have been delayed. Pat showed the ability to follow instructions and also that she was a good team worker.

Key term

CPR – Cardiopulmonary Resuscitation. This is an emergency procedure used to keep someone alive when their heart stops.

Positive criticism

Positive criticism is meant to help you develop. It is not meant to make you feel small. No one really likes criticism, but when we first start as a volunteer we don't know everything. Sometimes we need to be told what to do and how to do it better.

Key term

Criticism – feedback. It can be helpful (positive) or unhelpful (negative).

Most care workers are aware how criticism can affect people and try to give positive criticism, so you may hear things such as, 'Mary is shy but when she comes out of her shell she is very friendly.' This will encourage Mary to be more outgoing. It is important to realise that if someone criticises you they are doing it to help you improve. For this reason you should respond positively, smile and say, 'Thanks for that advice, I'll try that next time.' If you do this, an employer will be impressed that you are willing to learn.

P3 P4 P5 M2 M3 D2

Activity 4

Coping with criticism

1 How do you know you are doing a good job?

- Make a list of the top five things you would like to hear from your supervisor at placement (a pay rise doesn't come into this list).
- Compare your list with a friend. Have you got the same sorts of things?
- Did you list things such as hardworking, keen, and caring?
- What are the opposites of the words you listed? The opposite of 'hardworking' is 'lazy', and the opposite of 'keen' is 'not interested'.
- Which words are said about you? If it is the negative ones, try to turn them into the positive ones by changing your behaviour. Check your body language. Is it saying 'bored' when in fact you are shy?

2 One of the most difficult aspects of working is coping with criticism, especially if you feel it is negative or undeserved. If you get negative feedback saying what you don't do, look behind the words and ask yourself what they would like you to do. Sometimes it is as simple as asking 'Can I do something to help?' Make an action plan with SMART targets to improve your interpersonal skills. Keep a reflective journal to trace your improvement.

Using your skills will help towards evidence for P3 and P4. Discussing your overall performance helps towards M2, and discussing your interpersonal skills helps towards M3. An action plan will help towards D2. A reflective journal will help towards P5.

You may be able to use this as evidence towards these criteria and RL2, RL3, SM3, SM5, SM6, SM7, EP2.

Team working

Most care work is done in teams. Even the most famous surgeon can't work without a team of nurses to get the patient ready, or another doctor to give the anaesthetic, or a porter to bring the patient to the operating theatre, or the cleaner to clean the theatre. Team work is vital in all health and social care, and this is why employers look for this skill. If you are a good team worker you will work with others to get the job done. Even if you don't like someone in the team you will still work with them to make sure the patient/ service user/ resident is cared for.

Completing all tasks

Everyone has favourite bits of their job and the bits they don't like, but it's important to do your whole job well, not just the bits you like.

Duty of care

When we work in health or social care we have a 'duty of care', which means 'a responsibility to others to act in their best interests'. If Sarah has the best interests of the residents and her colleagues at heart she will report the wet floor and try to get it dried as soon as possible so that others don't have an accident.

Awareness of her own and other's safety

Sarah has an awareness of her own and other's safety. She knows that the residents are frail and can easily break a bone if they fall. She also knows that the carers are busy and may easily slip as they go from room to room. Sarah tells other staff at once about the wet floor, and goes to find the cleaner who has the key to the mop cupboard.

Understanding of the limits of own role

Sarah has an understanding of the limits of her own role. She knows she is not supposed to grab a handful of paper towels and try to dry the floor herself, because she might not dry it properly. The cleaner is trained to do the job, has the right equipment to do it properly and will place a 'Caution – wet floor' sign out until the floor has thoroughly dried.

Sarah has a good understanding of her role as a volunteer. She knows what she can and what she can't do.

M2 D2

Activity 5

Make a list of five risks there may be in a placement of your choice. For each risk, say what can be done to reduce the risk. Then say what the limits are of your own role in each situation. One example has been completed to start you off.

Hazard	Risk	How it can be reduced	Limit of own role as volunteer
1 Chips on the floor of the dining room.	A risk of slipping.	Pick up the dropped food.	A volunteer can pick up the dropped food but then should report it so the floor can be cleaned free of grease.
2			
3			
4			

Compare your list with a friend and discuss your limits. Do you agree about the limits of your role?

Join another pair so there are four in your group. Discuss one situation from each person. Do you still agree about the limits of your role?

This activity will help towards M2 and D2. It may also provide evidence for PLTS RL – reflective learners, TW – team workers, SM – self-managers and EP – effective participators (RL2, RL3, TW1, TW3, TW4, TW5, SM5, SM6, SM7, EP2).

Interaction with people and using a professional approach

In health and social care we need to interact with the people who use the services, with health and social care staff, and with other adults within the setting. Sarah understands her role. This helps in her interaction with people. She has a professional approach.

Let's look at what we mean by 'a professional approach'.

> **Key terms**
>
> Professional approach – the behaviour we would expect from a professional person such as a nurse, social worker, doctor.

 Case Study

Sarah has been volunteering one day a week at Sunnyside care home for over a month and is beginning to know the residents quite well.

Mrs Rose has dementia and is restless. She walks around the lounge and doesn't sit still for long. One day Mrs Rose asks Sarah to let her out of the front door.

What should Sarah do? Let her out or tell the staff? The professional approach is to tell the senior person on duty. This alerts the staff to the fact that Mrs Rose may need extra monitoring, and may need to have a carer stay with her. This is a good example of Sarah showing a **'duty of care'** to Mrs Rose. Letting Mrs Rose out would put her in danger.

Here are a few more examples to discuss. What should Sarah do to show a professional approach and duty of care?

1 A plumber arrives to fix a broken pipe. Should Sarah:

a ask him to wait in the hall and check with the person in charge?
b let him in and show him where the broken pipe is?
2 Mrs Rose's son arrives and starts asking about her treatment. Should Sarah:

a) tell him what he wants to know?
b) refer him to the person in charge?

Answers:

1 Sarah should ask the plumber to wait in the hall while she tells the person who is in charge.
2 Sarah should refer Mrs Rose's son to the person in charge.

Health and social care settings

Health and social care is provided in three ways:

> **Key terms**
>
> Statutory care – care provided by the state or the government. It is not intended to make a profit.
>
> Voluntary care – care provided by volunteers who work for charities. These charities have to raise funds themselves so they can offer the service. They do not aim to make a profit.
>
> Private settings – a care environment where people pay for the care and the owners make a profit.

- statutory
- voluntary
- private.

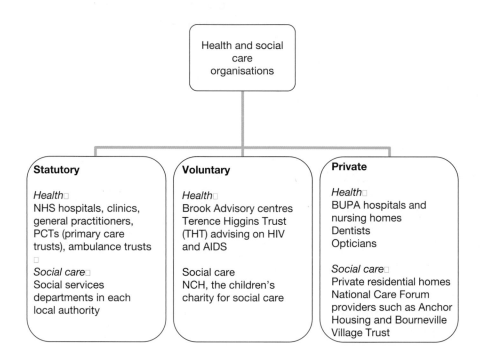

Health and social care organisations

Statutory

Statutory provision is provided by the state (another name for the government) – think 'stat' is in both statutory and state.

Statutory provision is paid for by taxes so you don't need to pay at the hospital or when you visit your doctor. In the health service, state hospitals, clinics and local doctors are part of state provision. In statutory social care we have local authority social services departments that employ social workers to assess the needs of older people, or people with mental health problems, or younger people who need social care.

Voluntary provision

Voluntary provision is provided by charities. It is paid for by donations from members of the public. When you see

Did you know...?

Before the UK had the National Health Service, if you needed to see the doctor you had to pay. Poor people could not afford to pay and so often did not get the health care they needed. Many people died because they were ill and poor.

people with collecting tins outside shops they are trying to raise funds for charities. People who use voluntary services sometimes make a small donation for the help they get, but often the help that is given is free.

Private provision

Private provision in health and social care is funded by charging fees. Some people use private health care because they can have it when they want it rather than having to wait. A health check may cost over £600. (See the BUPA website at www.bupa.co.uk/individuals/keeping-well/health-assessments.)

Private social care charges fees to residents. Many older people in residential homes pay over £400 per week to stay there. Some care home fees are over £800 per week.

(See the Care Quality Commission website at www.cqc.org.uk)

Different groups of individuals who use services

Health and social care covers a wide area. The Health and Social Care Act 2008 has these definitions:

> 'Health care' includes all forms of health care provided for individuals, whether relating to physical or mental health, and also includes procedures that are similar to forms of medical or surgical care but are not provided in connection with a medical condition.

> 'Social care includes all forms of personal care and other practical assistance provided for individuals who by reason of age, illness, disability, pregnancy, childbirth, dependence on alcohol or drugs, or any other similar circumstances, are in need of such care or other assistance.'

Source: www.cqc.org.uk/guidanceforprofessionals/socialcare/careproviders/legislation.cfm

There are many groups of people who use health and social care services. The Care Standards Act 2000 set up a National Care Standards Commission to register and regulate the following bodies:

- children's homes
- independent hospitals
- independent clinics
- care homes
- residential family centres
- independent medical agencies
- domiciliary care agencies
- fostering agencies
- nurses agencies
- voluntary adoption agencies
- local authority fostering and adoption services
- child minding or day care for children.

Groups include:

- adults
- children and young people
- people with mental health issues
- vulnerable adults.

Look again at the list of the bodies the Care Standards Act regulates and try to work out who might use each service.

Reasons for choice of setting

People choose the setting that will meet their needs. Some people live at home and need only day care. Others require residential care.

Adults and young people may have health and social care needs. People with mental health issues have specific needs and may also have health needs or social care needs (for example, someone with severe depression may also have broken leg). Some adults and some children are particularly vulnerable. A person with autism may not know how to relate to others and may need to be taught social skills at a day centre.

Older people may need nursing care but they may decide to stay at home and have someone come in to care for them. This is known as domiciliary care. They may also decide to go into a nursing home. Sometimes they need social care and don't have special health needs. They may live at home and attend a day centre, or they may decide to move into a residential home.

Children may be fostered, or live in a residential children's home. Many children are looked after by child minders while parents are at work.

There are lots of different groups who use health and social care services. Find out more about these groups from the Care Quality Commission website www.cqc.org.uk. Look for inspection reports on this website and see what inspectors think of the provision in your area.

Choice for the learner

Finding what is available in your area may help you to decide where you want to have your placement. Some people choose a placement because they already have some experience of working with people in health care or social care. Some people choose a placement because they have never worked in that area and want to know what it is like. It is a good idea to try something new. If you then decide to make your career in health and social care you will have broader experience on which to base your career choices.

3 Be able to demonstrate interpersonal skills in a health or social care setting

Interpersonal skills

'Interpersonal' means 'between people' so interpersonal skills are the skills that are used between people.

Verbal communication

Verbal communication (speaking) is an important way of interacting with others. Look back to the section on interview skills and remind yourself of what you already know about verbal and non-verbal communication.

Clear speech

Clear speech is important. If you mumble, the person interviewing you may not be able to understand you. If you are applying to volunteer or work with people who may have hearing loss, you may not get the job if you don't speak clearly. Many older people do have hearing problems and some children also have difficulty hearing.

Not using slang or jargon

Perhaps in your local area you use words that others may not understand. Sometimes people use slang with friends. For example, 'wicked' has a totally different meaning to older people. If you are asked at interview what you think of the care and you say 'wicked', you may not get the job. Can you think of any other slang words you use with friends that older people may not understand?

'Jargon' means specialist words. Often people use jargon to save time. For example, a doctor on a busy surgical ward may ask for 'U and E's.' It is a lot quicker than saying, 'Please get a blood sample and test it for urea and electrolytes.' Jargon is only useful when specialists are talking to each other, not when they are talking to members of the public. You should not use jargon. Aim to use words that everyone can understand.

Appropriate paralanguage

The term 'appropriate paralanguage' is in itself an example of jargon. 'Appropriate' is another way of saying suitable. 'Paralanguage' refers to the noises we make to show we are listening, such as 'Mmm', or 'Huh?' So *appropriate* paralanguage occurs if you are listening to someone and you go 'Mmm' and nod you head to show you agree. Not so difficult really!

Of course, it would not be appropriate if you waggled your head like it was on a spring, or if you nodded all the time and murmured 'Mmm' even if you disagreed. I'm sure you can think of other examples.

P4

Activity 6

Verbal communication

- Write a short account of how you have used verbal skills in your placement. Give three examples of using 'paralanguage' when communicating with people in placement.
- What was useful about using paralanguage?

This activity may help you towards P4 and PLTS (RL2, RL3, TW1, TW3, TW4, TW5, SM5, SM6, SM7, EP2).

Non-verbal communication

We have already mentioned non-verbal communication in the section on interview skills but it is worth exploring in a little more depth. Non-verbal communication is especially important if people don't speak the same language or if someone has hearing impairment. When you are communicating with someone who for whatever reason doesn't understand the words you are saying, non-verbal language becomes even more important.

Body posture

This tells a lot about someone. A person slumped in a chair or sprawled across a desk is not interested. A person who is sitting up, leaning forward, ready to join in is certainly interested. Watch a clip from one of the soaps with the sound turned off. Can you tell from the body language who is interested in whom, and who is not friends with whom?

Gestures

Gestures also tell us a lot. Gestures mean different things in different cultures. If you nod your head it can mean yes, but if the person you are communicating with is from Greece or Bulgaria, nodding the head means 'No'. Smiles mean different things in different cultures. In this culture, a smile usually means agreement or happiness, but in Japan, a person may smile when they are angry. In Asian cultures it is very rude to pat a child on the head. Be careful with what gestures you use – they must be appropriate and even then they may be misinterpreted.

Eye contact

Eye contact is expected in Western cultures. If someone can 'look you in the eye' they are seen as open and honest, In Asian cultures, eye contact may be considered rude – if a younger person looks an older person in the eye, they are seen as being disrespectful. In Western cultures it is rude to stare at someone, so make sure your eye contact doesn't turn into staring.

 ## Case Study

Nargus has a placement at Springfield Nursing Home. Mrs Brown, a resident, has age-related hearing loss. At lunch time, when Nargus helps Mrs Brown to cut up her food, she makes sure she sits facing her, so that Mrs Brown can read her lips. Nargus can make eye contact with Mrs Brown and communicate that way.

Facial expressions

Facial expressions are very important in health and social care. Sometimes, carers have unpleasant jobs to do. If a patient or resident has soiled the bed they will be very upset. If a carer then pulls a face and shows disgust, it adds to their misery. For this reason, carers must be very aware of their facial expressions.

P4

Activity 7

Everyone in the class writes a brief message on a piece of paper. The papers are folded and put into a hat. Each person then draws one folded paper from the hat. If they draw their own they have to put it back.

Work in pairs. Person A has to convey their message to Person B, without using words. Person B then has up to a minute to guess the message. They then change places and Person B has to convey their message to Person A without using words. Gestures, facial expressions and body language are allowed. The winning pair is the pair that guesses each other's messages correctly in the quickest time.

Try to communicate simple messages, such as 'I'm hungry' or 'I have a headache'. Messages like these are much easier to communicate than the story of the latest episode of a TV series.

This activity may help you to prepare evidence towards P4 and PLTS (RL2, RL3, TW1, TW3, TW4, TW5, SM5, SM6, SM7 and EP2).

Appropriate use of touch

Once again, note the word 'appropriate'. When we are with friends or family we may use touch, for example, giving someone hug, or tapping them on the arm to attract their attention. In your professional work as a carer, touch is often not appropriate.

 Case Study

Jenny has started her placement at a day centre for people with visual impairment. It is time to start putting away the activity they have all been working on that day. Should she go up to people and touch them to attract their attention? What do you think?
A better way might be to speak to each person individually, addressing them by name, or attract everyone's attention by clapping her hands and speaking loudly enough so all can hear. Just because someone has a visual impairment is no reason not to respect their rights.

Recognition of personal and public space

Personal space is the area around you that is *your* area. If others move into this space you feel uncomfortable. Of course it depends who it is – some people you allow to come closer than others. The important thing is that you control it. Watch what happens next time you get on a crowded bus. People move along to maintain their personal space, or if they can't move along and have to be close to a stranger, they don't usually make eye contact.

You have other personal space. Think of the space you have in your own room. Perhaps you allow only certain people in there.

When people move into residential care, their bedroom is their personal space but it is also the workspace for carers. Sometimes carers forget that Mrs Green's room is *her* space. A good carer will always knock and wait to be invited in before entering a resident's room.

Public space refers to areas such as the dining room or lounge, where anyone may go. It is public. Yet even here people like their own personal space. You may notice that in a care home, residents like to have their chair where they always sit. This is because even in a public space, everyone likes to keep their own bubble of personal space.

Listening skills

We have already mentioned listening skills in the interview section of this unit. The listening skills you use in interview are the same skills you need when working in health and social care. Active listening uses specific skills.

A good way to develop these skills is to remember 'SOLER'.

- Sitting attentively at a slight angle.
- Open body posture – don't cross your arms, legs or feet (may be seen as defensive).
- Lean slightly forward.
- Eye contact.
- Relax.

Practice using 'SOLER' when you next listen to someone.

P4

Activity 8

There are some fun ways to improve your non-verbal skills. Get a friend to video you. This works best if they do it without telling you when they do it. Play it back without any sound.

Look at your body posture, what gestures you use, what eye contact you make, and what facial expressions you use. Can your friends tell what you are communicating?

Are there any surprises? Does your body language give you away? When you are bored, do you start looking around or turn away?

This activity will help you improve your non-verbal communication. It may help you to prepare evidence towards P4 and PLTS (RL2, RL3, TW1, TW3, TW4, TW5, SM5, SM6, SM7 and EP2).

4 Be able to reflect upon own performance in a health or social care setting

Reflection is like holding a mirror up and seeing yourself. People who work in health and social care are expected to be 'reflective practitioners'. This means they are expected to look at what they do, why they do it, and improve on what they do.

In this section you will learn how to reflect on your own performance in placement.

Personal achievements

Make a list of your personal achievements. You may have passed your driving theory test, or learned how to find your way around the local area. You may have learned how to email or use a spell-check on the computer. Just finding out how to get to placement and being brave enough to go to a new place where you don't know anyone is a great personal achievement. List all your achievements.

Knowledge and skills gained

Now list all the knowledge and skills you have gained. Knowledge is what you know. Skills are what you can do. By finding your way to placement and meeting new people you may have gained knowledge about the bus timetable, and about the local geography. You may have gained skills asking directions. You will have gained confidence.

Perhaps you have gained knowledge of types of settings. For example, you may have discovered that a care home is residential care and a day centre is not residential. You may have learned that diabetic people have to be careful about their diet.

You might have learned new skills such as making birthday cards, or knitting as part of the activities at a day centre placement.

Activities undertaken

What activities have you undertaken? At first you might think you have done very little, but if you have given someone a cup of tea, or listened to an older person talk about when they were young, you have at least two activities to list. Keep adding to your list every week.

Personal strengths and weaknesses

List your personal strengths and weaknesses. If you are a college student, your tutor may already have a format for this and may use it in your personal tutorial. If you are not in that situation, make your own list. Be honest.

Here are some things to consider:

- Use of initiative – do you use your common sense or do you wait to be told what to do?
- Ability to follow instruction – do you do all that is asked, or do you skip the bits you don't like?
- How do you receive constructive criticism – ignore it, or listen and act on it?

Use of interpersonal skills

Look at your own interpersonal skills – see the section earlier in this unit if you can't remember what 'interpersonal skills' means. How have you used your interpersonal skills, such as verbal communication? Are you aware that you have used non-verbal communication at all? Most people aren't aware of how they use non-verbal communication. Hopefully you have smiled at people at your placement, and you must have made eye contact. How did this communication go – was it successful? If not, why not?

Recording reflections and building on them

Reflection is important but can easily be forgotten in a busy day. The best way to improve is to record your reflections. Most students have a log book in which to record what happens each week. Some people call it a diary. The important thing is to write down what happened. Be selective – put down key incidents. There is no need to record every week that you got the bus, arrived on time, spoke to the staff, but if for example, you spent half an hour listening to Mrs Grey talk about her childhood, you may wish to record that.

Once you have written down what happened, you can then reflect on it.

It is important to be honest when you reflect on your practice. There are many ways to reflect. One way is to use a reflective model such as Gibbs' Reflective Cycle.

1 Description
   - What happened?
   - How did it happen?
   - Who was there?
   - What did you do?
   - What did they do?
   - When did it happen?
   - Why did it happen?
   - Where did it happen?
2 How did you feel?
3 What was good about the experience? What was not so good?
4 Analysis – break it down into parts. What parts worked and what parts did not?
5 What else could you have done in that situation?
6 If it happened again, what would you do differently?

Another way to reflect is to use the 'conscious competence' model. It has four stages:

- Stage 1 – We don't know that we don't know something. So for example, you may not realise that you do not know the proper way to make a bed.
- Stage 2 – You watch a carer making a bed and realise you don't really know the proper way.
- Stage 3 – You practise and consciously make an effort to get it right.
- Stage 4 – You become so good at it that you do it right every time without thinking about it.

Try it out. Identify one thing you need to improve. Perhaps you are shy and don't

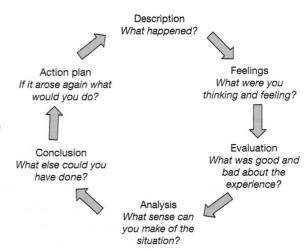

Gibbs' reflective cycle

know what to do at placement, so you sit in a corner and don't mix with others (unconscious incompetence).

The senior care assistant tells you to stop sitting alone and try talking to residents. You try but find it hard to start a conversation (conscious incompetence). Warning: many people stick at this point and give up (but they may not make good carers). You try again next time and ask Mrs Green about her knitting. She tells you all about her great-granddaughter and the cardigan she is making for her. You realise you can talk to older people and practise starting up conversations with them (conscious competence). Within a few weeks you forget you ever had a problem talking to people and you can chat easily to anyone (unconscious competence).

Another way to reflect on your performance is to use the Johari window (named after American psychologists Joseph Luft and Harry Ingham who devised it). A simple version is displayed below.

In the first column, 'they' can be anyone relevant to the situation. In this example, 'they' is your placement supervisor.

You may wish to draw your own. In Box A put the things you know about yourself and that others know. You may be good at time-keeping and at using your initiative or common sense. In Box C put some things you know but others don't. You may go to bed too late and not make time to do your coursework. Sometimes people know things about you that you don't realise yourself. This is Box B. But how do you find out what you don't know? Simple – you ask!

	Things I know	**Things I don't know**
Things they know	A I'm good at time keeping. I use common sense.	B
Things they don't know	C I go to bed late. I'm behind with my coursework.	D

This is a good way to find out.

In class, sit in a circle. Each person has a piece of A4 paper and writes their name on the bottom. Pass it to the person on your left. They pass theirs to the left, too. Your paper is now with the person next to you. They have to write a comment about you. Each person writes one comment at the top, then folds it over and passes it to the left. Eventually you will get your own paper back, folded over like a scroll.

You now have something to put in Box B. (Of course, to be really accurate it should go in Box A, but for now we'll keep it in Box B.)

Box D is the box for things you don't know and others don't know. This is how you react in a crisis. Perhaps Mrs Green starts to choke and you save her using your first-aid training, or you have to deal with an angry relative and you do it calmly. Only when the unexpected happens do you and others realise you have certain abilities. Box D is for these unexpected qualities you have.

So how can this help you improve your performance? Look at Box B. Is there anything you could improve on? Do you need a reality check? Does anything surprise you? Perhaps you thought you were quiet, but you find out that others find you noisy. Thinking about how you appear to others can help you to reflect on your own performance.

As you reflect on your work skills, your confidence will improve. Your logbook should be a record of your development on a regular basis – not something to fill in at the last minute. Make your own checklist if your logbook hasn't got one. How do you rate yourself at the start of the placement and then again at the end of the placement?

Use any or all of these reflective techniques and you will improve.

P5

Activity 9

Use Gibbs' reflective cycle, and write about one incident at your placement. Remember to write something for each section.

Description:

- **What happened?**
- **How did it happen?**
- **Who was there?**
- **What did you do?**
- **What did they do?**
- **When did it happen?**
- **Why did it happen?**
- **Where did it happen?**
2 **How did you feel?**
3 **What was good about the experience? What was not so good?**
4 **Analysis – break it down into parts. What parts worked and what parts did not?**
5 **What else could you have done in that situation?**
6 **If it happened again, what would you do differently?**

This activity will help you to providing evidence for P5 and PLTS (RL2, RL3, SM3, SM5, SM6, SM7 and EP2).

Career development plans/progression opportunities

When you have completed 60 or more hours in placement you will have a good idea of whether you want to work in health and social care. Your choices at this point will decide your career plans and the best way to progress.

If you decide that health and social care is an area you would like to work in, you have several choices. You can stay in full time education and apply for a Level 3 course. Many Level 3 courses ask for a merit or even a distinction on the Level 2 course, so work hard and keep focused to get good grades. A Level 3 course is often a BTEC National diploma. This is a two-year course, after which many people apply to go to university. Some people go to university to study nursing, social work, or midwifery. Others may apply to study youth work, social care or social policy. After university they may then go to work in the voluntary sector or work as health educators in the NHS.

If you decide that you like health and social care but don't want to stay in full-time education, you can look for a job as a carer. Some employers prefer to employ people over the age of 18, so they are able to do the full range of care work. Your career path may be influenced by your age. You may be required to undertake additional training to give you the skills needed for the job. Qualifications are changing so it is better to check with your local employer what they require when you apply for a job. They may ask you to build up qualifications based on the training they give.

If you decide that health and social care is not for you, at least you will have gained valuable work skills to take to another area. Connexions Direct and your tutor will be able to advise you where to get careers advice.

Activity 10

Write a report on your overall performance during your work experience. Be honest. If you have a report from a placement supervisor saying you are very quiet, there is no point saying in your own report that you are very chatty.

Points to consider:

1 Punctuality
2 Attendance
3 Ability to follow instructions
4 Responding to positive criticism
5 Team working
6 Completing all tasks
7 Timely reporting of incidents and accidents
8 Understanding of a duty of care
9 Awareness of own and others' safety
10 Understanding of the limits of own role
11 Your interaction with people who use services, health and social care staff, other adults within the setting
12 A professional approach
13 Verbal communication skills
14 Non-verbal communication skills
15 Other interpersonal skills.

It may help you to score yourself for each, as follows:

1 = excellent
2 = good
3 = satisfactory
4 = needs improvement.

You can then write about your strengths and areas to work on.

This activity may help you towards evidence for M3.

Summary

1 When applying for work experience, you will be judged on how you present your written application, and on your appearance and behaviour at interview.
2 In order to successfully complete a period of work experience in a health or social care setting you need certain work skills.
3 Know your responsibilities for health and safety.
4 Know what you can and cannot do.
5 Health and social care settings may be privately owned companies, state funded health centres or charities.
6 You can work with people of all ages and all abilities in health and social care.
7 You need to be able to show good interpersonal skills, both verbally and in your non-verbal communications.
8 You need good verbal communication – use clear speech, ask what you can do to help. Don't wait to be told.
9 You need good non-verbal communication – smile, look confident and be a good listener.
10 Reflect on your work experience. What have you learned? What could you do better? How does it link to your career plans?

Assessment and grading criteria

To achieve a pass grade the evidence must show that the learner is able to:	To achieve a merit grade the evidence must show that, in addition to the pass criteria, the learner is able to:	To achieve a distinction grade the evidence must show that, in addition to the pass and merit criteria, the learner is able to:
P1 complete an appropriate letter of application, with an attached CV, to a local health and social care setting [IE2,CT4, SM3] (see Activities 1 and 2)		

P2 plan appropriately for an interview at their work experience placement (see Activity 3) [RL2, RL3, EP2,]	**M1** demonstrate appropriate interview skills (see Activity 3)	**D1** assess the strengths and weaknesses of their interview skills (see Activity 3)
P3 carry out a period of work experience, using relevant skills, in a health or social care setting (see Activity 4) [RL2, RL3, TW1, TW3, TW4, TW5, SM5, SM6, SM7, EP2]	**M2** discuss their overall performance during the period of work experience (see Activities 4 and 5)	**D2** produce an action plan showing how they could have improved their work experience performance (see Activities 4 and 5)
P4 demonstrate appropriate interpersonal skills in a health or social care setting (see Activities 4, 6, 7 and 8) [RL2, RL3, TW1, TW3, TW4, TW5, SM5, SM6, SM7, EP2]	**M3** discuss own interpersonal skills used in a health or social care setting (see Activities 4 and 10)	
P5 complete a reflective logbook during their period of work experience in a health or social care setting (see Activities 4 and 9) [RL2, RL3, SM3, SM5, SM6, SM7, EP2]		

Further Reading

Mehrabian, A., 1981, *Silent messages: Implicit communication of emotions and attitudes*, Belmont, CA: Wadsworth
You may also like to visit Dr Mehrabian's website at: www.kaaj.com/psych/

Weblinks

www.bbc.co.uk/skillswise/
www.belbin.com
www.bupa.co.uk
www.businessballs.com/johariwindowmodel.htm
www.cqc.org.uk
www.kent.ac.uk/careers/sk/skillsmap.htm

Unit 6
Cultural Diversity in Health and Social Care

Cultural diversity in society is reflected in health and social care. This unit will help those who work in this area to develop their understanding of the value of cultural diversity and how this understanding can be used to help promote equality of opportunity for service users.

The unit provides an introduction to cultural diversity. It explores the diversity of individuals in society from a wide range of different religious and secular backgrounds, and their beliefs and practices. You will investigate the factors that influence equality of opportunity for individuals in society and the roles and responsibilities of service providers. The law dictates what rights people have in health and social care. We look at some of the legislation, conventions, regulations, codes of practice and charters that are relevant to cultural diversity.

The unit draws on all the other units and gives you a chance to put into practice all you are learning in Unit 1 Communication in Health and Social Care, Unit 2 Individual Rights within the Health and Social Care Sectors, Unit 3 Individual Needs in the Health and Social Care Sectors and Unit 9 Creative and Therapeutic Activities in Health and Social Care.

In this unit you can also work towards Functional Skills ICT and English at Level 2 and towards Personal, Learning and Thinking Skills.

> **Key terms**
>
> Cultural diversity – different traditions that people follow

Learning outcomes:

In this unit you will learn about:

- the diversity of individuals in society
- the beliefs and practices in different religious or secular groups
- factors that influence the equality of opportunity for individuals in society
- the role of legislation, codes of practice and charters in promoting diversity.

1 Know the diversity of individuals in society

What if:

- we all had to wear the same clothes?
- we all had the same hairstyle?
- we all had to eat the same food?
- we all had to live in the same type of house?
- we all had to have the same size family?

Just imagine not being able to choose what you wear, how you look or what you eat. In some countries, families are not allowed to have more than one child. In some countries, people are not allowed to say what they think.

> ## Key terms
>
> Diversity – difference or variety.

British society is not like this. It allows people to choose what to wear and how to live their lives, within reason, provided they stay within the law. This is why our society is so varied, or diverse.

Social, cultural and political diversity

The word 'social' refers to how people behave and interact. Social diversity refers to the different ways in which people behave towards each other. For example, some people respect and help older people, but others think that older people are 'past it' and should be pensioned off. This is an example of differences in beliefs. This translates into differences in behaviour, so a person who respects older people will listen to them. A person who does not respect older people will not listen to their views.

Cultural diversity is seen in the differences in how we behave, the food we eat, the way we dress, the way we spend our free time.

Politics refers to how we are governed. Political diversity is another way of saying differences in how we choose to be governed, what laws we should have and what plans should be made for the people in our country. Political diversity in the UK ranges from left wing to right wing.

Here are some left-wing views.

The *government* should:

- organise benefits for those who are sick
- help the unemployed with benefits
- provide free health care
- provide free education
- build council houses for people to rent.

Here are some right-wing views.

People should:

- have a private pension for when they are sick
- find another job if they are unemployed
- pay for their own health care
- pay for a good education
- buy their own house.

What do you think? Do you agree with the left-wing views or the right-wing views?

You probably found it hard to agree because you thought differently. This shows the diversity in your group. We can have different views because we have political diversity in our society. If we lived in a country where there was no choice and we were not allowed to discuss these matters, there would be less open political diversity. (People might still think differently but be frightened to express their views in case they were arrested and imprisoned for saying what they thought.)

In UK society there is diversity in:

- ethnicity
- religious beliefs
- secular beliefs
- social class
- gender
- sexuality
- age
- family structure
- disabilities.

'Ethnicity' refers to a person's ethnic group. It is sometimes used to refer to culture, or race or nationality. In fact, it is a term which changes its meaning. An ethnic group often defines itself by a common language or cultural heritage.

The Office for National Statistics in the UK uses the following terms for ethnic groups: white, mixed, Asian or Asian British, Black or Black British, Chinese and other. The groups have been subdivided into other ethnic groups so Asian or Asian British include Indian, Pakistani and Bangladeshi. In the UK, we have a census every ten years. A census is a way of recording and counting members of the population. Some people think the ethnic groups categories need to be changed by the time of the next census in March 2011.

The study 'UK resident population by country of birth' (Ellis, 2009) shows that in 2004, around 8.9 per cent of the total population was born outside the UK. By 2007 this had increased to 10.6 per cent.

> **Did you know...?**
>
> Nelson Mandela was charged with trying to overthrow the government of South Africa. He was imprisoned for 18 years on Robben Island because he wanted black and white people to have the same opportunities in South Africa. He said in his defence: 'I have cherished the ideal of a democratic and free society in which all persons live together in harmony and with equal opportunities.'

Table 6.01 Five most common non-UK countries of birth of people living in the UK, 2004 and 2007

2004	2007
India	India
Republic of Ireland	Republic of Ireland
Pakistan	Poland
Germany	Pakistan
Bangladesh	Germany

Source: www.statistics.gov.uk/articles/population_trends/PT135POPCOBARTICLE.pdf

One of the problems with using ethnicity as a term is that it makes some false assumptions. It assumes that place of birth, nationality and ethnicity are the same, but they are not.

Indian people are the largest minority group in the UK, but not everyone from India speaks the same language. There are over 14 official state languages. Many religions are practiced in India: there are Muslims, Christians, Sikhs, Hindus, Buddhists and Jains, to name just some. There is also huge variety in the food and customs of the people of northern India and southern India So you can see that to use 'ethnic group' in relation to all Indians isn't very useful. The census classifies Indian people together for convenience when collecting information, but in reality, Indians are very diverse.

Religious beliefs vary in UK society. Some people believe in one god and some believe in many. Atheists do not believe in any god. Agnostics say they we cannot know if God exists because we cannot prove whether there is a god or not.

The term 'secular' refers to non-religious beliefs. For example, many state schools in the UK are secular, i.e. not religious. Health care is also secular, as is the police force.

'Humanists' are secular. They believe that we are rational and logical beings who have the right and the responsibility to decide our own lives and shape our own society based on the ethics of human values.

Social class is one way people differ in UK society. We class people according to their job, wealth, power and education, how they dress and how they behave. A hospital doctor would have a higher social class

Did you know...?

Nationality is not the same as country of birth. For example, if British parents are working abroad, perhaps in the armed forces, the children born abroad will have British nationality.

Did you know...?

Ethics refers to values. *Ethnic* refers to racial or cultural origins.

than a factory worker because they have had a longer education and have better career prospects. In the long term they may earn a lot more and be able to afford a better house and better education for their children. Many people disagree with having social differences based on money and education, but such differences still exist in our society

The Office for National Statistics uses the following social and economic classifications:

1 Higher managerial and professional occupations.
2 Lower managerial and professional occupations.
3 Intermediate occupations.
4 Small employers and own account workers.
5 Lower supervisory and technical occupations.
6 Semi-routine occupations.
7 Routine occupations.
8 Long-term unemployed (including those who have never worked).

Why does social class matter to some people? In the UK, social class is linked to health. According to the 2001 census, the higher class you are, the healthier you are likely to be. People in the lowest classes are more likely to have long-term illness or disability. The government is concerned that there is such a difference in our society. Many government policies or plans aim to make things more equal. Working family tax credits are designed to help low-income families afford better food and a healthier lifestyle.

Gender or sexual category provides one aspect of our diverse society. Most people are born with either male or female sexual characteristics. Sometimes, people are transgender. In the UK there are about 5,000 people who fit into this category (Women and Equality Unit, 2005).

Sexuality refers to a person's sexual preference. Gay and lesbian couples now have rights to enter into a civil partnership that is legally recognised.

Age is another source of diversity in society. In the UK, fewer children are being born. At the same time, people are living longer. This means that the UK population is ageing. The number of people over 85 is the fastest-growing sector. The UK population aged 85 or over more than doubled from 0.9 per cent in 1971 to 1.9 per cent in 2004.

Family structure is now more diverse – 24 per cent (or nearly one in four) of families is a lone-parent family. Fewer children live in families with two parents. At the same time, more people are living alone – 7 million people were living alone in 2005.

Disabilities bring diversity too. The most common disability in people under 20 is now asthma. Autism and autistic

> **Did you know...** ❓
>
> Researcher Danah Boyd of the University of California found social class divides between users of FaceBook and MySpace. Originally, Facebook was limited to university students or those with an academic email address, whereas anyone could join MySpace. In the US military, officers mostly use FaceBook, whereas ordinary soldiers tend to use MySpace.

> **Did you know...** ❓
>
> You can see the census findings for yourself at www.statistics.gov.uk.

spectrum disorders and behavioural disorders are the main causes of severe disability. Statistics show that children of semi-skilled manual workers are more likely to have disabilities.

Activity 1

Work in groups of three. Take a set of index cards and three pens of different colours (felt tips are good). Use one colour for each factor, such as red for social factors, blue for political factors and green for cultural factors.

- Using the red pen, write on separate blank cards as many social factors as you can think of, such as managerial class, unemployed, large family, lone-parent family.
- Then take the blue pen and write cards for different political views, such as 'the council should build more houses', or 'buy your own house'
- Finally, take the green pen and write index cards for cultural factors, such as 'involved with music' or 'girls are expected to help in the house' or 'boys have more freedom'.

When you have several cards, mix them up then pick up one from each set and make up a person with those beliefs. So for example, you may have a person who is unemployed, involved with music and believes the council should build homes to rent. What might that person look like? Use your imagination. You may wish to draw them. Talk about your person with your group.

This activity will help you towards P1 and towards achieving PLTS (IE1, CT2, TW1, EP1 and EP5).

2 Understand beliefs and practices in different religious or secular groups

Range of religious and secular groups

In UK society today there is a range of religious groups. This has been the case throughout history. For example, the Romans brought a variety of religions when they conquered Britain. They had temples and shrines to different gods. The ruins of a temple to Mithras, the bull god, were found near Carrawburgh Fort on Hadrian's Wall in Northumberland.

Did you know...

According to the 2001 UK Census, the religious population in Great Britain is made up of 72 per cent Christians, 15 per cent no religion, 5 per cent belong to non-Christian religions, 8 per cent chose not to say.

of their life and that rational, logical thought provides a moral code to live by.

Jehovah's Witnesses

Jehovah's Witnesses are Christians. They are evangelical, which means they try to convert people to their religion. They believe that God is the only God and is called Jehovah, that Jesus Christ is his son and that the Holy Spirit is God's active force. They do not believe that Jesus died on a cross, but think he died on a stake or pole.

They believe the world will end soon, that the end times started in 1914 and that when 'the End' finally comes only 144,000 human beings will go to Heaven and rule the Earth from there with Christ.

Jews

There are Orthodox Jews and Reform Jews. There are 13 principles of Jewish beliefs:

1 God exists.
2 God is unique.
3 God is intangible, not a person or thing.
4 God is eternal.
5 We should only pray to God.
6 The words of the prophets are true.
7 Moses was the greatest of the prophets.
8 The first five books of the Bible, the written Torah and the oral Torah, which is in the Talmud, were given to Moses by God.
9 There is no other Torah.
10 God knows the thoughts and deeds of men.
11 God will reward the good and punish the wicked.
12 The Messiah or saviour will come.
13 The dead will be resurrected.

Muslims

The religion of Muslims is Islam. There are two branches of Islam – the Sunni (pronounced 'sunny') and the Shiite (pronounced 'shee – ite'). They have similar beliefs but have different views about who should have succeeded the prophet Mohammad.

The Five Pillars of Islam are the five things a Muslim should do. They are:

1 Shahadah: sincerely reciting the Muslim profession of faith.
2 Salat: performing ritual prayers in the proper way five times each day.
3 Zakat: paying a charity tax to the poor.
4 Sawm: fasting during the month of Ramadan.
5 Hajj: pilgrimage to Mecca.

Pagans

There are several beliefs that come under the name of Paganism. Ancient religions such as the Druids and Wiccans were in the UK before Christianity. Wiccan is another name for witchcraft. Most pagan religions believe Nature is sacred. Some believe in spirits. Shamans believe in contacting spirits for guidance and advice. Sacred Ecologists, Odinists and Heathens are also part of the pagan community.

> **Did you know...**
>
> Jews, Christians and Muslims form the Abrahamic religions. Buddhists, Hindus and Sikhs are part of the Indian tradition of religions.

Rastafarians

The Rastafarian movement arose from a Christian culture in Jamaica in the 1930s. Rastafarians assert that Emperor Haile Selassie of Ethiopia (who died in 1975) was a god. Marijuana is used in worship ceremonies: it is believed that users will be brought closer to Jah (God). Many Rastafarians do not cut their hair but instead wear it in dreadlocks – heavy matted coils.

Sikhs

The five Ks symbolise the Sikh religion and all Sikhs aim to maintain them:

- Kesh – uncut hair
- Kara – a steel bracelet
- Kanga – a wooden comb
- Kaccha – a cotton undergarment
- Kirpan – a ceremonial sword, which can be a few inches long or a full-size sword.

Male Sikhs are often called Singh, which means 'lion', as a middle or last name. Women do not change their name after marriage. Many Sikh women have 'Kaur' as one of their names, which means 'princess' or 'daughter'.

Beliefs and practices

There are many different types of religions. Within any one religion there are variations in beliefs, forms of worship and festivals. This unit is only an introduction. You may wish to carry out your own research to find out more about a particular religion or belief. Perhaps you already know about your own religion. If not, this is your chance to learn.

Religious festivals

The table below summarises the main religious festivals.

Table 6.02 The main religious festivals

Religion	Main festivals
Christians	Lent is a period of 40 days, not including Sundays, starting on Ash Wednesday, when Christians traditionally prepare for Easter with reflection and may give up certain foods. Lent ends with Easter, the most important of the Christian festivals. Easter commemorates the death of Jesus Christ and his rising from the dead (Resurrection). The date of Easter Sunday varies from year to year because it is based on the lunar calendar. It is celebrated on the first Sunday after the full moon, on or after 21st March. Christmas celebrates the birthday of Christ. Some Christians celebrate this on 25th December, and some celebrate it on 6th January. The period leading up to Christmas is called Advent.
Hindus	Holi is the Festival of Colours, which marks the coming of Spring in February/March. People celebrate it by throwing paint and coloured water and generally having fun. Bonfires are lit to symbolise the power of good over evil. Diwali, the festival of lights, is a five-day festival in October/November. The date changes because it is based on a lunar calendar, like the Christian Easter festival. Small lamps are lit and placed around the home as a welcome to Lakshmi, the goddess of wealth. Windows are opened and the home thoroughly cleaned. Gifts are given, and special food is prepared.
Atheists	Atheists do not have festivals.
Buddhists	Nirvana Day is celebrated on 15th February. It celebrates the death of the Buddha when he reached total Nirvana (perfect peace). Some Buddhists meditate. Some Buddhists celebrate this festival by taking food and presents to monasteries. Wesak or Vesak (Buddha Day) is on the first full moon in May and celebrates the Buddha's birthday, enlightenment and death. It is the most important day in the Buddhist calendar. Many Buddhists visit the temples early, clean their homes and decorate them, and give offerings to the temples.
Humanists	Although Humanists do not have religious festivals, they do have ceremonies to mark marriages, funerals and naming events.
Jehovah's Witnesses	Jehovah's Witnesses do not celebrate Christmas or Easter.
Jews	Passover (Pesach in Hebrew) is an eight-day festival when Jewish people remember how Moses led them out of slavery in Egypt. It is one of the most important Jewish festivals, and is celebrated with services at the synagogue on the first and last day. On the evening before the first two days, a special service, a Seder, is held at home over a meal. The festival is called Passover, because Jews believe that God passed over or spared them when he sent Plagues to the Egyptians.

	Rosh Hashanah in September marks the first and second days of the Jewish New Year. It is a time to think about the meaning of life. Special sweet food is eaten to look forward to a sweet new year. Bread is made as a circle to show the circle of life. Yom Kippur is ten days after Rosh Hashanah and is the Day of Atonement. People fast for 25 hours from sunset to sunset. In the time between Rosh Hashanah and Yom Kippur, people try to make up any quarrels they have had. Hanukkah is an eight-day holiday starting on the 25th night of the Jewish month of Kislev which is in December. The Jewish calendar is based on the moon – a lunar calendar. This means that festivals do not always happen on the same date every year according to the Western Calendar. Hanukkah celebrates a time over 2,000 years ago when the Temple in Jerusalem was destroyed but the oil lamp stayed alight. Families celebrate by giving gifts, sharing food and playing games with a spinning top called a dreidel.
Muslims	Ramadan is the ninth month of the Islamic calendar and a time when Muslims fast from sunrise to sunset for the whole month. Like other religions, the date is not fixed according to the Western calendar but is based on the moon. This is the month when Muslims are expected to reflect, pray and do good deeds. In the evening people visit friends and family and break their fast (breakfast) together. At the end of Ramadan, there is a big festival called 'Eid-ul-Fitr', the Festival of the Breaking of the Fast. Everyone gets new clothes and children are given presents. Everyone has to give to charity (usually one fortieth of what you have) so that all can celebrate, however poor they are. Eid-ul-Adha ('Celebration of Sacrifice'), also known as the Greater Eid, is the second most important festival in the Muslim calendar. It commemorates the time when God asked Ibrahim to sacrifice his son. Ibrahim loved God so much he was prepared to sacrifice the most precious thing he had – his son. God then sent a sheep to be sacrificed instead. This is the same story in Jewish and Christian belief, except that Ibrahim is called Abraham.
Pagans	Pagans celebrate eight festivals throughout the year; these are often called the Wheel of the Year. The year begins in February with Imbolc. Fires are lit to celebrate the increasing power of the sun over darkness. Approximately six weeks later the Spring equinox festival is celebrated with egg races, egg hunts symbolising the new fertility of the year. Beltane, six weeks later, is traditionally when people choose a marriage partner. Fires are again used to celebrate this but also people gather early flowers and dance around a maypole. Midsummer is the next festival, celebrating the longest day of the year. People go to Stonehenge to see the sunrise. Lughnasadh, in August, celebrates the first of the harvest, and is followed by the autumn equinox at the end of harvest.

	Samhain, the last festival of the Pagan year, marks the Feast of the Dead. It coincides with Halloween. Some pagans believe the worlds of life and death are closer at this point of the year. Older people are seen as wise. Death is seen as a natural end to life, and the spirits of loved ones who have died are often invited to join the celebrations. Fires are lit to celebrate the end of the year and each person takes some of the fire home to keep them warm through the winter months.
Rastafarians	Rastafarians celebrate festivals with music, poetry, vegetarian food and Bible readings. Rastafarian festivals include: Groundation day, 21 April, celebrates the visit of Haile Selassie to Jamaica in 1966 Ethiopian New Year's Day, 11 September, is celebrated because Rastafarians believe Ethiopia is their spiritual homeland Crowning of Emperor Haile Selassie, 2 November, celebrates Haile Selassie as the new Messiah Ethiopian Christmas, 7 January Ethiopian Constitution Day, 16 July Birthday of Emperor Haile Selassie, 23 July Marcus Garvey's Birthday, 17 August.
Sikhs	Baisakhi (Vaisakhi) celebrates the Sikh New Year and the beginning of the Sikh community. The Birthday of Guru Nanak celebrates the birthday of the founder of Sikhism. There is music and people recite the Sikh holy scriptures the Guru Granth Sahib. Sweet foods are eaten and people decorate Gurdwaras with flowers and lights. Diwali is also a Sikh festival. It celebrates the release from prison of the sixth guru, Hargobind, in 1619. Sikhs had celebrated Diwali for many years before that and the foundation stone of the Golden Temple at Amritsar, the holiest place in the Sikh world, was laid on Diwali in 1577.

Food

Food is a way of bringing a community together and often reflects underlying beliefs.

Buddhists, Hindus and Sikhs are often vegetarian because they believe it is wrong to kill. Rastafarians, Muslims and Jews do not eat pork because they believe it is unclean. Strict Jews will only eat meat that has been killed in a way that makes it Kosher, and strict Muslims will only eat meat that has been killed in a way to make it Halal. Both these methods mean it has been dedicated to God. This reflects their belief that everything is created by God. Muslims and some Christians do not drink alcohol because they believe it is disrespectful to get drunk and abuse the body God gave you.

REMEMBER

If you are caring for someone, always ask them what their dietary preferences are. Don't assume that you know what they want.

Religious symbols are powerful. They represent a set of beliefs. For example, Muslims use a crescent moon, many Christians use a cross and Jews have the Star of David.

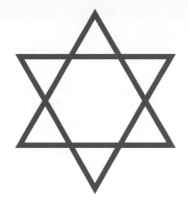

The Jewish Star of David

Forms of worship

Forms of worship vary. Some religions are very simple and their forms of worship reflect this. Some are more elaborate and include rituals, incense and complicated procedures. For example, Roman Catholic forms of worship may include a Mass, sung in Latin, with incense and a priest giving wine and bread to the congregation in memory of Christ's last supper. Some Christians such as Quakers have a very simple form of worship. Some Christians kneel to pray.

Muslims pray five times a day, as Christians used to do, but the form of worship is different. Muslims can pray anywhere but it is better to pray with others. They always wash before prayer. This is called wudu, and involves washing the hands, face and feet. They pray facing Mecca and kneel on the ground on a prayer mat, saying prayers in Arabic.

Muslims at prayer

Jews pray three times a day, and there are at least three types of prayer. As with Muslims, it is considered better to pray with others, so Jews try to pray in a synagogue. There are prayers of thanksgiving, of praise, and prayers to ask for things. Jews pray standing up. Sometimes they sway to help them in reciting their prayers.

Both Jews and Muslims have a call to prayer, but some Christians are summoned by church bells to tell them when it is time to go to church. There are many things in common between the Jewish, Christian and Muslim religion because they come from the same origin – the Abrahamic tradition.

Sikh worship can take place anywhere. They do not use images to aid prayer. There are set prayers a Sikh should recite in the morning, in the evening and before going to sleep.

Hindu worship is usually individual. People have shrines in their home and use images of gods to aid their prayer. Water, fruit and flowers are offered to the deity. They may attend a temple for a special festival.

Buddhists also have a shrine in the home, but with a statue of the Buddha rather than Hindu gods.

Health and medical beliefs

These may vary according to religion. Many people living in the UK are willing to accept western medical practices but some prefer not to use the medical services offered.

Some Christians believe in miracles, and go on pilgrimages to Lourdes in the hope of being cured of illnesses. Jehovah's Witnesses believe it is wrong to accept blood transfusions, even if it is the person's own blood that has been stored. Some people may try herbal remedies and alternative therapies. Pagans particularly have a tradition of using herbal remedies.

Hindu shrine

Activity 2

- **Choose two religions or secular groups from the following list: Muslim, Jewish, Pagan, Humanist, Jehovah's Witness, Christian, Sikh, Rastafarian, Atheist, Buddhist, Hindu.**
- **Make two small posters, listing the beliefs and practices of individuals from each group you have chosen. You may wish to decorate it with the symbol of that religion or group.**

This activity will help you towards P2, and towards PLTS (IE1, CT2, TW1, EP and EP5).

Activity 3

- **Using the posters you made in Activity 2, make notes about the similarities and differences between your two chosen groups.**
- **Divide a sheet of paper into two columns headed: 'Things That Are The Same' and 'Things That Are Different'.**
- **Look back at your posters and write down five things that are the same or similar in both groups.**
- **Look at the posters again and write down five things that are totally different between the two groups.**
- **Finally, use your lists to write a paragraph that describes the similarities and differences. Try to use sentences that begin with phrases like: 'On the other hand …' or 'In the same way …' and 'This**

is very different in ...'. Your tutor will help you with other phrases to show that you are comparing and contrasting the two religions or groups.

Make sure you describe in detail. Don't just list similarities and differences. This activity will help you towards M1.

3 Understand factors that influence the equality of opportunity for individuals in society

We have seen the variety of religious and non-religious beliefs that there are in the UK today. People's beliefs influence the opportunities they have. For example, a Rastafarian woman may not have the same chances as a Rastafarian man. A Sikh woman may have the same opportunities as a Sikh man in her own community. But what happens when people move outside their close communities? Other factors then influence the equality of opportunities. In this section we will examine the factors that influence life chances and how they do so.

Social, cultural and political factors

Whether people have the same chances as others depends a lot on the following factors:

- ethnicity
- religious beliefs
- social class
- gender
- sexuality
- age
- family structure
- disability.

In 2001 only 7.9 per cent of the population of the UK was from an ethnic minority. In reality, the bigger or more dominant a group, the more that services cater for them. So job adverts in the UK are written in the dominant language – English. If someone cannot speak or read or write English they have difficulty in getting work.

Religious beliefs can limit some opportunities. For example, in some circumstances a Muslim who wishes to pray five times a day may face difficulty when they need the time away from working in order to pray.

Social class is one of the main factors that limit opportunity in the UK, because it influences the amount of education and wealth a family has.

Children go to school in their local area, but where they live is determined by where their family can afford. People who own their own house may choose to live near a school that has good results, so their children can have a better education. A better education gives more choice of jobs.

Gender influences job opportunities and whether a person is willing to take the chances they are offered. Some jobs such as care work are dominated by one gender, for example only 10 per cent of nurses are men. Some women who are mothers leave nursing because they find it difficult to manage childcare responsibilities with long working hours.

Sexuality may influence the opportunities people are given. According to a report by Stonewall (www.stonewall.org.uk), 75 per cent of young gay people attending a faith school have been bullied and 97 per cent hear insulting remarks about gay people. Over half of gay and lesbian pupils feel unable to be themselves at school.

Age is a factor in whether people are given the same chances as others. People used to be discriminated against because they were seen as too young or too old for certain jobs. Older people were made to retire or were made redundant because of their age. Young people were told they did not have experience.

Family structure influences life chances. A single parent bringing up children will struggle to find the money for school trips or school uniform. According to a Labour Force Survey, in the three months to June 2007, 57.1 per cent of lone parents with young children were employed, compared with 71.1 per cent of married or cohabiting mothers (Source: www.statistics.gov.uk).

Disabilities may be physical or mental. Mental illness is a factor in how people experience opportunities. In a study of people with psychotic mental illness, in 2000, Maureen O'Brien found that 70 per cent of people with a psychotic mental illness were unemployed. Of those who did have jobs, half of them had part-time jobs. As a result, they experienced money problems.

Did you know...(?)

The Equality and Human Rights Commission (which replaced the Commission for Racial Equality, the Disability Rights Commission and the Equal Opportunities Commission) explains the rights people have under the law (www.equalityhumanrights.com).

Activity 4

- Working in groups of three, list the factors that may influence equality of opportunity. Write each factor on a separate card.
- Turn the cards face down.
- Take turns to pick up a card. When it is your turn you have to explain how that factor may cause a person to be disadvantaged in health or social care. Try to imagine a case study, or use a television character,

to talk about a person who might be disadvantaged by the factor and how it might affect them. (For example, you may imagine someone like Jake, who comes from a family of travellers and is called names by some people at school because of this.)

- When there are no cards left, shuffle them and place them face down, then take turns again. You are not allowed to give the same example twice, so if you had the card for disability last time and mentioned hearing loss, no one can use hearing loss again.

This activity will help you towards P3 and towards PLTS (CT2, RL1, RL5 and SM3).

Discriminatory practice

Discriminatory practice means how people are discriminated against. It happens in four ways:

1 Prejudice – or prejudging people without really knowing them. For example, a social worker may assume that all Asian families care for their old people, so Mrs Begum does not need home care.

2 Discrimination is favouring one person over another one, or being against someone for no reason. For example, a GP receptionist may think that anyone over 60 can have a day-time appointment because they assume that people over 60 do not work.

3 Stereotyping is classifying someone without really seeing them as a person. For example, an African-Caribbean man in casualty may be stereotyped as a porter, when he may in fact be a doctor.

4 Labelling – seeing only one part of a person, seeing their colour or disability rather than the whole person. For example, a person using a walking stick may be labelled as needing help but they may be perfectly independent.

Activity 5

Building on Activity 4, choose one example for each factor and discuss with your group how discriminatory practice can be avoided in each situation. You should aim for at least three ways to avoid discrimination.

This activity will help towards M2.

Effects of discrimination on an individual's health or well-being

When people are discriminated against it may affect them in the following ways:

- physically
- intellectually
- emotionally
- socially.

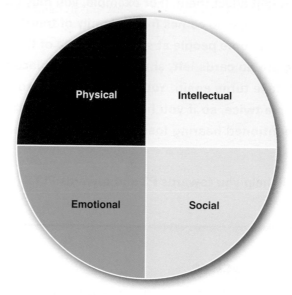

Think of pies as a way to remember these four things.

○ ## Case Study

Jared is 16 and lives in care. He comes to college. He is mixed race. Some of the other students get to know he is in care and start talking about him in the refectory. 'He must have done something wrong to be in care,' Sarah says. 'I'm not going to be friends with him – I don't want to mix with people like that. My dad says all the kids from that area are gangsters or druggies.' As Jared comes in they all go quiet. When he comes over they all look away and Jane puts her bag on the seat so he cannot sit with them. Later, Sarah's boyfriend and some mates wait for Jared and push him around as he walks to the bus stop.

- How is Sarah pre-judging Jared?
- How is she stereotyping Jared?
- How is she labeling him?
- Who is discriminating and how are they doing it?

The effects on Jared might be:

- physical – being pushed around now might lead to him being beaten up later
- intellectual – he might not want to come to class as the others are so unfriendly
- emotional – he may feel upset or scared and become withdrawn and depressed
- social – he may be lonely as people avoid him because they want to be friends with Sarah and her crowd.

We must not be like Sarah in the case study. We should see people as individuals.

Activity 6

Take one of your own examples and assess the possible effects of discrimination on the health and well-being of individuals you made up your case studies about. If you based it on a real person, make sure you maintain confidentiality.

Make a list and write an effect against each of the factors:

- physical
- intellectual
- emotional
- social.

This activity will help towards D1.

Individual worker responsibilities

An individual worker is responsible for their own actions. In health and social care you can never say 'I did it because s/he told me to.' If you hurt someone, you made that choice and you have to take responsibility for it. If you see discrimination happening, *never* join in. Ask why the person who is being discriminating thinks the way they do and ask them to see the person they are discriminating against as an individual, not a stereotype. Discrimination is never acceptable in care. We should challenge it and try to get it stopped.

Institutional responsibilities

Institutions such as care homes, day centres, hospitals and educational establishments have a 'duty of care' to protect people. There must be equal opportunities policies to guide staff about how to behave. The manager in charge must make sure all staff have training on providing care that sees the person first and does not stereotype. The staff then have individual responsibility to make sure they treat people fairly. The manager must have a complaints procedure so that anyone who feels they have been discriminated against can complain and have that complaint carefully investigated.

Working with colleagues

Not discriminating and treating people fairly extends to the people you work with. In health and social care, people must respect service users and also everyone they work with. It is important not to prejudge colleagues and not to discriminate against them in any way. Male nurses should not be given tasks such as heavy lifting just because they are male. They should not have to have a chaperone when with patients if a female nurse does not have to have a chaperone with patients.

Working with service users

When we are working with patients in health care and service users in social care we must not prejudge, stereotype, label or discriminate, but must treat each person as an individual and offer them the same opportunities. For example, always ask how a person would like to be addressed. Don't assume that because they are older they would like to be called 'Mr' or 'Mrs'. They may prefer to be called by their first name.

Materials

Equipment

The equipment we use must be suitable for all. The gown you offer a person in outpatients should be equally suitable for men and women. At a day centre, there should be equipment that can be used by everyone, not just a few. Mugs should have easy-grip handles so people with arthritis can enjoy a mug of tea with everyone else without needing a 'special cup'.

Activities

The activities provided should be suitable for everyone, or a choice of activities should be offered. Some men like knitting and some women like watching football or horse racing on television. In the care home, think of the people and their likes and dislikes. Don't assume you know – ask them! In the play corner of a nursery, provide a variety of activities for boys and girls. Some girls like to play with cars and some boys like to play at cooking.

Visual displays

These should represent a variety of people, of different ethnic backgrounds and genders. For example, don't just show female nurses and male doctors. The staff and service users of the day centre may well be from a variety of backgrounds and all should be represented.

Toys and books

Toys and books that provide positive images of gender and race should be part of the everyday equipment for children. There are many useful books that help children value themselves and avoid stereotypes (e.g. *It's OK to be Different* and *The Family Book* by Todd Parr, and *One Dad, Two Dads, Brown Dad, Blue Dads* by Johnny Valentine).

The role of the media

Our ways of thinking and behaving are formed by what we see around us. Sometimes we accept what we see without thinking but when we work in health and social care we need to ask why we think as we do. Sometimes we need to change.

Books can encourage discrimination or question it, for example *The Curious Incident of the Dog in the Night-time*, by Mark Haddon, tells the story from the viewpoint of someone with autism.

Leaflets sometimes stereotype people. Older people are shown as needing a stair-lift or a hearing aid. Some young people have hearing problems, but advertisements for hearing aids almost always use pictures of older people.

Newspapers may stereotype people as 'thugs', 'scroungers', 'hoodies' because sensational headlines sell newspapers. Magazines often show celebrities as people concerned with how they look. Some celebrities do a lot of good work but they don't always get noticed for that. Television programmes often stereotype people, for example as East End Cockneys or Australian surfers.

The Internet has opened up communication and possibilities for breaking down barriers between people. As it is not regulated it also opens up opportunities for prejudice and stereotyping. The individual has to choose how they use it. YouTube gives the opportunity to post a video. For example, 'Geriatric 1927' is a retired person who has his own site and presents the point of view of an older person; and The Zimmers, a group of older people, recorded a performance of The Who song 'My Generation', which challenged stereotypical views of older people.

4 Know the role of legislation, codes of practice and charters in promoting diversity

Roles and impact of the conventions, legislation and regulations

Conventions are laws that relate to several countries in a group. Individual countries ratify or sign up to the laws that cover their group. Sometimes individual countries decide not to ratify a law, which means they do not accept that law for their country.

The European Convention on Human Rights and Fundamental Freedoms 1950 bans torture and discrimination. Article 2 gives the right to life and Article 5 gives the right to liberty and security. Under this Convention it is illegal to tie residents in chairs as a means of restraint as this denies them their liberty.

The **Mental Health Act 1983** provides for the compulsory detention and treatment in hospital of those with mental disorders. A person may be admitted to hospital under Part 2 of the Act if there is a formal application by either an Approved Social Worker (ASW) or the nearest relative. The application must be supported by recommendations made by two qualified medical practitioners, one of whom must be approved for the purpose under the Act. Patients may apply to a tribunal to be considered for discharge.

The **Mental Capacity Act 2005** protects vulnerable people who are not able to make their own decisions. It makes clear who can take decisions, in which situations, and how they should go about this. It helps people to plan ahead for a time when they may lose the capacity to make their own decisions.

The **Mental Health Act 2007** amends the Mental Health Act 1983 and gives people a right to an advocate when they are detained, and protects children from being put on adult wards inappropriately. There are new safeguards over the use of electro-convulsive therapy, for people detained under the Mental Capacity Act.

> ### Key terms
>
> Legislation – laws passed by Parliament. Some laws are called 'conventions' or 'regulations'.

The Convention on the Rights of the Child 1989 includes rights to food, shelter, clean water, formal education and primary health care. There are rights that protect children from abuse, neglect, exploitation and cruelty. Other rights entitle children to express opinions and to have a say in matters affecting their life. Under this Convention children have a right to say who they prefer to live with if parents split up.

The Children Act 1989 brought together a lot of different laws about children and made local authorities responsible for fostering, child minding and day care as well as residential children's homes.

 ## Case Study – The Children Act 2004

There was public outrage at how the UK child protection system failed to protect eight-year-old Victoria Climbie, who was abused and murdered by her guardians in London, in 2000. A government inquiry was held and several recommendations were made which eventually were formed into a policy called 'Every Child Matters: Change for Children'. The aims of 'Every Child Matters' are:

- be healthy
- stay safe
- enjoy and achieve
- make a positive contribution
- achieve economic well-being.

You can find out more at www.everychildmatters.gov.uk.

Every Child Matters then led to the **Children Act 2004**. The aim of the Children Act is to streamline services for children so that different organisations caring for children will see the whole picture. This will improve the overall service for children through joint planning, buying-in and delivery of services. This should make everyone more accountable for their part in planning and delivering care. This was needed because professionals did not talk to each other enough, and as a result children were not always receiving the care they needed. Local authorities now have a duty to promote the educational achievement of children. There is now a Children's Commissioner who represents the views of children.

Race Relations Act 1976 and Race Relations (Amendment) Act 2000

The 1976 legislation made racial discrimination illegal. The 2000 amendment requires public bodies to promote race equality. Schools, local authorities and hospitals must all get rid of unlawful racial discrimination and promote equality of opportunity and good relations between people of different racial groups.

The Commission for Racial Equality (CRE) was set up to enforce the Race Relations Act. The CRE has now become part of the Equality and Human Rights Commission.

The Equality and Human Rights Commission (www.equalityhumanrights. com) acts for everyone in society and has new enforcement powers to guarantee people's equality. It must also promote understanding of the Human Rights Act.

Disability Discrimination Act 1995 and Disability Discrimination Act 2005

After the 1995 Act, it became illegal to refuse a job to someone because they had a disability. The Act gave people with disabilities rights in:

- employment
- education
- access to goods and facilities
- buying land or property.

The 2005 Disability Discrimination Act extended the powers of the 1995 Act. It became illegal for operators of public transport to discriminate against people with disabilities. This means that the rail service has to provide facilities so that disabled people can travel. This might mean ramps at stations or help from a guard. Buses now have lower platforms to enable people with disabilities to board. For the first time the definition of disability was extended to cover 'hidden' disabilities such as HIV, cancer and multiple sclerosis.

Human Rights Act 1998

Under the 1998 Act, human rights include:

- right to life
- protection from torture

- protection from slavery and forced labour
- right to liberty and security
- right to a fair trial
- no punishment without law
- right to respect for private and family life
- freedom of thought, belief and religion
- freedom of expression
- freedom of assembly and association
- right to marry
- protection from discrimination
- protection of property
- right to education
- right to free elections.

We all have a right to life, but under the Act we do not have a right to commit suicide or ask others to help us die. The Act gives individuals the right to challenge in the UK courts any actions or decisions of public authorities that they believe have violated their rights.

The Sex Discrimination Act was amended in May 1999 to protect trans-sexual people against discrimination in employment and vocational training.

Data Protection Act 1998

The Data Protection Act 1998 replaced the 1984 Data Protection Act (see the Information Commissioner's website at www.ico.gov.uk). The Act applies to 'personal data', about identifiable living individuals, and covers both personal data held electronically and manual or paper data held in structured files or easily accessible systems. The Data Protection Act gives rights to individuals about whom information is held. It also requires those who record and use 'personal information' to follow the eight principles of good information handling.

Data must be:

- fairly and lawfully processed
- processed for limited purposes
- adequate, relevant and not excessive
- accurate
- not kept for longer than is necessary
- processed in line with the data subject's rights
- secure
- not transferred to countries without adequate protection.

Data may be processed only where the individual has given their consent. The Data Protection Act 1998 gives individuals the right of access to information held about them but forbids releasing that information to anyone else without permission, unless there is a legal requirement to do so.

Care Standards Act 2000, Nursing and Residential Care Homes Regulations 1984 (amended 2002)

The Care Standards Act 2000 replaces previous legislation such as the Registered Homes Act 1984 and amendments. The Act established a new Commission for Social Care Inspection (CSCI). This has now ceased to exist and has been replaced by the Care Quality Commission.

The 2000 Act stated what must be done. This was in contrast to the 1984 legislation, which allowed flexibility of interpretation. The 2000 Act set out legally required national minimum standards. Some of these standards, such as minimum room size, were difficult for small homes to meet and thus many of them closed.

The Healthcare Commission, Commission for Social Care Inspection and the Mental Health Act Commission ceased to exist on 31 March 2009. It was replaced by the Care Quality Commission, which is the new health and social care regulator for England. They look at the whole picture of health and social care to ensure better care for everyone in hospital, in a care home and at home. You can find out more at www.cqc.org.uk.

Codes of practice and charters

Codes of practice are not the same as laws. A law is something everyone in the country must follow. Codes of practice apply to certain professions.

> **Key term**
>
> Code of practice – outlines how people should behave.

General Social Care Council/Care Council for Wales/Northern Ireland Social Care

The regulating body for social care workers is the General Social Care Council (GSCC). It produces a code of practice for employers and one for social care workers. Social workers must register with the GSCC. If they break the code they may be removed from the register, which means they cannot work as a social worker, or they may be suspended for a period or given a public admonishment. You can read why people get removed from the register on the conduct section of the GSCC website. For example, a social worker was recently removed from the register for breaking confidentiality and giving personal information to a third party who had no right to have it. Find out more at www.gscc.org.uk.

Some other codes of conduct and charters

The Nursing and Midwifery Council also has a code of conduct, which you can see on its website at www.nmc-uk.org.

Charters set out what is good practice and are often aimed at helping service users.

> **Key term**
>
> Charter – sets out what people would like.

For example, the Mencap families' charter was launched at the House of Commons on 17 April 2007 (www.mencap.org.uk).

Policies and practice

Organisational policies are written to help organisations comply with their legal duty. For example, the Health and Safety at Work Act states the legal duty of employers and employees, but every care organisation must have a health and safety policy saying how they manage health and safety in their workplace. The Equality and Human Rights Commission enforce all the laws about equality, but every organisation must have a policy saying what they do about equality in their organisation. Policies interpret the law for that particular workplace or organisation.

Procedures specify how the policies are put into practice. An equal opportunities policy may say the organisation does not discriminate. The procedure says how this happens, so the procedure for placing a job advertisement may be that it does not ask for any specific gender or age of applicant. A social worker will explain the complaints procedure so service users know how to complain.

Laws change and policies should be revised as the law changes. Procedures may also need to change. It is not easy to keep up-to-date with changes in laws. Listen to the news and check the government website (www.direct.gov.uk) to keep up to speed.

Activity 7

Research and produce a **PowerPoint presentation** or a **report** to outline *one* piece of relevant legislation and *one* code of practice or charter for a chosen health or social care environment that aims to promote diversity.

This activity will help you work towards P4 and PLTS (IE3, CT2,IE4, RL1, RL5, SM3, EP1 and EP5).

Activity 8

Describe how the legislation and code of practice or charter that you used in Activity 7 promotes diversity. Describe who it affects, how it works, where and when it applies, and if there is any overall body in charge of making it happen.

This activity will help towards M3.

Activity 9

Assess how effective the legislation and code of practice or charter that you used in Activity 8 has been in promoting diversity.

- First, make a list of 'what worked' and 'what did not work' for the piece of legislation and then for the code or charter. Give examples for each.
- Make a judgement about how effective the legislation (and then the code or charter) has been. You may decide it has been very effective, partly effective, or not at all effective.

This activity will help you work towards D2.

Responsibilities

In health and social care both employers and employees have responsibility to promote the rights of individuals. This is a 'duty of care'. Organisations that offer services such as health or social care are service providers.

Employers

Public authorities such as the NHS and social services departments must uphold and promote human rights in everything they do. They have legal duties relating to gender, race and disability.

Employers in hospitals, clinics, surgeries and day centres all have a duty to promote the rights of individuals. They do not have a choice. They must avoid discrimination in how they offer that service. They must not discriminate on any of the following grounds:

- disability
- gender
- race
- religion or belief
- sexual orientation.

Some exceptions

Very occasionally, it is lawful to discriminate, for example in the case of single-sex clinics such as a 'Well Woman' clinic, where it would be embarrassing for men to be present. The surgery can offer 'Well Man' clinics, so no one is deprived of a service. Another example is that of a care home with limited parking space. Spaces nearest the entrance are allocated for those with disabilities.

Employees

Employees working in health and social care must make sure they do not discriminate. As part of their induction, every care worker should have equal opportunities training and they must then practice this.

Summary

1 People differ in age, ability, social class, sexuality, and they come from different family types. This makes a diverse society.
2 Different religions have different beliefs but there are also many similarities between religions.
3 Some secular beliefs have ideas in common.
4 Some factors influence equality of opportunity positively, and some factors influence equality of opportunity negatively.
5 Discrimination can prevent equality of opportunity.
6 Health and social care workers must not discriminate.
7 Media such as television and newspapers can influence whether people are given equal opportunities. Materials can also influence whether people are seen as having equal chances.
8 Employers and employees have a responsibility to provide equality of opportunity.
9 Codes of practice and charters encourage equality.
10 Laws make equality a legal duty.

Assessment and grading criteria

To achieve a pass grade the evidence must show that the learner is able to:	To achieve a merit grade the evidence must show that, in addition to the pass criteria, the learner is able to:	To achieve a distinction grade the evidence must show that, in addition to the pass and merit criteria, the learner is able to:
P1 identify social, cultural and political factors that create diversity within society (see Activity 1) [IE1, CT2, TW1, EP1, EP5]		

P2 explain the beliefs and practices of individuals from two contrasting religious or secular groups (see Activity 2) [IE1, CT2, TW1, EP1, EP5]	**M1** compare the similarities and differences in the practices and beliefs of individuals from two contrasting religious or secular groups (see Activity 3)	
P3 explain factors that may influence the equality of opportunity for individuals (see Activity 4) [CT2, RL1, RL5, SM3]	**M2** discuss how discriminatory practice can be avoided (see Activity 5)	**D1** assess the possible effects of discrimination on the physical, intellectual, emotional and social health/wellbeing of individuals (see Activity 6)
P4 outline one piece of relevant legislation and one code of practice or charter for a chosen health or social care environment that aims to promote diversity (see Activity 7) [IE3, CT2, IE4, RL1, RL5, SM3, EP1, EP5]	**M3** describe how the legislation and code of practice or charter promotes diversity (see Activity 8)	**D2** assess the effectiveness of the chosen legislation and code of practice or charter in promoting diversity (see Activity 9)

Further Reading

Ellis, A., 'UK resident population by country of birth', *Population Trends*, 135, Office of National Statistics Centre for Demography, Spring 2009
'Gender Reassignment – a guide for employers', Women and Equality Unit, 2005 (www.equalities.gov.uk/research,_facts_ and_figures/reports_and_publications. aspx)

Weblinks

www.bbc.co.uk/religion
www.cqc.org.uk/
www.equalityhumanrights.com
www.dcsf.gov.uk/everychildmatters
www.guardian.co.uk/religion
www.gscc.org.uk
www.ico.gov.uk
www.mencap.org.uk
www.nmc-uk.org
www.statistics.gov.uk/
articles/population_trends/
PT135POPCOBARTICLE.pdf
www.stonewall.org.uk

Unit 7
Anatomy and Physiology for Health and Social Care

This unit provides knowledge and understanding about the way our bodies work. It looks at the systems within the body and the processes that are necessary to keep us alive. It also investigates potential malfunctions in the body (when the systems do not work correctly). The unit will also provide understanding about how to monitor body systems by recording routine measurements. We will also look at concepts of hazards and risk.

In this unit you can also work towards Functional Skills, ICT, English and Maths at Level 2 and towards Personal, Learning and Thinking Skills.

Learning outcomes:

In this unit you will learn about:

- the organisation of the human body
- the structure, function and interrelationship of major body systems
- carrying out routine measurements and observations of body systems
- the effects of malfunctions on bodily systems
- the routine care given to individuals with body malfunctions.

1 Know the organisation of the human body

Cells

All human bodies are made up of millions of cells and they all vary in size and shape depending on their function. A cell can only be seen under a microscope as it is incredibly small. However, all cells have:

- cytoplasm – this is a jelly-like structure that provides energy to keep the cell alive. Chemical reactions take place here
- a membrane – this is a thin wall that holds in the cytoplasm. It also controls the substances that enter and leave the cell
- a nucleus – this area controls cell division and is responsible for the function of the cell, e.g. a blood cell, a muscle cell or a nerve cell
- lysosomes – the main function is digestion. They can digest bacteria and viruses and are also capable of digesting damaged cells, hence they are called 'suicide bags'
- mitochondria – termed the 'power house' or the 'power plant' of the cell. This part of the cell converts sugars to energy
- vacuoles – the storage regions that save food, or where waste products become deposited.

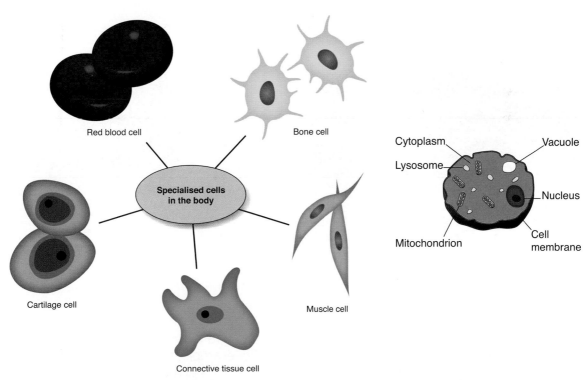

Specialised cells in the human body

Human cell

Tissues

Groups of cells work together in large numbers to perform specialised functions and are called tissues. There are four main tissue types found in our body, with special functions:

- Epithelial tissue is arranged in a single or multilayered sheet and usually covers internal and external surfaces of the body.
- Connective tissue is supporting; it has fibres in it that are tough and non-elastic. Examples include blood, cartilage, tendons, bone and adipose tissue.

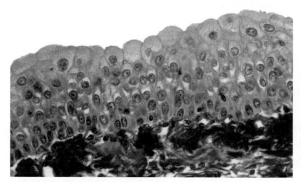

Epithelial tissue

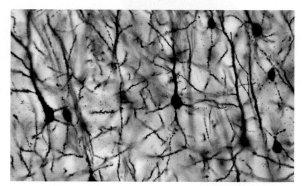

Connective tissue

- Muscle – found in all muscles and special muscles like the heart.
- Nervous – consists of neurons to form the nervous system.

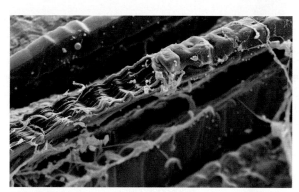

Muscle tissue

Nervous tissue

Organs

Several tissues can be grouped together to form a structure that carries out a particular function in the body: this is called an organ. For example, the stomach is an organ and contains epithelial tissue, muscle tissue and nervous tissue.

A group of organs that work together and whose functions are closely related is called a system. For example, the cardiovascular system is made up of blood vessels, blood and the heart. The nervous system is made up of the brain, the spinal cord and the nerves. These systems will be discussed later in this unit. To recap, examples of how a system is made are as follows:

CELL	↔	TISSUE	↔	ORGAN	↔	SYSTEM
MUSCLE CELL	↔	MUSCLE TISSUE	↔	HEART	↔	CARDIOVASCULAR SYSTEM

Activity 1

As a class, divide into small groups, each taking one of the organs listed below. Each group should draw the organ, label it and give a brief description of its function. On a large piece of paper, draw the outline of a simple 'gingerbread person'. Place your organ and description in its correct location. Display this in your classroom as help for P1 of your assignment.

- skin
- heart
- lungs
- brain
- eye
- ear
- stomach
- pancreas
- intestines
- liver
- kidneys
- bladder
- ovaries
- testes
- uterus

Visit www.bbc.co.uk/science/humanbody and follow the interactive body link to play the organs game.

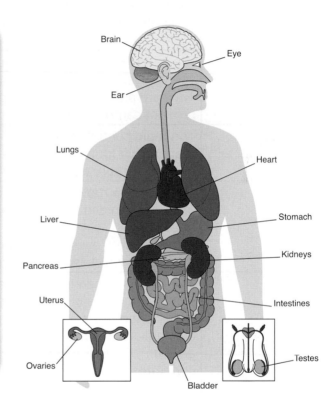

The organs of the human body

Table 7.01 The organs of the body

Organ	Main function	System
Skin	Protects the body from harmful bacteria with a waterproof barrier. It controls body temperature and has the ability to repair itself.	Excretory
Heart	A specialised muscle that contracts regularly and continuously, pumping blood to the body and the lungs. The pumping action is caused by a flow of electricity through the heart that repeats itself in a cycle.	Cardiovascular
Lungs	We have two lungs, which supply our bodies with the vital oxygen required for our bodies to function properly. They are also responsible for getting rid of the waste product carbon dioxide.	Respiratory
Brain	The main control centre for the body which is responsible for all functions within the body, whether under voluntary or involuntary control.	Nervous
Eyes	Our eyes are moved by muscles, which allow us to look up and down and from side to side without moving our head. Normally both eyes work together to form a picture on the retina, which is then interpreted by the brain.	Nervous
Ears	The organs of hearing and balance. Our ears have three sections: outer ear, middle ear and inner ear. Noise or sound waves enter our outer ear and are channelled down the canal until they reach our eardrum. Once the sound wave reaches our eardrum, it vibrates and the sound waves then pass into the middle ear. Our middle ear is an air-filled cavity that links the outer ear with the inner ear.	Nervous
Stomach	A food bag that stores, warms and softens food and drink. It is able to expand and contract in response to how much it contains. It converts solids into fluid to promote digestion, squeezes food towards its exit and then squirts it rhythmically into the next part of the intestine.	Digestive
Pancreas	Produces digestive juices (enzymes) that continue the process of breaking down foods which begins in the stomach. The pancreas also produces hormones and insulin, which controls the balance of glucose between the blood and the rest of the body.	Digestive

Intestines	In the small intestine the food mixes with vital enzymes secreted by the liver and the pancreas. Fats and proteins are mainly digested in the small intestine. The large intestine receives the end products of the digestion process where water and other nutrients are absorbed. Waste products to be excreted are stored in the end segment known as the bowel.	Digestive
Liver	The centre of your metabolism. Complex chemical processes take place in the liver and it controls the body's absorption of food. It carries out more than 500 separate processes concerned with regulating all the main chemicals in blood and many other life-supporting functions.	Digestive
Kidneys	Filter the blood, clean it and keep its composition balanced. They maintain appropriate levels of fluids, minerals and other substances, including salt and water. They react to hormones from the brain and produce vital hormones of their own.	Excretory
Bladder	Urine drains from the kidneys into the bladder via two tubes – ureters. It is then stored in the bladder. The bladder stretches and fills and at a convenient time is emptied via another tube (urethra).	Excretory
Ovaries	There are two ovaries, one at each end of the fallopian tubes. The ovaries are responsible for the storage and release of eggs (ova). They produce the female hormones oestrogen and progesterone.	Reproductive
Testes	Men have two testes, which are responsible for the production, storage and release of sperm. They produce the male hormone testosterone.	Reproductive
Uterus	Also known as the womb, it is a hollow, pear-shaped organ, which has a thick blood supply and allows the implantation and growth of the developing foetus.	Reproductive

Activity 2

P1

Draw a human body outline with a front and back view and identify the correct position of the following organs: skin, heart, lungs, brain, eye, ear, stomach, pancreas, intestines, liver, kidneys, bladder, ovaries, testes, uterus.

You may like to use a numbered key system to identify the organs more clearly. (P1)

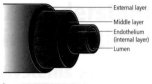

An artery

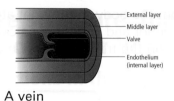

A vein

A capillary

Capillaries

Capillaries are thin-walled vessels that consist of a single layer of cells that allows oxygen, vitamins, minerals and water to be exchanged into the tissues to nourish the cells. Carbon dioxide and water then pass out of the cells to be excreted.

Blood

Blood is made up of 55 per cent plasma and 45 per cent blood cells. Plasma is the liquid portion of your blood. It has a number of vital functions in bleeding and infection control. It contains proteins and antibodies, which are produced by the immune system to fight diseases. Blood cells are suspended in the plasma. An average adult has around 5–6 litres of blood in their vessels.

Red blood cells make the blood look red and it's these that deliver oxygen to the cells in the body and carry back waste gases in exchange. The red blood cells look like tiny little inner tubes or doughnuts under a microscope. In the middle is where the oxygen sits.

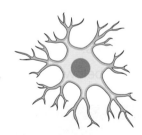

Red blood cell

White blood cell

White blood cells are part of your body's defence against disease. Some will attack and kill germs by devouring them and others will attack and kill by manufacturing and producing chemical agents against disease.

Platelets are other cells that help your body repair itself after injury. Platelets play an important role in blood clotting. When a small vessel is injured, platelets stick to each other and the edges of the injury and form a plug that covers the area. The plug or blood clot formed stops the loss of blood.

Platelet

The functions of blood

- Transportation – carries nutrients from the digestive system to the body cells. Carries oxygen from the lungs to the working muscles. Removes waste like carbon dioxide via the lungs and other waste products like excess water via the kidneys. Transports hormones to where they are needed.
- Protection – carries white cells to areas of infection. Carries antibodies to fight germs. Carries platelets to injured areas to form clots.
- Temperature regulation – carries heat away from working muscles and the centre of the body to skin. Maintains temperature within the body.
- Body equilibrium – reduces the effects of lactic acid that is produced in the muscles. Regulates fluid balance.

Respiratory system

The function of the respiratory system is to deliver oxygen into the body by breathing in and to remove waste carbon dioxide from the body by breathing out. These actions are called inspiration (breathing in) and expiration (breathing out).

The respiratory system consists of:

- mouth
- nose
- larynx (voice box)
- trachea
- lungs (x2)
- bronchus (x2)
- bronchioles
- alveoli.

The respiratory system has a similar structure to the trunk and branches of a tree. Oxygen is breathed into the body and carbon dioxide is breathed out of the body via the trachea and bronchus. These are similar to the main trunk of the tree. Adults breathe around 16–20 times per minute. As we breathe in, the air is warmed and moistened. As it travels down the trachea, bronchus and bronchioles, any particles of dust are trapped and tiny hairs that

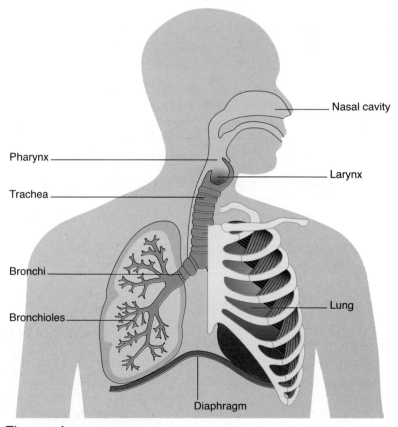

The respiratory system

line these tubes prevent this debris travelling to the lungs. The exchange of oxygen and carbon dioxide takes place at the end of the branches (bronchioles) in the alveoli. The alveoli are structures like bunches of grapes which allow maximum crossover of gases back and forth to make the process efficient.

Inhalation is the process of breathing in oxygen and exhalation is the process of breathing out carbon dioxide. This process is automatic – you don't have to think about breathing.

Muscles in the rib cage and a special muscle underneath the lungs called the diaphragm also help with the process of respiration.

Activity 4

Put your hands on your ribcage and feel your breathing. Can you explain what happens when you breathe in and then breathe out?

The nervous system

The main functions of the nervous system are:

- to *receive* information from our external and internal environment
- to *interpret* (make sense of) this information
- and then to *take actions* accordingly.

This could be actions like walking, talking or running away. Or it could be actions such as reducing body temperature, increasing heart beat or regulating water balance. In this way, your nervous system is similar to a telephone exchange: it receives messages from all over the body, interprets them and sends out messages with answers to make changes.

The nervous system is split into two parts: the central nervous system – brain and spinal cord – and the peripheral nervous system – nerves. All messages are sent from sensory receptors via a sensory nerve to the brain or spinal cord. The brain or spinal cord then interprets the message and responses are made by the motor neurones to the effectors to make the change or movement.

The brain

The brain consists of billions of nerve cells. It is responding all the time to external and internal messages – those outside you and within you. For example, as you are reading this book your brain is interpreting information and allowing you to understand new ideas and perhaps make pictures. It will also be responding to external things. For example, are you feeling hot or cold? Your brain adjusts the internal environment to help you to feel comfortable, as well as creating feelings or emotions.

Spinal cord

This runs from the base of the brain to the lower part of the back (lumbar region). It is a bundle of nerve fibres, nerve cells and blood vessels. The spinal cord is protected by the spinal vertebrae in the spinal column. The spinal cord is also protected by a tough outer membrane and between this and the spinal cord is a fluid that acts as a shock absorber called cerebro-spinal fluid.

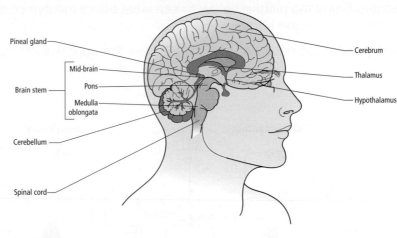

Pineal gland
Mid-brain
Brain stem
Pons
Medulla oblongata
Cerebellum
Spinal cord
Cerebrum
Thalamus
Hypothalamus

The brain

Nerves

There are 43 pairs of nerves that make up the central nervous system. Twelve of these pairs are the cranial nerves, which supply the brain, and the other 31 pairs are spinal nerves, which supply the rest of the body. Nerves vary in thickness and consist of bundles of nerve cells.

Nerves are made up of nerve cells or neurones and there are three basic kinds:

1 Sensory neurones relay impulses from the sense organs to the central nervous system.
2 Motor neurones relay the impulses from the central nervous system to the muscles or glands.
3 Relay neurones transport impulses between nerves.

- Reflex actions – these are movements that you do without thinking, such as blinking or your mouth watering. These actions are done in response to external stimuli, but you do not always have control over them. Have you ever tried not blinking for a few minutes?
- Voluntary actions – these are actions that we do have control over. You can decide to walk, run, sit down, read or write. These actions are under your control.

The autonomic nervous system

This part of the nervous system is not under our control. It has two parts, called the sympathetic and parasympathetic nervous systems, which together are responsible for maintaining vital organs and the stability of the body internally (homeostasis). This is discussed later in the unit.

The sympathetic nervous system prepares our bodies for fright, flight or fight situations, so this means our bodies will be prepared for immediate action. Study the picture below to see what effect the sympathetic nervous system has on the body.

The parasympathetic nervous system has the opposite effect.

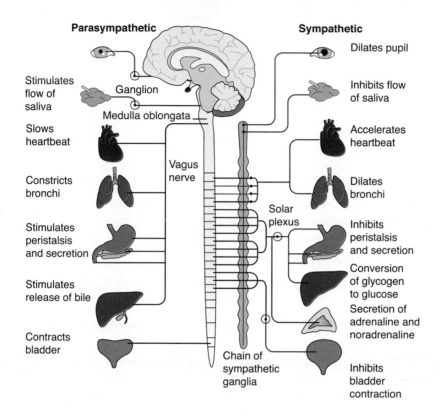

The nervous system

The endocrine system

The endocrine system produces chemical messages called hormones. These hormones are released by glands into the bloodstream. Once in the bloodstream, they target organs and can affect the structure and function of that part of the body. There are 39 hormones, which work with the nervous system to maintain homeostasis in the body.

The glands that secrete these hormones work in a system called negative feedback. Negative feedback means the gland is stimulated to produce more of the hormone when needed and to stop producing it when there is enough of the hormone in the body.

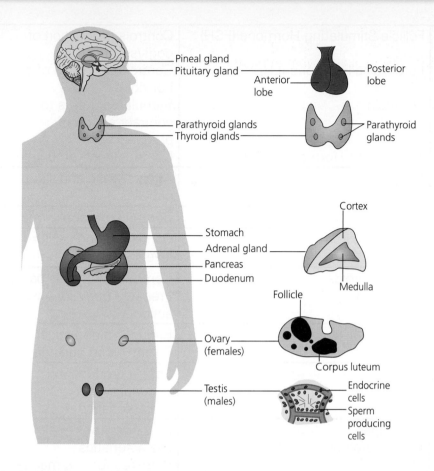

Table 7.02 Hormones and their effects

Name of gland/ organ	Hormone	Effect
Hypothalamus	The hypothalamus is a collection of specialised cells that forms the link between the endocrine system and the nervous system; it is situated in the lower central part of the brain. With the pituitary gland, it controls the amount of hormones in the bloodstream.	
Pituitary (master gland) Anterior lobe Posterior lobe	Growth Hormone (GH) Prolactin Thyroid Stimulating Hormone (TSH) Adrenocorticotropic Hormone (ACTH)	Stimulates growth of bones and muscles Stimulates breast milk production Controls secretion of thyroxine Controls secretion of adrenal glands

	Follicle Stimulating Hormone (FSH)	Controls production of eggs/sperm
	Luteinising Hormone (LH)	Controls secretion of sex hormone
	Oxytocin	Stimulates uterus to contract at end of pregnancy
	Anti-diuretic Hormone (ADH)	Controls urine production
Pineal gland	Melatonin	Affects wake and sleep patterns
Thyroid gland	Thyroxine	Controls metabolic rate
Parathyroid gland	Parathyroid hormone	Controls blood calcium levels
Adrenal glands	Corticosteroids Adrenaline	Controls chemicals balance Prepares body for physical action
Pancreas	Insulin Glucagon	Reduces blood sugar level Raises blood sugar level
Testes	Testosterone	Sperm production Secondary sex characteristics
Ovaries	Oestrogen Progesterone	Secondary sex characteristics Prepares for and maintains pregnancy

The digestive system

The digestive system or alimentary canal runs from your mouth to your anus and is approximately 8 metres long. Look at the picture below and see how many other organs in the body are involved in this system.

> **Key term**
>
> Hormones – these are chemical messages released into the blood stream to affect organs and their functions.

The digestive system consists of the mouth, salivary glands, pharynx, oesophagus, stomach, duodenum, ileum, colon, liver and pancreas.

Digestion takes place in two ways:

- physically – by your teeth and tongue, then the muscles in your alimentary canal break down the food into smaller pieces so that it is able to move through the gut
- chemically – enzymes and chemicals made by the digestive system are also responsible for breaking down the food.

Physical and chemical digestion take place at the same time – while the teeth and tongue are grinding and mashing the food, the enzymes can mix with the food to break it down even more.

To watch the digestive system in action, visit the website www.constipationadvice.co.uk and go to the section called 'How it works'.

The process of digestion is as follows:

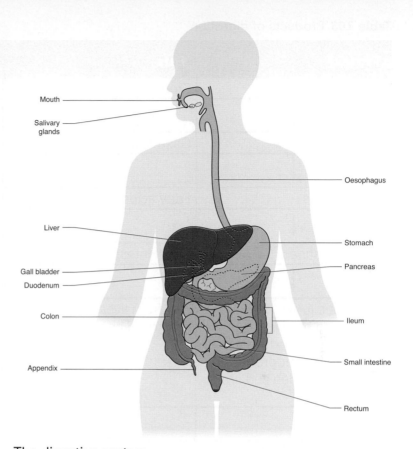

The digestive system

1 Ingestion – food is taken into the mouth and digestion starts. This is where chemical and physical breakdown of food takes place. Food is cut and ground into small pieces. The food is made into a soft bolus with the help of saliva, which is produced in the salivary glands in the mouth. The food is pushed to the back of the mouth and is swallowed; from here it travels into the oesophagus to the stomach by a process called peristalsis.

2 Digestion – when the food reaches the stomach it is further broken down by gastric juice, hydrochloric acid and enzymes and the churning motion of the muscles causes further breakdown. The food is now a thick liquid called chyme. Food stays in the stomach for around 3–5 hours.

3 Absorption – as the food is passed into the small intestine more enzymes from the pancreas further breaks down the food and bile from the liver breaks down fats. It is then taken from the gut wall into the bloodstream ready to be used in the cells.

4 Assimilation – this is the process where nutrients are used within the cells to convert to energy.

5 Egestion – this is when the food that has not been digested moves into the large intestine. The excess water is absorbed, which leaves a semi-solid mass called faeces. This moves along the large intestine and is eliminated via the anus.

Different enzymes are responsible for the breakdown of different nutrients along the alimentary canal.

Table 7.03 Products of digestion

Protein	Fats	Carbohydrates
Stomach	Stomach	In the mouth
↓	↓	↓
Pepsin	Gastric lipase	Salivary amylase
↓	↓	↓
Polypeptides	Fatty acids & glycerol	Dextin and maltose
↓	↓	↓
Small intestine	Small intestine	Small intestine
↓	↓	↓
Pancreatic juice Containing trypsin, chymotrypsin and elastin continue to split proteins into polypeptides and amino acids	Bile from liver emulsifies fats to aid absorption	Pancreatic amylase continues to split dextrin and maltose
↓	↓	↓
Peptidases separates amino acids	Pancreatic lipase continues to split fats into fatty acids and glycerol	Maltase, sucrase and lactase split maltose, sucrose and lactose into glucose

The excretory system

This is also known as the renal system. It is the filter system in the body which eliminates waste products from the blood.

The main waste substances are:

- carbon dioxide – from all respiration
- water – from cell respiration and digestion
- urea – this is from the liver after it has broken down amino acids
- mineral salts – for example, sodium chloride.

The kidneys

You have two kidneys, which filter the blood like a sieve. The kidneys keep in substances which are useful to the body and excrete waste substances together with water, which is called urine. Your kidneys also adjust the water, salt and acid balance of your blood through a process called osmoregulation. The kidneys are bean-shaped and are situated on either side of the vertebrae. They are about the size of a clenched fist. The right kidney is slightly lower than the left one, as it is below the liver.

The inside of a kidney has three regions:

1 cortex
2 medulla
3 pelvis.

The nephron is the working part of the kidney and spans all three regions of the kidney.

The ureters

These lead from each kidney and take urine to the bladder. They are long, muscular tubes that move the urine along by peristalsis. They are around 30 cms long.

The bladder

This is the muscular storage sack for urine and when full, an adult bladder can hold up to 500 ml. Emptying the bladder, or urination, is under voluntary control in most adults. It is triggered by the sensory nerves in the bladder, which send messages to the brain that the bladder is ready to be emptied.

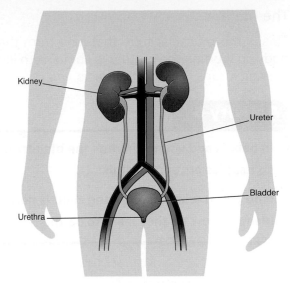

The renal system

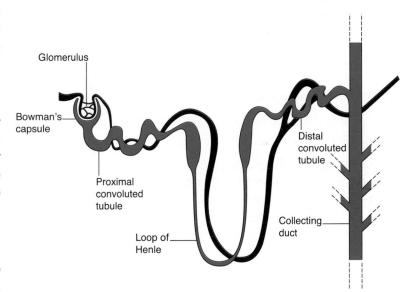

How a nephron works

The urethra

This is the muscular tube that runs from the bladder to the outside of the body. In women the urethra is about 4 cm long and in men it is about 20 cm long as it runs through the penis.

Activity 5

In babies and young children the bladder is not under voluntary control, so nappies are very useful!

Find out at what age a young child is normally able to control their own bladder. How do they learn to do this?

Reproductive system

This system is involved in the production of specialised cells called sex cells or gametes (eggs and sperm). It is in these gametes that the characteristics of each parent can be found and are transferred to the developing foetus. When an egg and sperm join together it is called fertilisation and the combined cells are known as a zygote. It now contains characteristics (genes) from both parents.

The male reproductive system

The male reproductive system has three main functions:

1 The testes produce sperm.
2 The penis deposits sperm inside the female reproductive system.
3 The testes produce the hormone testosterone (you will have investigated this in the endocrine system).

Sperm is produced in the seminiferous tubules testes, which are located in the scrotum. The testes are external organs

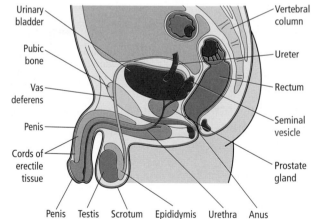

The male reproductive system

that keep sperm at a temperature lower than body temperature to keep it alive. Sperm is stored in the epididymis. When it is needed, it is released and travels along the vas deferens and past the prostate gland, where it receives nutrients and fluid to keep it alive. The sperm and fluid together are now called semen. In sexual intercourse, during ejaculation, sperm travels along the urethra of the erect penis and is deposited in the female vagina.

As we have learned from the endocrine system testosterone is responsible for the secondary sex characteristics in boys. Investigate what these are.

The female reproductive system

The female reproductive system has four main functions:

1 The ovaries produce eggs or ova.
2 The uterus provides a safe environment for the developing foetus where it can be nourished.
3 The ovaries produce the hormones oestrogen and progesterone (you will have investigated these in the endocrine system).
4 The mammary glands (breasts) produce milk for the newborn baby.

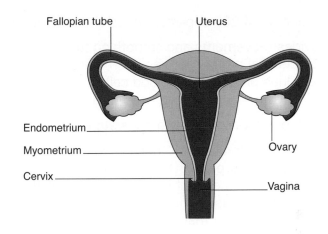

The female reproductive system is made up of two ovaries, two fallopian tubes, the uterus, the cervix and the vagina. Under the influence of oestrogen, ovum (eggs) are released from alternate ovaries each month (approxi-

The female reproductive system

mately every 28 days). The egg travels along the fallopian tube where it can be fertilised. When it is fertilised by a sperm, the ball of growing cells travels into the uterus where it embeds to begin the formation of a foetus. The pregnancy continues under the influence of the hormone progesterone.

If the egg is not fertilised it is shed with the monthly menstruation.

The diagram below shows the changes of the uterus lining during the menstrual cycle.

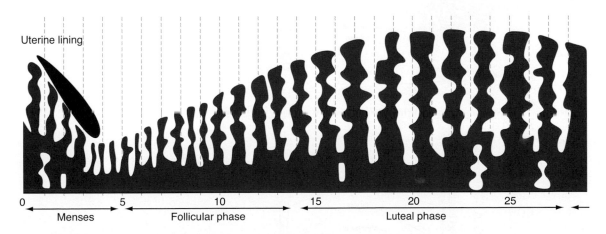

Changes in the uterus during the menstrual cycle

The musculoskeletal system

This system contains the muscles and bones of the body. Its function is to provide support and movement of the body as well as protection of vital body organs.

The skeleton

This is made up of 206 separate bones and has the following functions:

● It provides movements and something for muscles to attach to.
● It protects vital organs such as brain, heart and lungs.
● Some bones produce new blood cells.
● It assists with blood clotting, as it produces calcium.

The skeleton is divided into two separate parts:

1 The axial skeleton – skull, ribcage and backbone. Eighty of the 206 bones are in this part of the skeleton. In an adult, the skull consists of fused bones. The skull balances on top of the spine, which has 33 vertebrae and houses the spinal cord. In between the vertebrae are sections of cartilage that act as shock absorbers. The rib cage protects vital organs like the heart and lungs. The ribs assist with the breathing mechanism as they have attached muscles, which expand and contract during breathing.

2 The appendicular skeleton – pectoral girdle and the pelvic girdle, the arms and the legs. The other 126 bones are contained within this part of the skeleton. The pectoral girdle attaches the arms to the main skeleton

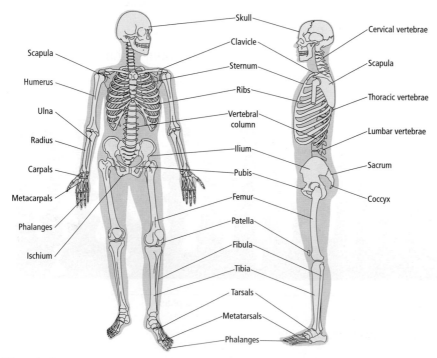

The skeleton

frame and the pelvic girdle attaches the legs to the main frame of the skeleton. The shape of the pelvic girdle differs in males and females – the female being wider and flatter to cope with childbirth.

Joints

Where the ends of two bones meet is called a joint. There are over 200 places where this happens in your body. There are three types of joints:

1 Moveable joints, e.g. shoulder, elbow, knee.
2 Slightly moveable joints, e.g. spine.
3 Immoveable joints, e.g. skull.

Activity 6

Joints can also be classed according to how they move. Investigate the following types of joints and explain their movement, giving an example within the body:

● **hinge joint**
● **ball and socket joint**
● **sliding joint.**

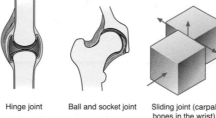

Hinge joint   Ball and socket joint   Sliding joint (carpal bones in the wrist)

Bones are held together with ligaments. These are pieces of strong connective tissue. Ligaments contract and extend, in order to allow movement of the bones.

The three types of joint

Muscles

Muscle makes up a large percentage of our body weight. There are three different types:

1 Striped, skeletal muscle or voluntary muscles – these are attached to the bones and appear striped under a microscope. They are responsible for movement. They can tire easily. We have to tell this muscle what to do.
2 Involuntary or smooth muscles – these are found inside organs like the digestive organs, blood vessels and urethras. They are responsible for contracting and relaxing and moving food, blood and urine through them. They work constantly and never tire.
3 Cardiac muscle – this is found only in the heart and contracts at least 70 times a minute, constantly.

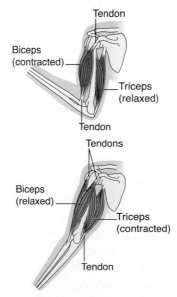

Muscle pairs flexing and extending a bone

How muscles work

Muscles are controlled by nerves and always work in pairs. This is because muscles pull bones: they do not push bones so they have to work together to make movements.

Activity 7

Look at the pictures below and explain how muscles move bones.

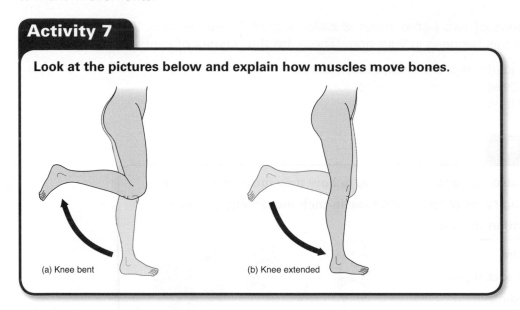

(a) Knee bent   (b) Knee extended

Interrelationship

Although the systems you have just read about all work to provide a main function for the body, it is clear that their job cannot be done without the help of other body systems. Therefore systems within the body rely on each other to maintain correct body functioning. For example, the cardio-vascular system relies on the respiratory system to provide oxygen from the lungs to give to the heart to pump around the body. The cardiovascular system then returns deoxygenated blood to the heart, then the lungs, to drop off the carbon dioxide and pick up new supplies of oxygen.

Here are two other examples of systems working together:

- The reproductive system is controlled by hormones, which are produced by the endocrine system.
- The movements of the musculoskeletal systems are controlled by the nervous system.

Homeostasis

Homeostasis is the mechanism in our bodies which regulates and maintains a stable and constant internal environment. To help us under-stand homeostasis, imagine your body is similar to your home and your homeostatic mechanism is your central heating system. Within the system is a thermostat which regulates the heating system, similar to the hypothalamus in our brain, which regulates our internal environment. The hypothalamus is the control centre.

Our bodies are continuously making adjustments to regulate normal body functions. Fortunately these adjustments are done automatically; otherwise we would be very busy people, regulating our internal environment frequently.

Homeostasis is described as a negative feedback system. This simply means that the system is able to take corrective action to maintain a constant environment. This can be further explained in the diagram.

Homeostasis is responsible for maintaining the constant level of many body functions, for example:

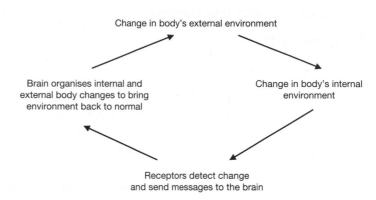

Homeostasis: a negative feedback system

- body temperature
- blood pressure
- oxygen supply
- blood glucose levels.

Body temperature

Homeostasis cannot take place without detectors and correctors. Look at the diagram opposite and corrective action the body takes to maintain a constant body temperature.

There are also behavioural actions that we take in response to a rise or fall in body temperature, for example:

- have warm or cold drinks
- put on or take off clothing
- take exercise
- switch on a fan.

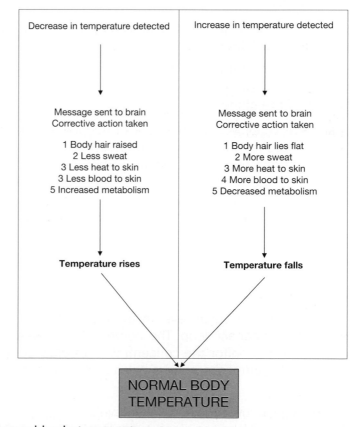

Normal body temperature

Blood pressure

The heart rate and blood pressure are under the control of the autonomic nervous system and also are affected by hormones so are under the control of the endocrine system. The system also follows the principles of the negative feedback system. We do not tell our heart rate to increase or slow down.

What makes our heart rate change?

1 Exercise
2 Fear
3 Excitement.

The cardiovascular centre in the brain controls the heartbeat, which affects the blood pressure. If the heart rate needs to increase, messages are sent along the sympathetic nervous system and the heart rate increases. If the heart rate then needs to slow down, messages are sent along the parasympathetic nervous system and the heart rate decreases. The detectors that send these messages back and forth are chemical receptors in the heart, blood vessels and brain. These detectors constantly monitor the blood and the level of carbon dioxide and oxygen. When necessary, adjustments are made to correct to the normal rate – arteries widen to lower the blood pressure or narrow to increase the blood pressure.

Oxygen supply

Respiration or breathing rate is controlled by nerve impulses from the respiratory centre in the brain. It controls:

- the rhythm of breathing
- the depth of breathing
- the rate of breathing.

This centre also follows the principle of negative feedback and stimulates a change in respirations when receptors in the blood sense a decrease or increase in the amount of circulating carbon dioxide. For example, during exercise when the receptors detect a high level of carbon dioxide in the bloodstream, they send messages to the brain to increase and deepen the breathing rate in order to expel carbon dioxide and replenish oxygen.

Our breathing rate is also under voluntary control – we can alter our rate of breathing or hold our breath if we wish!

Blood glucose level

The control of blood sugar level in the blood follows the same principle – the negative feedback loop. The control centre here is in the pancreas where receptors monitor the concentration of glucose in the bloodstream and hormones control the correct balance. The hormones are responsible for the control of:

1 Insulin – which lowers blood sugar levels.
2 Glucagon – which raises blood sugar levels.

Study the table below to understand the body response after a meal (i.e. high blood sugar level) and when hungry (i.e. low blood sugar level).

Eating	Hungry
Carbohydrates in food digested and changed to glucose	Low blood sugar level
Glucose high in blood	Pancreas produces the hormone glucagon
Pancreas produces insulin	Changes glycogen from the liver into glucose so it can be used in the body
Some glucose stored in liver as glycogen, some used by cells	Blood glucose level rises to normal
Blood sugar level decreases to normal	Pancreas stops producing glucagon

Activity 8   P2   M1   D1

For P2, choose two major body systems and illustrate with diagrams their structure, function and how they work together; you may like to choose the cardiovascular and respiratory system for this task.

Structure – what is it made from (shape, colour, size, position)?

Function- – what is the job of this system?

For M1, discuss how the structure of each system helps it to carry out its function, for example the muscular walls in the heart and its specialised tissue enable it to beat regularly.

For D1, you need to explain how your chosen systems work to maintain homeostasis, for example the respiratory system works harder as the high carbon dioxide levels in the blood are detected thereby stabilising blood gas levels. As the breathing rate is increased so is the heart beat. This circulates oxygen to the cells with the help of the cardiovascular system.

3 Be able to carry out routine measurements and observations of body measurements

As a professional in a health and social care setting it may be necessary for you to measure and record how the main body systems are functioning. To do this you need to know the following:

1 How to measure the system accurately.
2 What equipment to use and how to use it safely.
3 What the normal measurements are for that system.
4 How to record the measurement accurately.

Observations

It is important to establish what is called a 'baseline set of observations' to give to the doctors or supervisors in the care setting. This gives information to professionals to be able to treat and diagnose service users and to follow improvement or decline of their condition. The observations will then be taken at regular intervals to show a pattern of measurements. We must remember that not all service users are the same. Many factors will alter readings and these have to be taken into account when taking observations from service users.

Skin colour and texture of the skin

When caring for service users we should be looking at other signs, rather than just focusing on a reading from a machine. This means we should be communicating with our service users and watching their responses. Is their speech difficult, slurred or incoherent? Is their skin colour normal? It could indicate breathing or circulation problems if it is pale or if the service user is bluish around the lips or on nail beds. Skin colour could also indicate a raise in body temperature. Service users who are dehydrated may have very dry skin that lacks elasticity. This is common in elderly service users.

Sweating and temperature of the skin

Not only is it important to note the colour of the skin but also the temperature of the skin. Obviously this can be done using a thermometer but can also be done simply by touching the service user. This is also useful when caring for a service user who has a darker skin pigment. Touching the service user on the forehead is preferable as feet may feel cold as a result of a high temperature.

Cold skin can be an indication of many disorders so it is important to combine your findings with other symptoms. If your service user is showing, for example, cold, clammy skin which is also pale and associated with breathing problems these symptoms could indicate blood loss, shock or heart conditions.

A service user who is hot and then cold may have an infection. Cold skin can also be a sign of hypothermia from prolonged exposure to cold weather or a poorly heated living environment.

Breathing rhythms

Breathing difficulty or any kind of shortness of breath is a potentially life-threatening emergency. It can indicate numerous dangerous causes such as a heart attack, pneumonia or pulmonary embolism. There are other, less serious causes, but these highly dangerous conditions need to be considered if so these symptoms need to be diagnosed immediately by a medical professional because they can represent a life-threatening emergency.

When you are taking measurements it is important to listen for any abnormal breathing rates or noises which should be noted and reported to supervisors or medical practitioners.

Breathing difficulties or wheezing may also be due to chest infections or chronic conditions such as asthma or emphysema. This is discussed further in the unit.

Thirst

This symptom is usually linked with other factors, for example, excessive drinking and urination can indicate diabetes.

Thirst can also indicate shock from conditions associated with blood or fluid loss from major bleeding or severe burns.

Coughing

Dry cough

A dry cough occurs when the throat and upper airways become inflamed. It is non-productive, which means that phlegm/sputum (thick mucus) is not produced.

The common cold or flu causes a dry cough because the brain registers the inflammation in the throat and upper airways as a foreign object and tries to remove it by coughing.

Dry coughs are usually felt in the throat as a tickle, which sets off the coughing.

Chesty cough

A chesty cough usually produces phlegm. The cough is helpful, because it clears the phlegm from your lung passages.

If the phlegm/sputum is a green/yellow colour it could indicate a chest infection, which may need medical treatment; if it is blood-stained it may be a more serious condition, such as tuberculosis, a malignancy or a chronic lung infection.

Routine physiological measurements
Pulse rate

The pulse is the rhythmical beat from the heart as the arteries expand and contract. It gives an idea of how well the cardiovascular system is working.

A pulse can be felt anywhere in the body where an artery travels over a bone. The most common places for feeling a pulse are wrist-radial pulse and neck-carotid pulse.

The pulse is recorded in beats per minute (bpm). When taking a pulse rate, the beats should always be counted for a full minute.

When taking a pulse rate it is important to assess if the beat you are feeling is regular. Some medical conditions can affect the rhythm of the heartbeat. It is also important to note whether the beat is strong or weak. Abnormalities should always be noted and reported.

In an adult normal pulse rate is 60–80 bpm.

Activity 9

Discuss the factors in the diagram. Would they increase or decrease the pulse rate?

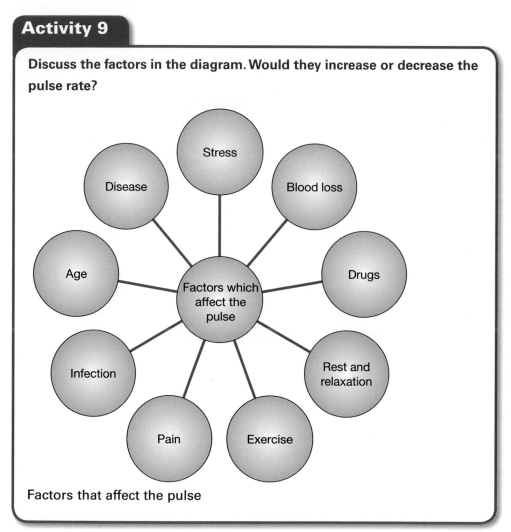

Factors that affect the pulse

Blood pressure

Blood pressure is the force exerted by the blood on the vessel walls. Again, this is a measurement to monitor the cardiovascular system. Blood pressure can vary over the body depending on where the pressure is taken.

It is usually measured in the arm with a machine and an inflatable cuff. Nowadays these are very often battery operated and will display the pulse rate as well (older styles tend to be manually operated).

Normal blood pressure reading for an adult can range between 110/60 mmhg–140/90mmhg (millimetres of mercury).

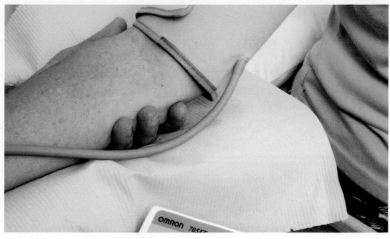

A person having their blood pressure measured

Activity 10

From the diagram below, pick out the lifestyle factors that may affect blood pressure. Discuss how they can be altered.

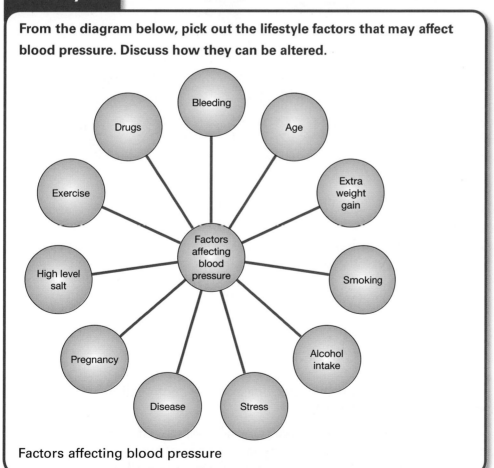

Factors affecting blood pressure

Breathing rate

Breathing is the process by which the body gains oxygen and gets rid of carbon dioxide. Breathing rate is measured by watching the movement of the chest – one breath in (inspiration) and one breath out (expiration) are counted as one respiration. When measuring breathing rate, it should be counted for a full minute. Occasionally respirations may be shallow, so it may be necessary (with permission) to rest your hand lightly on the person's chest. Again, it is important to note and report the strength and rhythm of the client's breathing rate. The normal respiration rate for an adult is 16–20 respirations per minute.

Peak flow

Peak flow monitors the respiratory system. A peak flow meter is a small device that you blow into and is used commonly with asthmatic service users. It measures the fastest rate of air (airflow) that you can blow out of your lungs. It records airflow in litres per minute (l/min). A single reading is not very useful in helping decide how well the lungs are functioning – it is advisable to take three readings of peak flow and record the highest. The client usually is in a standing position to make the best possible reading. A normal reading for an adult is 400–700 litres per minute.

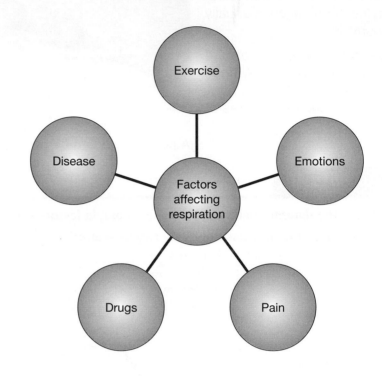

Factors affecting respiration

Body temperature

The temperature of the body needs to be kept fairly stable as dramatic changes can seriously affect the body's systems. Body temperature monitors how effectively the homeostatic mechanisms are controlled in your body. Temperature is measured in °C.

There are different ways to measure a temperature as well as different places on the body where temperature can be taken:

- tympanic thermometers – in the ear
- liquid crystal display (LCD) strip thermometers – on the forehead
- digital thermometers – in the mouth or under the arm.

Normal temperature for an adult is 36–37.2°C.

Different types of thermometers

Blood glucose levels

Blood glucose (sugar) readings are usually done for those service users who have diabetes. Blood sugar levels monitor how effective the pancreas is at producing and using the hormone insulin. The blood sugar level is the amount of glucose (sugar) in the blood, expressed as (mmol/l).

To check blood sugar level, put a small amount of blood on a test strip. Now place the strip into the glucose meter. After about 30 seconds it will display the blood glucose level. The best way to take a blood sample is by pricking your finger with a sharp lancet that is designed to penetrate the skin only as far as needed to draw a drop of blood. However, new devices have been produced which avoid the need to pierce the skin. These are called non-invasive methods. For example, see http://staffnurse.com/nursing-news-articles/non-invasive-blood-glucose-test-1668.html

The normal blood glucose level for an adult is 5–8 mmols per litre of blood.

Activity 11

Get into small groups and look into the following procedures. Find out all the important points and prepare an information leaflet for a care worker. Make sure you give them clear instructions about how to measure the following:

pulse rate	breathing rate	temperature
blood pressure	peak flow	blood glucose level.

Include the following information and draw up clear diagrams:

- how to position the service user
- how to take and record the above measurements
- what the normal range is for an adult
- what equipment you may need.

Stroke (cardiovascular system)

A stroke can be described as an interruption to the blood supply in the brain. This can be caused when a blood vessel is blocked by a clot or the blood vessel bleeds so the brain tissue is not fully supplied with oxygen and nutrients. Strokes can cause loss of movements, which can be isolated to one side of the body and also can cause confusion and speech difficulties.

Visit this website for further information on risk factors and treatments: www.nhs.uk/pathways/stroke/Pages/Landing.aspx

High blood pressure (cardiovascular system)

High blood pressure (hypertension)

High blood pressure or hypertension is usually described as having a blood pressure of 140/90mmHg or above for a constant period of time.

High blood pressure often causes no symptoms or immediate problems, but it is a major risk factor for developing a serious cardiovascular disease, such as a stroke or heart disease.

In high blood pressure, your heart has to work harder to pump blood around your body. This can weaken it and over time can lead to life threatening conditions. The increased pressure can damage the walls of arteries, which can result in a blockage or cause the artery to split (haemorrhage). Both of these situations can cause a stroke.

Asthma (respiratory system)

Asthma is a condition that causes the airways of the lungs (the bronchi) to become inflamed and swollen. It is a very common lung condition. Most cases begin in childhood.

The lungs become irritated by common triggers, which cause an allergic response in the tissue linings of the muscular bronchi in the lungs. When the bronchi are irritated, they become narrow and the muscles around them tighten, which can increase the production of sticky mucus, or phlegm. This makes it difficult to breathe and causes wheezing and coughing, and it may make the chest feel tight.

Visit this website for further information on risk factors and treatments: www.nhs.uk/conditions/asthma/Pages/Introduction.aspx

Emphysema (respiratory system)

This is a chronic lung condition, which means the lungs have been damaged over a long period of time. It is unlikely to make significant improvements as the lung structure has been damaged, which affects how efficiently the lungs work. In emphysema the air sacs, or alveoli, at the end of the bronchiole tree become over-stretched and lose their elasticity. This results in less oxygen and carbon dioxide being exchanged, so the service user is usually very breathless.

Emphysema and chronic bronchitis both come under the commonly used term chronic obstructive pulmonary disease (COPD).

Visit this website for further information on risk factors and treatments: www.nhs.uk/conditions/Chronic-obstructive-pulmonary-disease/Pages/Introduction.aspx

Chronic bronchitis (respiratory system)

The term bronchitis refers to inflammation of the air passages in the lungs. This can be acute, which means a short illness which can usually be treated and relieved. Chronic, as we learned earlier, means over a long period of time, so if the lungs have been inflamed over a long period of time this can be from irritants like smoke or from repeated lung infections.

Visit this website for further information on risk factors and treatments: www.nhs.uk/conditions/bronchitis/pages/symptoms.aspx

Diabetes (endocrine system)

Glucose is absorbed from the blood by a hormone called insulin, which is secreted from the pancreas. In diabetes mellitus this process does not work, so cells cannot take in glucose and the blood glucose remains high.

There are two types of diabetes:

Type 1 diabetes (insulin-dependent diabetes)

This form of diabetes occurs from damage to the pancreas from infections or occurs genetically. The pancreas does not produce any insulin at all so the service user will always require insulin injections to control their blood glucose levels. This type usually occurs in younger people.

Type 2 diabetes (non-insulin diabetes)

This form of diabetes is more likely to occur in people who are overweight; the pancreas does not produce enough insulin or the cells are resistant to insulin. Type 2 diabetes is more common and increasing in society today, but the symptoms can be controlled with a healthy diet and exercise.

Visit this website for further information on risk factors and treatments: www.nhs.uk/conditions/Diabetes/Pages/Introduction.aspx

Crohns disease (digestive system)

This can affect any part of the digestive tract from the mouth to the anus. It is an inflammation of the wall and lining of the digestive tract. It most commonly occurs in either the small or large intestine. As the lining is inflamed, correct absorption of nutrients is impossible and the person may suffer weight loss, diarrhoea, abdominal pain and, if not treated over a long period of time, may become malnourished. Although this condition is chronic, people may have long periods of time where the symptoms do not occur. This is called remission. The condition can affect anyone but is more common in people aged 16–30 years.

Visit this website for further information on risk factors and treatments: www.nhs.uk/conditions/Crohns-disease/Pages/Introduction.aspx

Renal failure (excretory system)

This condition occurs when the kidneys are no longer able to carry out their job of filtering the blood. It is possible to live with one kidney if one is damaged. However, if the damage is due to a chronic disorder like diabetes or high blood pressure, it is likely that both kidneys will be affected. This condition is incurable and may require dialysis or even a kidney transplant. Treatment of the underlying condition is necessary to relieve symptoms and so reduce damage. Acute renal failure can arise from an accident or an injury and can usually be treated.

Visit this website for further information on risk factors and treatments: www.nhs.uk/conditions/Kidney-failure/Pages/Introduction.aspx

Osteoarthritis (musculo skeletal system)

Osteoarthritis is a condition that affects the joints. It is the most common type of arthritis in the UK, with an estimated 8.5 million people affected by the condition.

There are three characteristics of osteoarthritis:

- it causes damage to cartilage – the strong, smooth surface that lines the bones and allows joints to move easily and without friction
- it results in bony growths developing around the edge of the joints
- it causes mild inflammation of the tissues around the joints.

Osteoarthritis mostly occurs in the knees, hips and small joints of the hands, but almost any joint can be affected.

Visit this website to find out more about risk factors and treatment: http://www.benefitsnow.co.uk/health/oadef.asp

Parkinson's disease (nervous system)

Parkinson's disease is a chronic neurological condition that affects around 120,000 people in the UK. The condition is named after Dr James Parkinson, who first identified it in 1817.

The average age at onset is 60, although people have been diagnosed as young as 18. Parkinson's is a disorder of the central nervous system that results from the loss of cells in various parts of the brain. This causes symptoms from memory loss to dementia and it also affects coordination and movement. The classic symptom of Parkinson's is tremors but it can also affect facial expressions and people with Parkinson's can suffer from mood disorders, for example, depression and anxiety.

Visit this website to find out more about risk factors and treatment: http://www.michaeljfox.org/living_aboutParkinsons_parkinsons101.cfm#q

Multiple sclerosis

Multiple sclerosis is the most common neurological condition among young adults in the UK, affecting approximately 85,000 people. It is possible for multiple sclerosis to occur at any age, but in most cases symptoms are first seen between the ages of 20 and 40. Women are almost twice as likely to develop it as men.

Multiple sclerosis is a condition of the central nervous system which controls the body's actions and activities, such as movement and balance.

Each nerve fibre in the central nervous system is surrounded by a substance called myelin. Myelin helps the messages from the brain travel quickly and smoothly to the rest of the body. In multiple sclerosis, the myelin becomes damaged, interrupting the transfer of these messages.

Visit this website to find out more about risk factors and treatment: http://www.nhs.uk/Conditions/Multiple-sclerosis/Pages/Introduction.aspx

Potential risk

A risk factor is something that increases your chances of getting a disease. Sometimes, this risk comes from something you do. For example, smoking or a poor diet can increase your chances of developing colon cancer. Therefore, smoking and a poor diet is a risk factor for colon cancer. Sometimes, there is nothing you can do about the risk – it just exists. For example, people aged 50 and older are more likely to develop colon cancer than people under 50. So, age is a risk factor for colon cancer.

The websites provided earlier in the unit give up-to-date researched information about the conditions, risk factors and treatment and preventative care to assist you with your assignment.

Lifestyle factors

Lifestyle factors include:

- smoking
- excessive intake of alcohol
- illegal drug taking
- lack of exercise
- poor diet
- poor sexual health.

Environmental factors

Environmental factors include:

- housing conditions
- air quality

- water quality
- employment status
- financial status
- education
- political climate
- access to health care and transport
- peer pressure.

Key term

Inherited – genetic characteristics passed down to the next generation.

Inherited factors

Genetic abnormalities include Down's syndrome, cystic fibrosis, sickle cell disease and phenylketonuria. These are genetic factors which cannot be changed as they are inherited from parent genes. Some conditions are extremely rare and are not apparent in a parent, but it is only when two rare or recessive genes meet that the children are affected.

If parents are aware of genetic disorders either from family history or from previous affected children, then genetic counselling can be provided to assess the chance of new pregnancies being affected.

Age

This is a risk factor associated with degenerative disorders and we can be said to be more at risk of suffering from conditions like malignancies, heart disease diabetes, high cholesterol, which all have age-related components. Musculo skeletal problems or neurological disorders like dementia and Alzheimer's disease are also more prevalent in ageing service users. As we age, we may experience a loss in function decline due to changes in our bodies and brain. These changes can be difficult to cope with. A healthy lifestyle will prevent or lessen many of the most typical types of functional decline.

Some factors cannot be changed and so you may be more at risk because of age or gender.

Genetic abnormalities include Down's syndrome, cystic fibrosis, sickle cell disease and phenylketonuria.

Activity 13

Investigate the regulations under the Health and Safety at Work Act.
Find out which parts are relevant to your work setting.

Activity 14

P4 P5 M2

For P4, briefly outline one malfunction for each of body systems you have discussed in P2 and P3.

For P5 identify potential risk factors for each of the suggested malfunctions; for example, if you have chosen heart attack some of the risk factors associated with a heart attack that you may identify are high fat diet, smoking and a sedentary lifestyle.

For M2 you should describe what effect the malfunction will have on the routine measurements and observations which you have already suggested in P3; for example, in the case of heart attack you could mention why the pulse rate would be raised or irregular and why the service user may look pale, cold and clammy.

5 Know routine care given to individuals with body malfunctions

Routine Care

As a care worker, it is important that you always treat individual service users with dignity and respect. Remember, you are not just treating the symptoms of a disease – you are caring for an individual's holistic needs. In other words, all the parts of an individual are important: we should not just focus on the disease.

Routine care considerations	Care given

Monitoring of body systems	Regular measurements of the affected body system to observe improvement or decline in the condition.
	    Changes in lifestyle, for example, improved diet or help to stop smoking, increased exercise.
	    Use of aids to improve lifestyle, for example, hearing aids or mobility aids.
	    Empowerment of the service user by teaching self administration of medication, for example, asthmatics using inhalers, and diabetics checking blood sugar levels and administering medication accordingly.

Summary

After completing this unit you will have an understanding of all the major systems within our bodies and you will be able to understand where they are positioned and how they work together to perform major functions, for example breathing.

This unit will help you to understand why routine measurements are important and how to carry out these routine measurements for service users.

At the end of this unit you will be aware of what can go wrong in major body systems and will be able to identify, with the help of routine measurements, some important conditions which may cause those systems to malfunction.

This unit will give you the knowledge and information about the skills required to be able to give appropriate care to service users which is appropriate for their condition so they are able to resume a healthier lifestyle.

This unit outlines the importance of individualised care for service users which meets the needs of their condition.

It is important for carers to understand the organisation of the human body and the workings of the body in its normal state, as this will help us understand and identify when things go wrong.

Assessment and grading criteria

To achieve a pass grade the evidence must show that the learner is able to:	To achieve a merit grade the evidence must show that, in addition to the pass criteria, the learner is able to:	To achieve a distinction grade the evidence must show that, in addition to the pass and merit criteria, the learner is able to:
P1 identify the organisation of the human body and the position of the main organs of the body (see Activity 2) [IE2, IE3, CT1, CT3, SM2, SM3, SM5]		

P2 illustrate the structure and function of two major body systems and how they interrelate (see Activity 8) [IE2, IE3, CT1, SM2, SM3, SM5]	**M1** discuss, for each system, how its structure helps it to carry out its functions (see Activity 8)	**D1** explain how systems interrelate to maintain homeostasis (see Activity 8)
P3 carry out routine measurements and observations used to monitor the two body systems (see Activity 12) [IE2, IE3, RL2, RL3, TW4, TW5, SM2, SM3, SM5]		
P4 outline a common malfunction in each of the two body systems (see Activity 14) [IE2, IE3, RL2, RL3, TW4, TW5, SM2, SM3, SM5]	**M2** describe how the presence of the malfunction might affect routine measurements and observations of each body system (see Activity 14)	
P5 identify potential risk factors for each of the two malfunctions (see Activity 14) [IE2, IE3, CT1, SM2, SM3, SM5]		
P6 identify the routine care given for each malfunction (see Activity 15) [IE2, IE3, RL2, RL3, TW1, TW2, TW4, TW5, TW6, SM2, SM3, SM5, EP1, EP4, EP5]	**M3** describe the routine care for each malfunction (see Activity 15)	**D2** explain how the routine care given for each malfunction affects the body (see Activity 15)

1 Know developmental changes that occur at different life stages

All human beings start from the moment of conception – when a sperm meets and fertilises an egg – but not all human beings develop in the same way. Many factors influence the rate and type of growth and development. These are factors not just from our genetic make-up but also from external influences around us. There is a pattern to human growth and development but we do not all follow the same pattern at the same rate.

Growth is not the same as development. Some people grow but do not develop. Sometimes babies are born with brain abnormalities and do not develop the skills of walking and talking. A pregnant woman who gets German measles (Rubella) may feel unwell. If she is in the early stages of pregnancy, the virus can cause severe damage to the unborn baby. For more on this, see the Medinfo website (www.medinfo.co.uk/ conditions/rubella.html).

> **Key terms**
>
> Growth – this can refer to an increase in size, weight or height.
> Development – this relates to acquiring skills and knowledge to perform tasks.

Activity 1

Human development can be divided into four different areas:

1 **physical**

2 **intellectual**

3 **emotional**

4 **social.**

Below is a list of explanations for PIES. Can you match them to the development areas above?

A – Problem solving, language development, reading and writing skills, memory, concentration and creativity.

B – Getting on with others, how to behave in different situations, becoming part of a group and making friends.

C – Development of the body structure and its systems, how the body works, how each part of the body relates to other parts.

D – Developing feelings towards each other, making sense of your own feelings, becoming aware of your identity and self-image.

Answers:

1 – C, 2 – A, 3 – D, 4 – B.

Lifestyle and key aspects of development

Conception

A woman is usually fertile around two weeks after her menstrual period. An egg is released from the ovary and travels along the fallopian tube. If sexual intercourse takes place, it is in the fallopian tubes that fertilisation will take place by the male sperm. The man releases millions of sperm during ejaculation, although only one sperm is needed to fertilise a female egg.

When the egg and sperm meet, they start to divide and quickly become a ball of cells. Over a few days, this ball of cells travels into the uterus and attaches itself to the uterus wall, where it starts to develop into a new human being. This process of the egg and sperm joining and starting to divide is known as fertilisation – 23 chromosomes from the sperm and 23 chromosomes from the egg join and provide the genetic make-up for a new human being.

Activity 2

Go to www.babycentre.co.uk/pregnancy – this website gives information and pictures from Week 4 to Week 40 of pregnancy.

In small groups, choose a stage of pregnancy and investigate what is happening to the baby and the mother. You may like to display your findings in a poster, highlighting each month's development.

Birth and infancy 0–3 years

A normal pregnancy is around 40 to 42 weeks long. As we noted earlier, our development can depend very much on internal and external factors. Pregnancy is the first important stage, when many factors can affect the growth of a baby.

Activity 3

Get into small groups within the class. Put some ideas together and suggest why growth and development can be affected by internal and external factors. Try to think of positive and negative factors. Here are some ideas to start with.

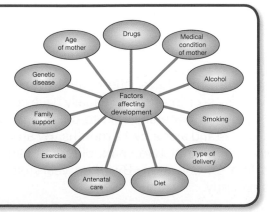

Physical development

Babies are born with a set of primitive reflexes, which are sometimes called survival reflexes. Some of these automatic responses stay with us for life and some disappear as the natural body responses take over. This set of reflexes indicates that the newborn's central nervous system is in good working order.

Reflexes include:

- Rooting reflex – this causes the baby to turn their cheek in the direction of touch and helps them to direct their mouth towards their mother's breast.
- Sucking reflex – this causes the baby to suck any object that touches their lips or enters their mouth and enables them to feed from birth.
- Moro reflex – this causes the baby to fling their arms outwards, arch their back then bring their arms together as if they were holding something and occurs in response to a loud noise.
- Grasping reflex – this causes the baby to curl their fingers tightly around any object placed in their palm.
- Tonic neck reflex – this causes the baby to turn their head, arms and legs to one side when laid on their back; they flex the limbs on the opposite side.
- Stepping reflex – this causes the baby to lift their legs as if about to walk when held upright.
- Babinski reflex – this causes the baby to fan then curl their toes when the bottom of their foot is stroked.

At this development stage, physical development is rapid. The physical increase from newborn to three years old is tremendous. Physical development can be split into two categories:

> **Key term**
>
> Reflexes – these are actions which are not under our control. Babies have primitive reflexes which disappear; they protect the baby in the first few months of life.

- gross motor skills – large movements: kicking, hopping, skipping, jumping, running, walking
- fine motor skills – small movements: threading, picking up small things, holding objects.

Gross motor skills

When babies are born, they have little control over their head if an adult does not support it. By six months they usually have complete head control. By nine months they are generally able to pull themselves up to a sitting position, and then to stand alone by 12 months. By around 15 months most babies can walk alone and at two years old most can walk up and down stairs with two feet on one step. By three years old, most children can climb the stairs properly.

Do remember, babies and children may develop crawling and walking skills earlier or later than others. These development stages are just average guidelines for parents and professionals – it is perfectly normal for babies to develop at different rates.

Activity 4

Study the pictures. Put an age to each child and suggest which gross motor skills are being displayed.

Fine motor skills

Newborn babies keep their hands closed most of the time. They have an automatic grasp reflex, which usually disappears by about three months old. By six months a child will generally voluntarily grasp an object or toy and hold it. The movements in the hands become more refined by nine months and most children can use finger and thumb to hold objects. By 12 months they can usually hold a crayon using the 'palmar grasp'. At 15 months they can usually take a spoon to their mouth and by two years old they may begin to dress themselves.

Activity 5

Study the pictures and put an age to each child. Suggest which fine motor skill they are displaying.

Intellectual development

This area of development is rapid and includes development of language. Think of a newborn and how they attract people's attention, then think of a three-year-old and how they attract people's attention. They have gone from crying to talking, often in full sentences. Intellectual development also includes using the senses.

Newborn babies use their senses to explore their surroundings. They are aware of bright colours and sounds. By six months old they are beginning to tell the difference between familiar sights and tastes. Have you noticed babies always put objects straight in their mouths? Why do you think this might be?

From six months onwards they repeat actions, like dropping a toy from a pram, but they have only a short attention span. From 12 months onwards they are beginning to understand the world around them and have increased curiosity. By the age of two they can usually point to familiar parts of the body and do simple jigsaws. By the age of three they will generally start to understand the concepts of over, under and behind and they enjoy listening to stories.

Emotional development

Emotional development is encouraged and supported if the baby has a constant caregiver. This provides them with a firm feeling of stability and attachment. This sense of attachment is called bonding. Newborn infants may cry if they are left alone too long or not held firmly because they do not feel a sense of security.

John Bowlby was a well-known theorist in this area and he considered that all infants needed one main caregiver to ensure that attachment and bonding was established. If this attachment from the main carer was removed, his research showed, then the infant would suffer emotionally. Further work in this area has been done by Mary Ainsworth and Michael Rutter, which contradicts Bowlby's research. Their work states that so long as relationships are secure, a range of caregivers in an infant's life will not have a detrimental effect.

As they reach three months old, babies can wriggle with pleasure and show happiness. At six months old they may show anxiety towards strangers and at 12 months old they can show emotions like anger, for example if a toy is taken away from them. At two years old they may start to have tantrums – you have probably heard of the 'terrible twos'? However, at this age they are trying to become more independent. By three years of age they may copy the moods or behaviour of adults around them, so having positive role models is very important.

Social development

Between the age of birth and three months, babies will start to smile at familiar faces. By the age of six months they may get upset when their mother leaves the room and may not be confident with others. At 12 months they enjoy being with familiar people and they usually enjoy mealtimes. At two years they often enjoy helping others and they may show concern for other children who may be upset. By three years old they will probably begin to take turns when playing with other children and are becoming more independent.

Activity 6

One stage of social development is learning to play between the ages of 1 and 5 years. Investigate the following stages of play:

- **solitary play**
- **parallel play**
- **on-looking play**
- **associate play**
- **cooperative play.**

Explain each one and suggest an age at which it occurs.

Childhood: 4–10 years

Physical development

In this life stage, children's physical development is showing strength, agility and dexterity. The rate of growth is now steady.

By the age of four, gross motor skills have usually improved and they will be able to stand, run, and walk on tiptoe. Their ball skills will have improved and they should be able to catch, throw, bounce and kick. By the age of six or seven they will be able to ride a bicycle and their stamina will be increasing. They will have more ability to climb, manoeuvre and run fast during team games.

By the age of four, fine motor skills are also rapidly improving. They should have mastered pencil control and be able to thread a string of small beads. Hand-eye coordination improves and children begin to show the ability to manipulate small objects.

Intellectual development

At the age of four, when a child's concentration span is much longer, children in the UK usually begin their full-time compulsory education. By the age of five they may start to draw quite detailed pictures and even enjoy solving problems. Moving towards the age of ten, children will start thinking in a more complex way and be able to perform simple tasks while listening to instructions. Language development is also an important aspect: four-year-olds start to talk in full sentences.

Language development

By age four, children will be asking many questions, using why, when and how and understand the answers. They may be able to tell long stories and enjoy simple jokes. They start to recognise some word patterns, for example the past tense. For example, they may say 'I walked', which is correct, but as they don't yet know the exceptions to the rule they may say 'I runned' and 'I goed' instead of 'I ran' and 'I went'. By the age of five, their speech is mostly grammatically correct. By the age of eight or nine, most can use and understand complex sentences and speak expressively. By the age of ten, most children will be fluent talkers and show an understanding of others' points of view.

Another important part of intellectual development is moral development. This means that, as children grow up, they start to develop an understanding of the differences between right and wrong. Parents and carers are the main influence on children's moral development.

Two important theorists, Piaget and Kohlberg, have discussed the development of 'moral thinking' and published their ideas about the links between intellectual development and morals.

Activity 7

Visit the website below and make some brief notes on the thoughts of Jean Piaget and Lawrence Kohlberg.

www.open2.net/healthliving/family_childdevelopment/morality.html

- Do you feel that moral development is influenced by anything else?
- Role models in the media, friends and family can affect how children see what is right and wrong. What do you think?
- Should politicians, pop stars and TV personalities behave in a positive way?

Emotional development

Emotional development is about developing the ability to understand and control one's emotions. As children grow up, they start to understand more about their feelings and the feelings of others. This is a gradual process throughout childhood – and it carries on for most of our lives!

From the age of five, children start to become more confident and want to do well at school and in games. A six-year-old may show signs of frustration when they fail at something. In this life stage children's behaviour may be difficult to handle at times because they are developing control over their emotions. By the age of eight, they are becoming more emotionally stable. There are also other important factors that can affect children's behaviour – see the diagram below.

Social development

The four-year-old child still depends on their parents and carers to provide social activities for them and to help them with the new social skills they are learning. For example, they still need help with dressing, eating with a knife and fork and going to the toilet. They will start to learn norms of behaviour (the acceptable values, beliefs and patterns of behaviour) for example manners, appropriate dress and method of speech. As they grow, most five- and six-year-olds like to choose their own friends and decide on play activities. By the age of ten they will generally develop much

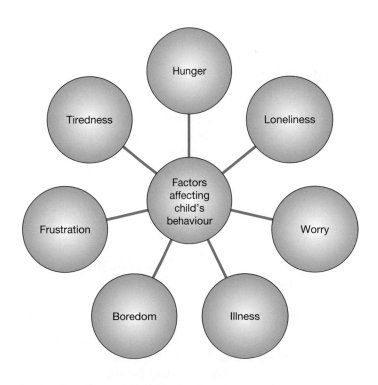

Factors affecting a child's behaviour

fuller awareness of social skills and also be aware of rules and the need to cooperate with others. This is called primary socialisation and we will look at this later in the unit.

Adolescence: 11–18 years of age

This life stage is the change from childhood to adulthood.

Physical development

During this life stage girls and boys start puberty. During puberty, physical changes prepare the body for sexual reproduction.

Female changes	Male changes
Breasts develop	Facial hair
Pubic hair grows	Pubic hair grows
Weight gain	Growth spurt
Growth spurt	Growth of penis and testes
Periods start	Voice deepens

These physical changes are due to growth and maturity of the reproductive organs (discussed in Unit 7). The reproductive organs produce hormones, which initiate secondary sex characteristics. The changes have a great effect on the other developmental areas of the adolescent.

Intellectual development

During this life stage, adolescents study for formal examinations at school and may choose to study further subjects at the age of 16. Vocabulary increases, and as young people start to develop a sense of values and beliefs they may question the world around them. Adolescence can be a very impressionable age – young people often make lifestyle choices that have positive or negative effects on their future.

The theorist Piaget believed that problem solving becomes a skill during adolescence. It may not be as refined a skill as in adulthood, but young people have the ability to think deeply and make judgements. They are often aware of the need to find out enough about an issue to allow them to make good decisions.

Emotional development

This stage of development for adolescents can be described as an 'emotional rollercoaster'. They are coping with major physical changes to their bodies. Socially, they strive to be accepted by their peer groups. Emotionally and physically, they may be attracted to the same or the opposite sex and they are also faced with issues of self-esteem and self-concept (discussed later in this unit).

They may be studying for important exams, leaving home, forming important emotional relationships, becoming independent and moving from education to the world of work. Think about your own adolescence. Would you agree that it is an exhausting time?

Social development

This is a crucial stage for making relationships and fitting in with peer groups. It is a time to establish identity and explore sexuality. Young people may experience conflict with parents as they begin to form their own ideas about the world and how to be independent. They may be entering the world of professional employment as well as establishing relationships in other areas.

It is at this stage that young people become less dependent on their families and are influenced by teachers, peers and the media. This is called secondary socialisation, which is discussed later in this unit.

Adulthood between 18 and 65 years

It is difficult to say what marks adulthood as it can vary in different cultures. In the UK, we are able to vote at the age of 18 and also legally buy alcohol. However, you can legally marry at 16 with your parent's consent and join the Armed Forces. You can also finish compulsory education and go into employment at 16.

Activity 8

Has anyone ever said to you: 'Let's talk about this like adults?' or 'Grow up, stop acting like a child!'

When or what makes you an adult? Discuss this with your classmates.

The life stage of adulthood can be split into further categories:

- young adulthood
- middle adulthood
- late adulthood.

Physical development

Young adulthood is often a time of high physical fitness in men and women. Women are most fertile at this time and many have their children in their twenties and thirties. High-risk pregnancies increase with the age of the mother. Between the age of 45 and 55, women reach the menopause. A reduction in hormones causes the woman's periods to stop. This in turn can cause a reduction in calcium production and so bones may eventually become brittle – a condition called osteoporosis.

As middle adulthood approaches, some people notice a decline in their sensory abilities. For example, they may need to wear glasses or may not be able to hear certain sounds or noise pitches. Hair loss in men is common. Adults at this life stage may be less active, so may gain weight. This is not an inevitable part of ageing. It happens when we eat the same amount of food, but have lower activity levels. In late adulthood there is an increased risk of health problems associated with age.

Intellectual development

In young adulthood, students complete their full-time education and may go on to study for other qualifications or complete specialist studies at college or university. They usually have a good memory and long concentration span. By late adulthood, we have acquired many complex intellectual and social skills, as well as plenty of life experience and wisdom to pass on to others.

Emotional development

During adulthood, most people's self-esteem and confidence increase, providing that emotional factors in their lives are positive and their personal relationships are stable.

Most adults will have experienced both positive and negative emotions during their lives, and many are able to deal with emotions well and show empathy towards others.

Social development

New social relationships are made through the world of work. Many young adults meet their life partner through work. Later in adulthood, social relationships may be put under pressure as marriage and parenting play their part. It is possible that the family income may reduce when one parent cuts down their working hours or leaves work to bring up the children. Family life can be quite tiring or stressful when work and family responsibilities are high. Later on, in middle adulthood, as children grow up, responsibilities usually lessen. Some adults feel at a loss as their children leave home – sometimes known as 'empty nest syndrome'. This is most common in autumn, when vast numbers of teenagers have just left home for college or university.

It can also happen when a child gets married, because matrimony is a clear signal that parents are no longer needed in the same way.

Older people may lose some social relationships on retirement, or if their partner dies. However, for many people social activities increase as they have the extra time and money to enjoy their retirement.

Older people – 65 years onwards

Around the age of 65 many people retire from full-time work, or reduce their employment commitments. However, owing to the fact that the population is living longer, people are now working longer. Also, because of healthier lifestyles and medical progress, a lot of older people can maintain good health. Therefore a 65-year-old may not see themselves as 'old'. It can be a time of life to begin new challenges, rather than for slowing down and taking life easy.

Physical ageing

During the ageing process, cell and tissue repair is slower and major body systems begin to slow down or suffer malfunctions (as explained in Unit 7, some malfunctions are more likely to occur during the ageing process).

Physical changes that may occur include:

- greater susceptibility to illness
- slower recovery times
- slowing down of physical responses.

Physical health can vary from person to person and is dependent on many risk factors (as shown in Unit 7). Older people should always be encouraged to be as physically active as they can to avoid deterioration of body systems, such as the cardiovascular, musculo-skeletal and nervous systems.

Intellectual development

Although it may take longer to learn new skills there is no reason to stop learning. Older people who keep their mind active and continue to learn may become able to advise younger members of society with wise decisions and a deep store of knowledge.

Emotional development

This can be affected by life events and can lead to the loss of self-esteem or self-confidence.

These include:

- isolation from peers, family, and community
- loss of independence
- progressive deterioration of health
- loss of significant other
- loss of friends
- being ignored despite their wisdom and experience.

On the other hand, many older people gain strength from their experiences and are involved positively in their lives.

Social development

Some older people may suffer isolation because they have suffered bereavement or they may not be able to get out as much due to illness or physical limitations. This may affect their confidence and desire to join in with social activities. Some older people may be very proactive in maintaining a social role in the community or family, which enables them to keep in touch with others.

Activity 9

P1   **M1**

For P1: Design a chart or table that identifies the key aspects of each life (0-3, 4-10, 11-18, 19-65) in each development area (PIES).

For M1: Outline details of each development stages. For example, in stage 0-3 years you will have mentioned that newborns have survival reflexes. For M1, you need to say what these reflexes are.

2 Know positive and negative influences on individuals at different life stages

Socio-economic factors

Income and expenditure

Income is the money that comes into the home. This may be from paid employment, from savings, investments or inheritance or from benefits that come from the government if a person is unemployed or has a disability. Expenditure is money spent to provide for living needs. Clearly, the amount of expenditure is determined by the amount of household income.

A high income allows a better choice of housing, education, health services, diet, clothes, transport and so on. However, we should remember that a higher income does not always mean that better lifestyle choices are made.

Government and other research shows that people on a lower income are more likely to suffer ill health. In areas where income is low, the choice of housing may be limited. There may be a higher than average incidence of crime, which leads to stress in the family. Groups of people on a low income include unemployed people, some single-parent families, people with long-term illnesses, disabled people and older people.

Housing

Poor housing can lead to an increased risk of physical illness (e.g. damp increases respiratory problems) and the stress of living in poor housing can increase the risk of mental illness such as depression. Vulnerable people such as young children and older people are particularly at risk from health problems caused by poor housing.

Environment

The environment is the surroundings in which a person lives. It refers not just to a house, village or town, but the wider environment, such as the area or country. If the country someone lives in is at war, or politically unsettled, then it will affect many areas of their lives, including their safety, education, health and freedom of movement.

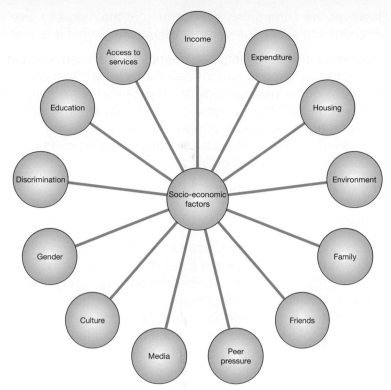

Socio-economic factors

Family, friends and peer pressure

Our family can have a positive influence on our growth and development (as discussed in more detail later in this unit). Our family is responsible for our early socialisation, which can be positive or negative depending on our role models. Peer pressure means the influence that people similar to ourselves, such as friends or co-workers, have on our behaviour. For example, we could be influenced to study, work hard and achieve or we could be influenced to make choices like smoking or taking illegal drugs. Both these choices can dramatically change our growth, development and health.

Media

The media (forms of mass communication such as television, books, magazines, newspapers and the internet) has a huge influence on our attitudes and behaviour.

The positive aspects of the media, for example in delivering education, are clear. Television programmes can also have a positive effect. For example, if sport is presented as positive in a popular programme, viewers are more likely to want to take part in sports. The result is that we have fun with friends and are healthier because of the exercise we are doing.

However, we sometimes put our trust in the media to give us news, entertainment and education without questioning what it is that we see or hear.

The media makes billions of pounds through advertising sales. We are constantly exposed to and influenced by advertising. We buy what we see on television, in newspapers or magazines – especially products that are endorsed by celebrities that we like. The constant exposure to violent and sexual images, to advertisements for junk food and the influence of the fashion industry to be thin as a result of extreme diets can all have negative influences on lifestyle choices.

(The role of the media is also discussed in Unit 6.)

Culture

Culture includes common factors that bring a group of people together. It is a term for a way of life and a set of norms by which a group or society is held together. In the UK, we live in a society that includes a wide range of cultures. This can be very positive as we can learn and appreciate aspects of the cultures of others, for example, food, dress, music and religion, so giving us a tolerance and acceptance of our differences. The negative affect of culture is when people do not accept others' differences, which could lead to discrimination against a minority group. (This is discussed in Unit 6.)

Gender

Gender is to do with being male or female and can influence our development and how we see society. Women now have equal rights in employment and education under the Sex Discrimination Act 1975. However, statistics show that women still have a large proportion of the lower-paid jobs and are the main carers in the family, taking time off work to care for children or older relatives. Traditional roles are changing and it is now not unusual to see men having paternity leave and women in powerful jobs. These role models have a huge influence on how people see society and how it can change.

Discrimination

Discrimination occurs when people are treated unfairly because of their differences. (Discrimination is discussed in Units 2 and 6.)

Education

Education benefits everyone. It can lead to a better quality of life and increased choice. Lack of education or a poor education will lead to poorer job prospects, which as already mentioned, may lead to a low income and poorer standard of living. (Education is discussed further in Unit 2.)

Access to services

Growth and development can be affected by an individual's ability to access the health services they need. For example, if a person is unable to travel because of disability, age, geographical location or lack of money, their quality of care could be affected.

Life events

During our lifetime many events will occur that may change the course of our lives.

These events can be either predictable (we know they will happen or we choose them) or unpredictable (unexpected events).

These life events may cause short- or long-term effects. These can be stressful to the individual and to those around them. For example, can you remember when you started school or nursery? It may have been upsetting for you to leave your parents and your brothers and sisters. But also it may have been an exciting time, meeting new friends and doing new activities every day. For your parents it may have been a time when they could resume employment, so household finances would be easier. They may have felt a sense of loss as you left for school, seeing their child grow up. It may also have been a relief if they were struggling with difficult childcare arrangements.

So each life event, whether predictable or unpredictable, can bring both positive and negative effects in our lives.

Predictable life events	Unpredictable life events
Going to school/nursery	Birth of brother/sister
Employment	Divorce
Leaving home	Redundancy
Marriage	Serious injury
Parenthood	Abuse
Retirement	Bereavement
Ageing	

Activity 10   P2

Read through the five case studies given below and state for each one the life events that have occurred, whether they were predictable or unpredictable, and the socio-economic factors involved (positive or negative).

This will help you to formulate the information need for P2.

Case Study 1

Judith is a single mother living in a small flat with her three-year-old son Thomas. Judith tries to budget on her low income but sometimes is forced to cut back on fresh fruit and vegetables. Sometimes she has to buy more expensive food from the local store as she cannot afford the bus fare to the supermarket, where cheaper brands and offers may be available to her.

The local environment where Judith lives has high unemployment and so it is hard for her to find part-time work. She also struggles to afford suitable childcare arrangements. She has a small, reliable network of friends.

Case Study 2

Eva and Stephan have recently moved to England from Poland with the hope of finding well-paid employment. They have been highly educated in Poland, so possess many skills.

At the moment their English-language speaking is limited. They are renting a house close to a large town. They are expecting their first child and so they need to find appropriate healthcare services and education services to support their changing lifestyle.

Case Study 3

Mark and Susan live in a large detached home in the suburbs of a town. Mark earns a high salary but his work takes him away from the family for most of the week. Susan works part-time and is able to take and collect her teenage daughter Louise from high school. Their lives are extremely busy and have little routine. Susan buys a lot of convenience foods to save time on cooking but she always provides a hot meal for her daughter. Mark eats out a lot while entertaining clients in restaurants. He sometimes misses meals because of his work commitments, or eats 'on the go' while travelling. Although he works very hard and is hardly ever at home, he feels it is worth it to provide money for family holidays abroad twice a year.

Case Study 4

Gemma and Christopher are three-year-old twins. Their mother works full time as a nurse and their father takes care of the household and childcare duties. They have a strict routine, with mealtimes and bedtime always at the same time. They all sit down together to enjoy a family meal once a day. Dad enjoys watching television while the twins are playing but Mum is worried about how this may influence the twins. They play regularly with children from next door whose rules and manners are not as strict as theirs. Occasionally the twins are confused when they see other children doing things they are not allowed to do.

 ## Case Study 5

Len has just retired from the mining industry after working for 45 years. Unfortunately his health is not good. He attends regular hospital appointments to treat his chronic lung condition. Len's wife died a year ago and he is finding socialising very difficult. Len relies on his son Joseph, who lives nearby, but he is away on business a lot.

3 Know the factors that can influence an individual's self-concept

Self-concept is a person's idea or picture of themselves. It is often formed from other people's opinions. Self-concept includes:

- self-esteem – our self-worth or value
- self-image – how we see ourselves in relation to others.

Self-concept

The way we see ourselves may be completely different to how others see us. Imagine looking at yourself in the mirror. How do you see yourself? Is it different to how other people see you?

Many factors can affect our self-concept, either positively or negatively. When a person feels good about themselves, they feel the world is a good and happy place to live in. Having a good self-concept helps us to succeed in education and society.

A person who does not feel good about themselves sees the world as an unhappy place. Poor self-concept may lead to fear, anxiety and low achievement in education and society.

Self-concept can alter from day to day, depending on what situation you are in, and it can be influenced by many factors. Children and young people should have positive experiences around them to help develop their self-esteem and reinforce a positive self-image. This should enable them to grow up to be happy and active members in their society.

Our self-concept can also be influenced by factors around us. These factors change over our life stages depending on the life events we come across.

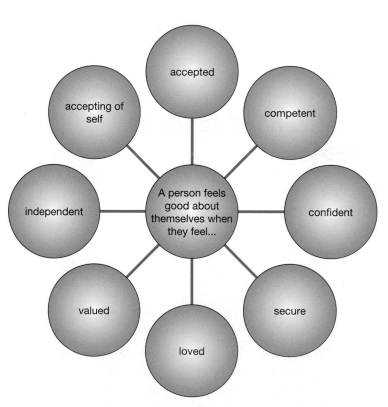

Table 8.01 Factors that can affect self-concept

Factor	Influence
Age	Our view of self-concept changes throughout our lives. Young children are able to recognise themselves from around 18 months and then the socialisation process begins to allow the child to have either a positive or negative view of themselves. Self-concept can be affected in teenage years by peer pressure but usually as we enter adulthood we have a greater understanding about ourselves and who we are. In older adulthood we have often developed wisdom and knowledge about ourselves and the world around us.
Appearance	This can be affected positively and negatively by peer pressure and the media. Young people become aware of their appearance and are affected by opinions of others. Appearance may be constructed from images in the media of how we should look which again can be harmful (e.g. 'size zero' models encourage young women to try to be very thin). On the other hand, appearance can be influenced positively by sports images and the portrayal of healthy lifestyles. Appearance may also influence people to keep up with the latest fashion.
Gender	As men or women we have expected roles in society. These roles are influenced by our socialisation process and also by the culture we belong to. Stereotypes of men's and women's roles in the media still influence our behaviour, although many changes have taken place since the late twentieth century.
Culture	Cultural diversity can have a positive influence if we embrace the differences of others, but if differences are used to discriminate against others, it is harmful.
Relationships + family	Self-concept is affected by our relationships with our family, friends and the outside world. Positive comments will lead to self-confidence and a positive self-image and we will also learn to be positive to others. When we receive negative comments or constant criticism about aspects of our lives we may develop low self-esteem.
Abuse	There are many forms of abuse. Abuse causes both short- and long-term harm and can vary from person to person. (See also later in this unit.)
Income	Income can influence many aspects of our lives, including housing, education and health. Level of income allows or restricts choices we can make in our lifestyle.
Media	Media influences individuals at different life stages. There is much debate about whether media influences extreme behaviour, such as excessive dieting or violence.

Education	A good education can lead to a positive self-image, self-confidence and play a part in secondary socialisation. Lack of education may affect a person's self-esteem.
Emotional health and wellbeing	Being emotionally well means having a positive attitude and belief in ourselves, being in control and having the ability to make informed decisions about our lives.
Socialisation	Socialisation is a general term for the many different ways and processes by which children come to be able to function as members of their social community. (See also later in this unit.)
Environment	The immediate and wider environment plays an important part and can influence self-concept. In our society we have freedom of speech and live in a relatively stable environment. If you live in a war zone or in an area of political unrest, freedom to do anything may be difficult and so can cause problems with self-concept.

Socialisation

All humans are social creatures. A large part of what goes on between parents and their children, in all cultures that have ever been studied, is to do with 'training' children in the ways of the culture. Parents teach their children ways of relating to others – including learning the culture's language – and the wide variety of skills needed to function in society, for example, mealtimes, bedtimes and the rituals and general routines of family life.

Socialisation is quite a long, drawn-out process and in some respects it continues throughout our lifetime. Consider, for example, when adults travel abroad and interact with people from unfamiliar cultures. Even when we meet a new social group within our own culture, for example at college or in the workplace, we may need to adjust to new ways of behaving.

Primary socialisation

In primary socialisation, a child begins to learn from their family group. This is where they are usually taught the values, expectations and customs of their family group and culture. It all happens from a very early age.

Secondary socialisation

Later on, children learn about how society works from influences like teachers, the media and friends they meet.

Both processes have positive and negative influences on the way we develop and see the world.

Abuse

When working in health and social care it is important for the wellbeing of the service users to be aware of signs and symptoms of abuse and to know what to do if you have suspicions. Vulnerable people are especially prone to abuse. This includes children, older people and those with physical and learning disabilities.

Abuse can take many forms, including physical, emotional, sexual, mental or social.

The NSPCC defines **physical** abuse as including hitting, shaking, kicking, punching, scalding, suffocating and other ways of inflicting pain or injury to a child or other individual; **emotional** abuse as when a parent or carer behaves in a way that is likely to seriously affect their child's emotional development; **sexual** abuse as forcing or tricking a child or other individual into taking part in any kind of sexual activity.

Source: www.nspcc.org.uk

Abuse could also be **financial**, which may include using a person's money without their knowledge or understanding, or theft of an individual's money and possessions. Abuse can take the form of **neglect**, which means depriving a vulnerable person of what they need, such as food, warmth, medication or activities.

Abuse occurs for a variety of reasons. It may be due to someone trying to take power and control (intentional abuse), or it could be unintentional abuse that arises from work-related issues or exhaustion. People may also be unaware of the effect they are having on someone else.

Possible signs of abuse

What to do: Any suspicion or disclosure of abuse must be taken seriously and be properly looked into. You must report any allegation of abuse to your line manager as soon as possible. You have a legal responsibility to report it. You should also record in writing exactly what the conversation was, rather than rely on your

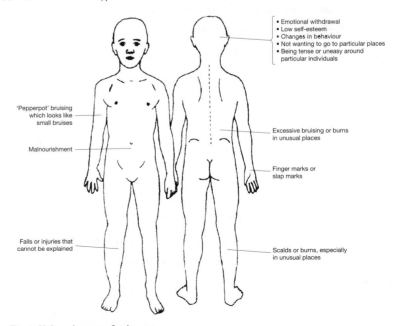

• Emotional withdrawal
• Low self-esteem
• Changes in behaviour
• Not wanting to go to particular places
• Being tense or uneasy around particular individuals

'Pepperpot' bruising which looks like small bruises

Malnourishment

Excessive bruising or burns in unusual places

Finger marks or slap marks

Falls or injuries that cannot be explained

Scalds or burns, especially in unusual places

Possible signs of abuse

memory. You should not discuss the disclosure with the person who is alleged to be the abuser or with other members of the staff team. You should avoid saying that you 'won't tell anyone' if the person disclosing it asks you. Even though they may be seeking this reassurance from you, withholding the allegation may result in more harm.

Writing the report: When writing your report of the allegation, you should ensure that the information is exactly what the person said to you rather than your interpretation of it. It must be an accurate account and it should also record the time and place of the conversation and any other relevant details.

What happens once an allegation has been made? Each workplace will have its own policies and procedures on addressing allegations of abuse and it is these which will be followed in the event of a disclosure. The allegation should always be taken seriously and investigated thoroughly. Support will be offered to the individual who is making the allegation and all those involved in the investigation.

All of these factors may have implications in the short-, medium- and long-term.

Activity 11

P3   M2   D1

Do the first part of this activity with one other person.

1 Look at the diagram and imagine yourself in the middle.

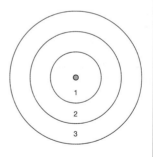

1 = Factors about self: age, gender, culture, appearance, health status.

2 = Factors in our immediate environment: family, abuse, relationships, socialisation, income.

3 = Factors in our wider environment: media, education, societal norms and values.

Consider all the factors that can influence your self-concept:

- Have any changed?
- If so, has your self-concept changed?
- Would you like to change any of the factors?
- How would your self-concept alter?

2 On your own, make a list of factors affecting self-concept. Then write it up as a report.

P1 asks you to identify factors affecting self-concept. If you outline these factors you will achieve M2. If your factors include description then you have achieved D1.

For example, income is a factor that influences an individual's self-concept; a positive effect is being able to afford good housing and a good diet; this will positively influence a person's lifestyle and health. On the other hand, a low income may give rise to unsafe and unhealthy housing conditions and a poor diet, which could lead to ill-health.

4 Understand different care needs of individuals at different life stages

Issues around life stages

Changing care needs at different life stages

When we are assessing care needs we should always treat the client as a whole (holistic care). For example, if someone has a broken leg they will need pain relief and possibly a plaster cast. We also need to think about their mobility – for example, how they will get to work, how they will get upstairs at home and whether they have any support. (This is discussed further in Unit 3.)

As we grow from very dependent babies to independent adults, our care needs will vary. We all have different requirements that need to be met to enable us to live and survive. As conditions, our environment and our age changes, so do our needs. For example, we all need to be in a safe environment, but the way we equip a baby's environment and an older service user's environment will be very different. A service user who has a disability may require specialist assistance to meet their particular needs.

The following chart covers a range of basic needs for all life stages. Specific needs will be met according to individualised care planning by the multi-disciplinary team.

Table 8.02 Basic needs at different life stages

Life stage	Physical care need	Intellectual care need	Emotional care need	Social care need
Birth and infancy 0–3 years	Healthy diet. Safe environment. Hygienic environment.	Communication to acquire language skills.	Bonding with main carer. Love and affection from carers in a secure environment.	Play activities. Role model to show social skills. Primary socialisation.

Childhood 4–10 years	Healthy diet. Safe and clean environment. Adequate rest and sleep. Activities to encourage physical skills.	Appropriate toys and activities to stimulate the acquisition of new skills and knowledge. Appropriate environment for education.	Opportunities for expressing emotions appropriately.	Reinforcement of social skills, values, belief and norms. Personal safety issues to be addressed.
Adolescence 11–18 years	Healthy diet – encouragement to make healthy choices. Regular exercise. Regular sleep and rest patterns.	Education and training to gain and improve knowledge and skills. Various learning experiences.	Emotional support to fit into social groups and establish own self-image.	Secondary socialisation.
Adulthood 19–65 years	Healthy diet. Regular exercise to fit around busy lifestyle.	Extension of knowledge and skills already acquired. Opportunities for career change or career break.	Positive relationships.	Taking part in social groups to maintain identity.
Older people 65 years+	Safe environment according to needs (e.g. reduced mobility). Appropriate aids and assistance. Opportunities to promote independence. May require assistance with hearing and vision.	Opportunities to learn new skills and refresh existing skills in a supported environment.	Good self-esteem from positive care in all environments.	Social opportunities to maintain self image and promote independence.

Providing for care

All service users need to have an identity and to feel valued. It is the role of the caregiver to ensure that this happens. We should always deliver care to our service users with all their needs in mind.

- Individual care – care that suits an individual's needs.
- Holistic care – care that includes all an individual's needs.

Care needs can be wide-ranging and can also differ at different life stages. As care workers we need to be skilled at identifying service users' individual care needs and then planning appropriately for their care. Follow the cycle below to identify needs and plan care for individuals.

The care planning cycle

This cycle should be followed in all care establishments in some way. The Community Care Act 1990 states that all service users have the right to have their needs assessed and planned for.

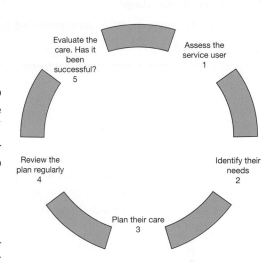

The care planning cycle

Evaluate the care. Has it been successful? 5

Assess the service user 1

Review the plan regularly 4

Identify their needs 2

Plan their care 3

Activity 12

Investigate your work setting and see how care is assessed and planned for. Share this with your class and see how care assessments vary in different settings. Many professionals may have input into a service user's care so that all the needs are fully met. For example, a service user may see a general practitioner, a physiotherapist, a pharmacist and a nurse. This is called multi-disciplinary care.

Activity 13   P4   M3   D2

For P4 – using the following case studies, explain the differences in the care needs at the different life stages. For M3, you should discuss the care needs and for D2 you need to say why (justify) the care is different for each life stage.

- To start this piece of work, read the first case study.
- Next, draw a mind-map stating what life stage the study is about and the care needs that the service user has.

- **Do the same for the other two case studies.**
- **When you have done this for all three case studies, explain and then discuss the differences in the care needs that you have highlighted at each life stage.**
- **Finally, say why the care provided to each of these service users is different.**

Case Study 1

Mary is a 74-year-old widow who is recovering from a stroke. She is spending some time in a residential care home before returning to her own home. The stroke has left Mary slightly weakened down her left side and she occasionally needs assistance with mobility.

Mary's daughter lives close by and Mary also has a good network of friends.

Case Study 2

Mohammed is 17 years old and is attending his local hospital as he is a newly diagnosed diabetic. He has been given a lot of information about his condition but is finding some of the medical terminology difficult to understand. He is going to take a friend with him to help him translate some of the information. He is very worried about his visit and how to adapt his lifestyle to his condition.

Case Study 3

Sara is about to return to work after having her first baby, Holly. Holly is 12 months old and is going to attend the local nursery. She has just started walking and enjoys playing with large, wheeled toys. Sara is worried about leaving Holly as she has been used to a home environment.

Remember, we must always treat service users with dignity and respect, irrespective of their age, gender or culture.

Summary

After working through this unit you should understand the development process through the life stages and be able to appreciate that not all individuals develop at the same rate as others. This will help us to understand that there are both positive and negative influences which affect this important process.

It is our role as carers to understand that care can be delivered in different ways to different service users dependant on their needs.

We will be able to understand that the development of self-concept is extremely valuable and therefore provide care and support accordingly.

Assessment and grading criteria

To achieve a pass grade the evidence must show that the learner is able to:	To achieve a merit grade the evidence must show that, in addition to the pass criteria, the learner is able to:	To achieve a distinction grade the evidence must show that, in addition to the pass and merit criteria, the learner is able to:
P1 identify key aspects of physical, intellectual, emotional and social development at each of the life stages (see Activity 9) [IE1, SM2, SM3]	M1 outline key aspects of physical, intellectual, emotional and social development at each of the life stages (see Activity 9)	
P2 state positive and negative influences on growth and development (see Activity 10) [IE3, IE5, SM2, SM3]		
P3 state factors that influence an individual's self concept (see Activity 11) [IE3, IE5, CT4, SM2, SM3]	M2 outline how factors can influence the development of an individual's self concept (see Activity 11)	D1 describe how factors can influence the development of an individual's self-concept (see Activity 11)

P4 explain potential differences in care needs of individuals at different life stages (see Activity 13) [CT1, CT2, SM2, SM3]	**M3** discuss potential differences in the care needs of individuals at different life stages (see Activity 13)	**D2** justify care provided to an individual at their different life stages (see Activity 13)

Further Reading

Meggitt, C. and Sunderland, D., (2000) *Child Development: An Illustrated Guide*, London: Heinemann

Meggitt, C. and Thomson, H., 1997, *Human Growth and Development for Health and Social Care*, London: Hodder Arnold

Child Care, Health and Development (Blackwell publishing)

Weblinks

www.babycentre.co.uk/pregnancy
www.medinfo.co.uk/conditions/rubella.html
www.nspcc.org.uk
www.open2.net/healtheducation/family_
childdevelopment/morality.html

Unit 9
Creative and Therapeutic Activities in Health and Social Care

This unit looks at how service users can benefit from creative and therapeutic activities. To complete this unit, you must plan, carry out and then review an activity.

Creative and therapeutic activities can benefit all service users and can assist with rehabilitation, acquiring skills or maintaining skills.

This unit will help you to understand the legislation required to plan and implement appropriate activities in a range of care settings. The unit will highlight how important the care provider is in supporting these activities.

Learning outcomes:

In this unit you will learn about:

- different creative and therapeutic activities and their benefits
- legislation and regulations relevant to the implementation of creative and therapeutic activities
- the role of the professionals in supporting individuals who undertake creative and therapeutic activities
- implementing creative and therapeutic activities.

1 Know different creative and therapeutic activities and their benefits

Creative and therapeutic activities

There are many different activities that may have benefits for service users. Some examples are given below.

Expressive art can be used as a way of communicating. There is a British Association of Art Therapists (see www.baat.org), which provides more information. Art therapy can enable service users to make changes through using art materials.

Craft activities, such as card making or jewellery making, can be undertaken with a variety of service users.

Photography is a popular activity, particularly using digital cameras, which enables service users to see their pictures immediately. Also, with a little technical knowledge, they can alter and improve the image. Photography is also useful when capturing service users enjoying other creative and therapeutic activities to keep as a memory.

> ### Key term
>
> Therapeutic – this refers to actions or activities that are particularly designed to provide benefits to an individual or group.

Gardening can be enjoyed by a range of service users and can be a pleasurable activity. It can be used for learning with younger service users and can be adapted to suit most settings, whether indoor or outdoor.

Music may involve making music, listening to music or even music therapy, which uses music for therapeutic benefits.

Dance – there are numerous types of dance, from ballroom to belly dancing, all of which have their own benefits and can be appropriate for all ages of service user, depending on their needs. Visit the following weblink for further information: www.aarp.org/health/fitness/get_motivated/lets_dance_to_health.html.

Movement is activity with a beat or rhythm and exploration of space and body awareness, not necessarily dance. It can be beneficial to all ages of service users. Follow this weblink to read further articles about movement: www.madacademy.com/music-and-movement/default.htm.

Drama therapy uses drama as part of a therapeutic process. Drama allows service users to explore stories and express feelings. The British Association of Drama Therapists states that drama therapy can be used to assist service users in making 'psychological, emotional and social changes'. Drama therapy can include roleplay and mime. Drama therapists work in a variety of settings, including schools, and with a wide variety of service user groups, such as children with autism or older people with dementia. For more information, go to www.badth.org.uk.

Cookery can be enjoyed by a range of service users and adapted to meet specific needs. Obviously health and hygiene are important during this activity. Cold cookery can be enjoyed if the setting does not have cooking facilities – for example, icing biscuits, sandwich making and cake decoration.

Exercise may involve outdoor exercise such as walking, playing games or using the gym. Exercise has numerous benefits and can be undertaken by a variety of service users.

Games and quizzes can be used by a variety of service user groups. They could be physical games such as cricket or rounders, or mental games such as quizzes or crosswords.

Sports can be played in teams as well as individually. There are all-round benefits to playing sport and activities can be chosen to suit many different types of settings. Watching sports activities can also be beneficial and interactive for some service users.

Swimming enables service users with limited mobility to enjoy freedom of movement. Swimming is suitable for all ages, obviously with supervision. Hydrotherapy is a treatment process and differs from swimming because it involves special exercises that take place in a warm-water pool, usually within a hospital physiotherapy department.

Horse riding is a physical activity that can be beneficial to many service users. Horse riding must be carried out with authority and supervision, and using the correct equipment. Enjoyment of the surroundings and open air can be hugely beneficial.

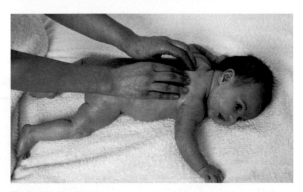

ICT can be used as a form of expression and discovery for all ages.

Yoga is described by The British Wheel of Yoga as a 'holistic approach to mind, body and spirit'. Classes generally exercise, stretch and flex the body and offer relaxation. For more information, go to www.bwy.org.uk.

Baby massage

Massage is the manipulation of soft tissues, which can make changes in the body's surrounding structures. It can also provide relaxation benefits and is a popular therapy for babies. See the following weblink for more information: www.urban-kneads.com/Benefits.html.

Multi-sensory stimulation can be used for service users who have impaired senses or who suffer from dementia. It stimulates different areas of the brain to offer a sense of calm and improve mood. This therapy should be carried out only by a specialist therapist because adverse effects may occur if over-stimulation is offered. See weblink for further information: www.nhs.uk/Conditions/Dementia/Pages/Treatment.aspx.

Animals can provide companionship for older service users, particularly those living alone. However, animals can provide benefits to all age groups. See weblink for further information: www.maturetimes.co.uk/node/9315.

There are many different settings where activities may take place. Some examples are given in the diagram.

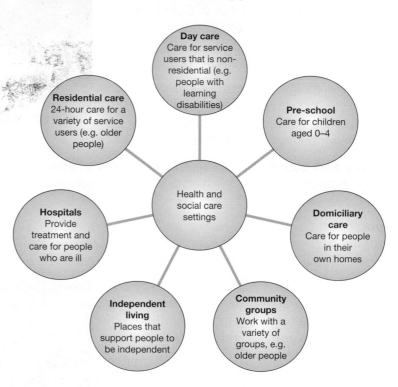

Different health and social care settings

Activity 1

In pairs, discuss any work experience placements you have had in health and social care settings. What types of activities did the service users carry out? Can you think of any creative or therapeutic activities that could be introduced into your care setting?

Service users may have a variety of needs, which may mean they could benefit from creative and therapeutic activities. These needs can be remembered as PIES!

- **P**hysical – to do with the body. A person may have had a stroke, which could have left them with a weakness on one side of their body, or they may have had an accident that has caused them to lose a limb. Any activities that exercise the body would count as physical.

- **I**ntellectual (cognitive) – to do with the brain, thinking or learning new skills. Intellectual needs may include activities that relieve boredom. They can also help prevent memory loss. Any activities that stimulate the brain or get people thinking are ideal for meeting intellectual needs. Language – to do with how we communicate with each other. A service user could have lost the ability to speak or a child may learn new words.
- **E**motional – to do with how we feel about ourselves or our ability to express emotions. A service user may have poor self-esteem or may be depressed, or they may be bereaved or separated from loved ones.
- **S**ocial – to do with friendship groups and working with other people. A service user could be new to the area or have few friends.

Activity 2

Read the three case studies below and identify the PILES needs of those involved.

Case Study

- Sally is a 70-year-old woman. Her husband died recently and she is lonely. A lot of her friends have either moved away or died. As she is older, she has poor mobility and finds it difficult to get out and about.
- Nine-year-old Jodie is in hospital because she is having surgery. She sometimes finds it difficult to communicate her needs. As she has spent a lot of time in hospital, she has not had the opportunity to develop many friendships with other children.
- Rob has always been dependent on other carers and is now trying to increase his own independence.

Benefits of creative and therapeutic activities

There are a number of benefits that service users may gain from creative and therapeutic activities. Some of these are listed below.

- New skills can be developed or existing skills can be maintained (individuals can stay physically or mentally active). Benefits could also include promoting independence or being supportive.

- Physical benefits may include improving fine motor skills, such as dexterity (e.g. picking up small objects), or gross motor skills, such as moving major muscle groups in legs or arms. Physical benefits may include a general increase in fitness (such as in games). Physical activity is often shown to be a very important factor in good mental health as well as physical health.
- Intellectual benefits may include developing imagination (e.g. making up stories), problem solving (e.g. crosswords) or developing language (such as games you may play using new words with children). Communication skills may be developed or improved.
- Emotional benefits may include improved self-esteem for the individual or social benefits, such as developing friendships and cooperation.
- Social benefits will include development of new friendship groups and learning to cooperate with others.

Activity 3

Choose one of the following activities and identify the benefits of that activity using PIES.

1 **Playing football**
2 **Cooking**
3 **Playing a board game**
4 **Listening to a story**
5 **Playing bingo**

So why are these benefits so important? If you think about your own experiences, you will soon realise that all individuals need to engage in activities that they enjoy and that stimulate them. Service users who can communicate well, or can join in with games or play, or simply have good friends, are likely to feel more positive and happy. Some of these benefits may interlink – for example, an increase in fine motor skills and agility may improve confidence, which in turn will boost an individual's self-esteem.

Activity 4

P1 **P2** **M1**

Prepare a presentation to inform new carers about creative and therapeutic activities. Check your presentation includes the following:

For P1, a list of various activities that could be carried out in a range of health and social care settings.

For P2, identification of the benefits of the activities you have listed in P1.

For M1, an outline of these benefits.

Use the example below to help you.

The benefits of a quiz:

- Physical – using fine motor skills when controlling pen to write answers.
- Intellectual – using knowledge or learning new knowledge from answers known or learned. Learning new words or vocabulary.
- Emotional – may relieve boredom and can help people to relax, which will decrease stress levels. Also helps them express their thoughts, feelings or worries.
- Social – meeting new people and maintaining friendships. This also promotes a sense of cooperation and teamwork.

2 Know legislation and regulations relevant to the implementation of creative and therapeutic activities

Before carrying out any activity, it is crucial to consider any health and safety implications. This is to ensure the health and well-being of service users, staff, other people and the general environment. You may carry out a risk assessment, which looks at what hazards there may be, what may occur as a result of this hazard and then what measures are in place to reduce the possibility of this occurring.

Key terms

Legislation – this is law that has been passed by parliament.

Regulation – this is an enforceable guideline that must be followed in an organisation.

Policy – this is a set of statements which outlines values and principles within an organisation; it may include instruction as to how to carry out actions to achieve the policy requirements.

Table 9.01 Example of a risk assessment

This is the probability of the risk happening with the control measures in place.

A Activity	B Hazard	C Hazard rating	D Person at risk	E Control measures in place	F Likelihood with control measures in place	CxF
Making cards with children aged 7 years.	Children could swallow glue.\n\nCuts from scissors.	1	Children	Non-toxic glue. Supervision of children by staff. Use suitable scissors.	1	1

Here you list all the risks from the hazard.

This is about how severe the hazard will be. 1 is the lowest whereas 3 is the highest.

What measures are already in place or can you put in place to reduce the risks.

There is legislation around health and safety. A brief overview is provided below, but for more information, see Unit 4 (Ensuring Safe Environments in Health and Social Care).

Table 9.02 Health and safety legislation overview

Health and safety legislation	Brief description	Example of activities that this law may relate to
Health and Safety at Work Act 1974	Main piece of legislation covering workplaces. Both employers and employees have responsibilities to ensure health and safety.	All activities in workplaces
The Food Standards Act 1999 and General Food Regulation 2004	Cover all aspects of food (e.g. storage, cooking, serving).	Any activities using food, e.g. cooking

Manual Handling Operations Regulations 1992	Relates to any activities that may involve moving objects (including people).	Any activities that may involve heavy objects or moving a patient.
Control of Substances Hazardous to Health 2002 (COSHH)	Ensures substances are kept safe. This includes storage, use and disposal. There should be guidelines and risk assessment in place.	Activities that involve the use of substances such as glue or paint.
Reporting of Injuries Disease and Dangerous Occurrences Regulations 1995 (RIDDOR)	Ensures that accident books are monitored and completed. Certain aspects are reportable under RIDDOR.	Accident books should be kept. Any reportable occurrences should be notified to the Health and Safety Executive.

As well as these laws, there may be specific policies (such as the confidentiality policy) that you should observe. There may also be other codes of practice. Before undertaking an activity, you should consider any possible hazards and how the impact of these can be reduced. For example, the hazard could cause injury to the service user or to the member of staff involved. There may also be hazards in the environment or from equipment, for example when a young child using scissors would be at risk of cutting themselves – this is the hazard. Therefore, they should use scissors designed for use by young children.

Activity 5

Add this information to the presentation you started in Activity 4.

For P3, your presentation should identify legislation relating to the delivery of activities in health and social care settings (this information should be general to all activities and settings). You should list the legislation, policies and guidelines you need to consider prior to carrying out activities.

For M2, your list should include a brief outline of the legislation, policies and guidelines you have considered.

For D1, your presentation should describe why these legislation, policies and guidelines are important.

3 Understand the role of the professionals in supporting individuals who undertake creative and therapeutic activities

Principles and values

As a health and social care professional, your values and principles when carrying out activities should always be paramount. These important guidelines are discussed in Unit 2 (Individual Rights within the Health and Social Care Sectors).

Whatever our role is with the service user, we should always uphold anti-discriminatory practice and provide opportunities that offer choice and support independence. So careful selection of activities should ensure equality and empowerment of our service users.

> ### Key terms
>
> Empowerment – this is a process whereby service users who have previously been dependent on care and support are enabled to make decisions and choices to take control of their own lives.

Supporting inclusion

Inclusion is a basic human right and all service users should be embraced, irrespective of race, gender, culture or age. For care workers to be 'inclusive' in their practice with service users, they should give equal access to all activities and opportunities. This removes barriers and promotes new experiences, friendships and encourages communication.

Supporting activities

While planning and carrying out therapeutic activities, care workers should be part of the activity; this ensures health, safety and security and allows the carer to motivate and encourage reluctant service users, offering physical and practical help when needed.

As health and social care workers, we are responsible for providing adequate and

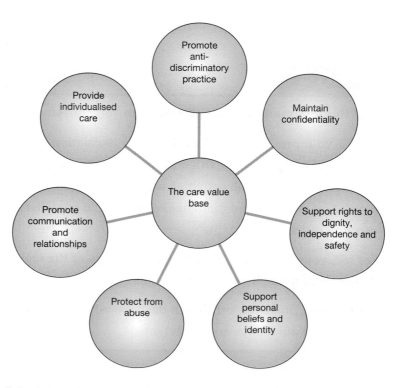

Principles that underpin health and care practice

appropriate resources for the service users (this is discussed later in this unit).

Activity 6   **P4**

Prepare an information leaflet that explains the role of professional health and social care workers when planning and carrying out creative and therapeutic activities.

---

4 Be able to implement appropriate creative and therapeutic activities

Factors affecting choice of activities

When choosing, planning and implementing an activity, it is crucial to consider the needs of service users. You could find this out by asking them directly or by speaking to carers or family. You can then start to develop activities that will have maximum benefits for the individual service user. There are also a number of factors that you should consider during this process.

Potential benefits

When selecting activities for the service users, we should make sure they are going to enjoy them. However, therapeutic and creative activities are carried out as they provide a range of benefits. Think about PIES (discussed earlier in this unit). Also, skills can be regained, improved and developed, depending on the age and type of service user you are planning for.

Interests and preferences

The activity will be more beneficial if the service user is interested in your choice. Older service users may be reluctant to participate if they do not understand the activity, but young children may be more adventurous.

Age and ability

This is an important factor to consider because the activity should be appropriate for the age and development stage of children. An activity should meet these needs, not only physically but also intellectually. Older service users should not be stereotyped into activities because of age, but safety should be considered at all times. Remember that all your activities should be adapted to suit the abilities of your service users to support inclusion.

This will mean you checking your service users' needs and matching your resources to them. For example, if you are carrying out a cooking activity with service users who have problems with their joints, make sure the utensils have large handles or grips.

Culture

Consider the cultural background of all your service users because you may exclude someone if their beliefs or traditions do not meet with the requirements of the activity. For example, before making Christmas cards, make sure the service users are happy to join in because it may be a festival they do not wish to celebrate.

Gender

Most activities should be enjoyed by all genders to promote inclusion, but there may be cultural reasons that may affect who takes part in the activity. For example, a sporting activity that involves showing parts of the body (e.g. swimming) may exclude some females because of their religion.

It is not professional to choose activities for females or males only, so again think about your selection carefully.

Table 9.03 Needs of the individual

Need	Points to consider when planning an activity	Some suggested activities
Physical	What stage of development are children at? Does any equipment need to be adapted? Is the environment safe? Do any service users have physical restrictions? Are you trying to enhance small physical skills or gross physical skills?	**Large physical movements**: Team games, sports activities, dance, gym equipment, ball games **Small physical movements**: Sewing, knitting, art and craft, jigsaws, board games, computers
Sensory	Is a hearing loop required or hearing appliances? Do instructions need to have enlarged print? Do instructions need to be in Braille? Which sensory area are you hoping to improve/stimulate?	Music and dance, light rooms, talking books, sensory books

Social isolation	Activities should be done in small groups to avoid isolation and encourage friendship and communication.	Cooking activities, team games, outdoor visits
Learning disability	Activities may need to be short and repetitive to assist learning. Activities may need to be delivered in different formats to suit learning needs. Activities may require skills to develop independence.	Music activities, art and craft, social outings
Depression	If service users are depressed, they may not want to take part in complex activities, so consider activities in small groups to encourage communication and build self-esteem.	Art and craft activities, yoga/massage, photography, gardening
Developmental	What developmental stage is service user at? Which development area are you focusing on? Is the service user developing, regaining or maintaining particular skills?	Activities should be selected according to developmental area/stage
Communication	Activities in small groups or one-to-one will encourage communication.	Drama/roleplay, board games, quizzes

Planning creative and therapeutic activities

As well as the above factors, you should also consider the following points.

Timing

Time of day should be considered. For example, a photography session that requires light should be carried out in the morning or early afternoon. Younger children may benefit from a sports or drama activity in the afternoon when their concentration span may be low – physical activity may restore their energy levels.

The length of the activity should be considered. Do you have enough time to complete the activity? You may have to repeat it several times for large groups. An activity that has been rushed may not serve any purpose at all.

Is the activity too long? Will the service users be bored? Consider the concentration span of the service users – short activities may be beneficial for younger children as well as older people who may have memory difficulties.

Resources

When planning creative and therapeutic activities, health and safety considerations (covered earlier in this unit) are an important part of selecting suitable and appropriate resources. Consider the following:

- Is there enough space?
- Is there sufficient seating for all service users?
- Is the space and equipment accessible to all participating service users?
- Do you have enough material resources?
- Do you need other health and social care workers with you to support the activity and service users?

If you are cooking with 20 children, do you have enough oven space for all their cakes and biscuits?

Before the activity, make sure all your resources are working, in date, suitable and adapted to meet individual needs.

Service users who have a disability may need some of the following to ensure they can participate:

- easy grip tools or equipment
- hearing loops/talking books
- alternative written instructions in Braille, a different language or large print.

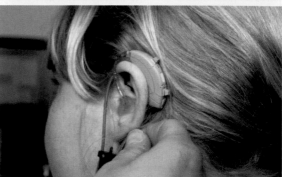

Equipment that can be used to support service users: easy grip tools, hearing loops, Braille books

Activity 7

You are going to carry out an activity with service users in your health and social care setting.

For P5, using the format in the table below, plan an activity for an individual in your setting.

For M3, carry out your planned activity.

For D2, present your evaluation with information from your supervisor, service users and your own thoughts, including your own effectiveness and how your service users have benefited holistically. Use the list of questions below to help you with your evaluation.

Table 9.04 Plan for a creative or therapeutic activity

Setting name	
Activity	
Date	
Time/duration	
Service user group	
Service user number	
Specific service user needs	
Resources needed	
Health and safety considerations, including risk assessment	
Physical benefits	
Intellectual benefits	
Language benefits	
Emotional benefits	
Social benefits	
Outline of activity, including your role and what you hope to achieve	
Evaluation of activity	

Evaluation of activity

To help you complete your evaluation, you should ask a manager or supervisor to write a written testimony as evidence of your completed activity. Any points raised here will help you with your evaluation. You could also ask the service users about the activity. Their feedback will also help you to evaluate your activity.

Ask yourself the following questions, which will help you formulate your evaluation.

- Was the setting/environment suitable?
- Did I have sufficient time?
- Did I have enough resources?
- Was health and safety adequate?
- Did the service users participate and enjoy the activity?
- Did I meet all service users' needs?
- Did I achieve what I set out to do?
- Would I do this activity again?
- How might I change it?
- Did I enjoy it?

REMEMBER

Prior to carrying out your activity, make sure you have consent from your setting's supervisor, manager or teacher to ensure health and safety considerations are made and consent is obtained from service users if required.

Summary

By the end of this unit, you should be able to identify appropriate creative and therapeutic activities for your service users and tailor them to their needs. First of all, you need to understand that your service users have needs and also that your activities have various benefits. These benefits can be realised by choosing and matching activities sensitively to your service users.

You will be aware of the variety of activities that can be selected and also in what settings they can take place.

As you plan and carry out activities, you will understand the need for risk assessment and your role within this area to deliver and evaluate the activities from your point of view and the service user's experience. This will help you to plan for the next time and evaluate how effective your role has been.

We should always reflect on our practice and strive to give our service users the best care and experience they can possibly have.

Grading grid

In order to pass this unit, the evidence that the learner presents for assessment needs to demonstrate that they can meet all the learning outcomes for the unit. The assessment criteria for a pass grade describe the level of achievement required to pass this unit.

Assessment and grading criteria

To achieve a pass grade the evidence must show that the learner is able to:	To achieve a merit grade the evidence must show that, in addition to the pass criteria, the learner is able to:	To achieve a distinction grade the evidence must show that, in addition to the pass and merit criteria, the learner is able to:
P1 identify creative and therapeutic activities for people using health and social care services (see Activity 4) [IE3, TW1, SM3]		
P2 identify the benefits of creative and therapeutic activities for individuals using health and social care services (see Activity 4) [IE3, TW1, SM3]	**M1** outline the benefits of creative and therapeutic activities for individuals using health and social care services (see Activity 4)	
P3 identify legislation, guidelines and policies relevant to the implementation of creative and therapeutic activities (see Activity 5) [IE2, SM3]	**M2** outline legislation, guidelines and policies relevant to the implementation of creative and therapeutic activities (see Activity 5)	**D1** describe the importance of relevant legislation, guidelines and policies relevant to the implementation of creative and therapeutic activities (see Activity 5)
P4 explain the role of the professional when planning creative and therapeutic activities in a health and social care environment (see Activity 6) [IE2, IE3, SM3]		
P5 plan a creative or therapeutic activity for an individual using health or social care services (see Activity 7) [IE2, CT1, CT5, RL4, SM3, EP3]	**M3** carry out a planned creative or therapeutic activity in a health or social care environment (see Activity 7)	**D2** present an evaluation of the effectiveness of your planned activity to meet the holistic needs of an individual (see Activity 7)

Further Reading

Agar, K. (2008) *How to Make your Care Home Fun: Simple Activities,* London: Jessica Kingsley Publishers.

Banks, B.W. (2008) *Activities for Older People,* London: Butterworth Heinemann.

Beckerley, T. (2008) *Fun with Messy Play Ideas and Activities for Children with Special Needs*, London: Jessica Kingsley Publishers.

Weblinks

www.cot.co.uk – College of Occupational Therapists

Unit 10
Health and Social Care Services

People who work in health and social care need to understand how the services are organised at local and national level, together with how services are provided and delivered. The requirements for different job roles in health and social care are explored and the nature and purpose of multi-disciplinary and inter-agency working is also considered, including how it affects practitioners and service users. As some people experience difficulties in accessing health care, consideration is given to the ways in which practitioners in health and social care work in partnership with others to try and overcome this.

Learning outcomes:

In this unit you will learn about:

- the key elements of health and social care services
- the barriers to accessing health and social care services
- the principles of partnership in health and social care
- the requirements for job roles in health and social care.

1 Know key elements of health and social care services

Health and social care services provide one part of what can be thought of as 'the welfare state', which includes health and social care services for everyone, as well as financial support (state benefits) for the unemployed, the old and infirm. (The modern-day equivalents are currently Jobseeker's Allowance, State Pensions and Disability Living Allowance, etc.) The welfare state was introduced fully following World War 2 in Britain with the aim of providing services 'from the cradle to the grave', i.e. from birth to death, and, most importantly, free 'at the point of use'; that is, no one using them had to pay cash, as the government funded the provision of services from the tax revenues collected from everyone. It has been estimated that around 80 per cent of the costs of health services are paid through taxation, and of this about 60 per cent of the cost is used to pay staff (see www.nhs.uk/NHSEngland/thenhs/about/Pages/overview.aspx).

> ## Key term
>
> Services – the organisations and people supplying a particular need.

The NHS is the biggest employer in the UK and has its own *constitution*; however, it is important to understand that there are other models of providing care. In France, for example, services are funded through compulsory insurance paid in part by government and in part by service users. In the USA, health care is currently funded entirely through private insurance. People who cannot afford medical insurance have to pay the full cost of treatment, which can run into thousands of dollars; however, some provisions for the poorest are likely to be made law.

During the intervening years, there have been numerous changes to the way health and social care services in the UK have been organised and provided as they have responded to changes within society – for example, changes in the birth rate and the number of people living longer. There have also been huge advances in drug treatments and medical technology, which has allowed people to cope with long-term health problems and have increased life expectancy.

Currently, there is much more emphasis on health and social care services working together and, in terms of services for children and young people, working with the education sector, with the aim of improving the life chances and outcomes for children and young people. (For further information, go to www.everychildmatters.gov.uk.) For example, the school health services might provide *drop-in centres* in secondary schools, providing information on sexual health as well as general health advice for young people.

This section looks at key parts of the current health and social care provision in England, Wales and Northern Ireland.

Organisation of health care

The Department of Health (DH) is responsible for the provision of health in the UK. The DH is part of the government, headed by the Secretary of State for Health, who is a government minister (and therefore a Member of Parliament), appointed to the role by the Prime Minister and therefore answerable to Parliament. The role of the DH is to ensure better health and well-being of the population. It does this by deciding on policy goals and priorities and supporting service delivery, in effect leading on health and well-being on behalf of the government.

Minister/Secretary of State for Health – decides policy (appointed by the Prime Minister and part of the government)

Permanent Secretary – runs the department (a civil servant, permanently employed; non-political post)

NHS Chief Executive – leads the NHS and is chief advisor to the minister on NHS issues

Chief Medical Officer – a qualified doctor responsible for protecting public health and providing leadership to the regional directors of public health; chief advisor to the minister on medical issues

Key people in the Department of Health

The DH has a presence in each of the nine government office regions – North East, North West, Yorkshire and Humber, West Midlands, East Midlands, East of England, South West, South East and London. The department has responsibility for the whole of the UK and works closely with representative governments in Scotland, Wales and Northern Ireland and represents the UK with international bodies such as the World Health Organisation and the European Union.

The DH oversees health and adult social care; it is important to recognise that they do not directly deliver health care or social care services to the public. The Department of Health works with the National Health Service (NHS) and the different agencies and organisations that work together to provide health care. The DH also works with social care, mainly through local government (local authorities) to provide adult social care. (More information on local authorities can be found on the website of the government at www.direct. gov.uk.) Another government department, the Department for Children, Schools and Families (DCSF), leads on social care for children as well as education. Both the DH and the DCSF work closely with the organisations responsible for regulating the professions and health and social care organisations.

Key
Government office regions

Statutory provision

Statutory services must be provided in law (i.e. through an Act of Parliament). The government funds (pays for) statutory services for health under the NHS and for adult social care through Local Authority Social Services (LASS) departments. Social care for children and young people is funded by DCSF, which also has responsibility for education services. The NHS and LASS do not necessarily provide all the services themselves, but they must provide access to services, which they can do through contracting arrangements with individual specialists and organisations.

Government office regions

Source: www.statistics.gov.uk

Statutory health services

Statutory health services are provided under the NHS. It is important to recognise that the NHS is not one organisation, but made up of several different strands and it provides a whole range of services to promote and support health as well as dealing with ill health. These include hospital and community services, general medical services provided by general practitioners (GPs), dental services and optical services.

The National Health Service was set up in 1948, based on the ideal that good health should be available to all. The NHS was based on three core principles:

- to meet the needs of the whole population
- to be free at the point of care
- that treatment be based on clinical need, not ability to pay.

This means that the government will only pay for what it considers to be essential *services* (i.e. essential work carried out under an NHS contract and based on clinical need). This is why, if you go to the dentist for something that is not covered under the NHS contract such as teeth whitening (cosmetic dentistry), you will have to pay for the full cost of treatment. This is because the cost of NHS services is paid for through taxes and everybody contributes, so it would not be fair for people to receive non-essential treatments such as cosmetic surgery on the NHS. However, if you went to the dentist with toothache and had to have a filling, the NHS would pay for this. Similarly, if you are going on holiday and you need to have some immunisations, your GP may charge you a fee, as such treatment is considered non-essential – it is your choice to holiday abroad. However, if you have a baby, the immunisations are provided free of charge as this is considered essential to protect the baby's health from serious diseases in the years to come.

The structure of the NHS changes over time to meet the needs of governments and populations, but currently it is organised as follows.

- Strategic health authorities – these oversee and manage local health provision on behalf of the DH and the Secretary of State. They are responsible for implementing government health policy at local level and are located in the Government Office Regions. They make sure that government priorities for improving health are included in the plans of local health trusts (e.g. programmes for improving cancer services). They also have responsibility for helping to increase the capacity of local services so that they can deal with more patients effectively.
- Primary care trusts (PCTs) – these are locally based and have to make sure there are sufficient services in the local area to meet the needs of the local population, including hospitals. They are responsible for providing access to everyday healthcare services, such as doctors, dentists and opticians and preventive services in the community. PCTs control 80 per cent of the NHS budget and commission services on behalf of the population. There are currently 152 PCTs in England; slightly different arrangements are in place in the other UK countries.
- Acute NHS trusts – these provide hospital and immediate treatment services, such as accident and emergency, surgery and acute medical services. They employ the majority of health staff, including medical and non-medical staff, and are responsible for ensuring that hospitals provide high-quality care and manage their finances efficiently.

Some of the larger NHS trusts are national or regional centres for specialist care and may be linked to a university to help to train health professionals.

- Foundation NHS trusts – these provide similar services but they have much more financial freedom; they are run by a board made up of local managers, staff and members of the public so that they can provide services to meet the specific needs of the local community.

- Ambulance trusts – these provide emergency access to health care and employ ambulance staff and paramedics. There are 12 ambulance trusts in England and they respond to emergencies categorised by the control room receiving calls into Category A emergencies, which are life threatening, or Category B and C, which are urgent but not life threatening. They have rapid response vehicles, which are equipped to provide emergency treatment at the scene (e.g. at a car accident or fall).

- Mental health trusts – these provide health and social care services for people with diagnosed mental illness. Some of this treatment is provided in hospital but the majority is in the local community through the GP or community nursing service. Some services are provided through local authority social service departments.

- Care trusts – these are relatively new and are set up when health and social services decide to work together to provide integrated or shared services for the local community. These organisations share budgets and exchange information and expertise to benefit people using their services. An example would be services for children and young people with long-standing health conditions who are looked after at home.

- Children's trusts – these bring together health, education and social services for children and young people in an area. They aim to improve the health outcomes for all children and young people by integrating services, sharing information about vulnerable children and young people and providing early intervention services. For more information, go to www.dcsf.gov.uk/everychildmatters/about/aims/childrenstrust/childrenstrusts.

Other NHS provision includes NHS Direct, which is a 24-hour telephone helpline service that anyone can access. Trained health professionals provide information and advice and may suggest you call the out-of-hours service, for example, which provides access to GPs in the evening and weekends for emergency care.

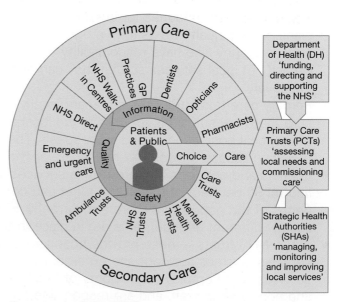

Structure of the NHS

Activity 1   P1

Healthcare provision in Wales, Scotland and Northern Ireland is slightly different from England. Working in groups, research the healthcare provision using the following websites:

- www.wales.nhs.uk
- www.show.scot.nhs.uk
- www.n-i.nhs.uk.

Compare the care provided in the different regions and discuss this with the rest of the class.

Statutory social services provision

Social services departments are one part of local authorities, which typically have responsibility for some or all of the following in a defined local area:

- education
- social services
- planning
- waste disposal, recycling and collection
- trading standards
- emergency planning
- roads, highways and transportation
- housing
- environmental health
- parks, open spaces and countryside
- markets and fairs.

Each local authority has elected representatives, called councillors, who have responsibility for the budget. They employ other people to carry out the day-to-day running of the council's services – namely a chief executive, directors of each service area (e.g. planning, environment or education) and council officers. Local authorities are funded partly from central government and partly from local council tax.

Social services are the responsibility of the director of social services, who is answerable to the chief executive. The role of social services is to look after the welfare of vulnerable people – for example, people with disabilities, people with mental health problems, children in need (as defined within the Children Act 1989 and 2004) or older people – and each local area has its own social service office.

Qualified social workers are employed to assess the requirements of vulnerable people and arrange services to meet their needs, usually through contracting arrangements with service providers. For example, social workers may arrange residential accommodation for a person who is no longer able to live at home, or arrange for agency carers to support relatives who can no longer cope with caring for a relative suffering from the effects of an illness, such as Alzheimer's disease. People needing social services may be asked to contribute to the cost of the services provided, depending on their income and individual circumstances.

Social services departments also have responsibility for child protection in the local area, so if there are concerns about children, such as suspected abuse, this will be referred (passed on) to social services for investigation. There is often partnership between health, social services and education – for example, where families need support to cope.

Activity 2   P1

Investigate your local authority (LA) and find out what services are provided in your local area. Find out what social care facilities are available for older people or disabled people and how they are funded. For example, does the LA pay for them outright or give them a grant?

Non-statutory provision

These are health and social care services that are provided by a range of different organisations and individuals to meet non-essential or specific needs that are not catered for by the local health and social care provision; for example, cosmetic surgery, osteopathy, psychological therapies and self-help groups. However, the NHS and LASS sometimes make a financial contribution or pay for treatment or care from some of the organisations through contracting arrangements. For example, cosmetic surgery may be funded in rare cases where it is having a psychologically damaging effect on the person's mental health and well-being – for example, a woman with a large disfiguring 'port wine' birthmark on her face. Similarly, if someone was in need of home care but could not afford to pay for it because their income was too low, social services may provide funds – for example, if they were receiving minimum state benefits.

Private provision

Private health and social care provision is sometimes known as the independent sector, since it does not receive any direct government funding. Such services must be paid for, either directly by the patient or through insurance arrangements. Private healthcare organisations providing treatments include private hospitals and clinics, including beauty clinics. Residential and nursing care homes are examples of private social care provision; they are usually owned by an individual, a consortium or national organisation that may have many homes. It is common for local authorities to pay some or all of the cost of residential care for a vulnerable older person, depending on individual circumstances. In some cases, (e.g. where there is an underlying health condition), the NHS will pay for a place in a nursing home.

Voluntary sector provision

This refers to the provision offered by charitable organisations, which have usually been set up to provide services and facilities for a specific group of people where statutory provision is thought to be insufficient (e.g. Alzheimer's Society). Charities have a particular organisational structure, which includes a board of trustees, and their funding comes primarily from donations. Some charities do receive funding in the form of grants from local authorities to provide specific services, however, and others are able to bid for contracts to deliver services on behalf of health or social care providers. For example, foster care agencies may help to provide and train foster parents for children in need on behalf of the LASS department, who may have given the charity responsibility for providing all foster carers in the local area (this is called outsourcing).

Informal provision

This refers to care provided by friends and family. Although they do not usually receive funding, people needing care services are increasingly being given their own budget to buy in their own care, rather than having social services organise care on their behalf. This allows the service user to choose who cares for him or her and pay them, including family members, who may have had to give up work to care for their relative. It is important to remember, however, that funding will only be provided if the person meets the LASS criteria (i.e. they have been assessed by the social worker as vulnerable and in need and haven't enough money); usually they will be receiving benefits.

P1

Activity 3

Read the following case study and identify the services provided and which of the sectors outlined above they fall into (statutory, private, voluntary, informal).

 ### Case Study

Jane is a 70-year-old woman who has Alzheimer's disease. She lives in her own home. Jane's care is provided by her husband, Terry, her daughter Ann, who visits her parents every day, and the We Care nursing agency, which is paid for by Terry, Jane and Ann. The family also receive support from a local society. Jane's medical care is provided through her local GP and medical specialists.

The way healthcare services are organised is sometimes categorised as primary, secondary or tertiary health care. However, it is important to recognise that the gradual move towards providing more integrated care means that there is less distinction between these categories than was previously the case.

- Primary care is essentially preventive and aims to either prevent disease or catch it in the early stages when it is more easily treatable; breast screening and immunisations are examples of primary care.
- Secondary care provides treatment for existing conditions and is often provided in hospitals – for example, surgery or hospital admission for investigations or treatment.
- Tertiary care is provided at home, in the community or in residential accommodation. Tertiary care includes rehabilitation services (e.g. following stroke) or management of long-term conditions, such as diabetes or dementia.

Health and social care settings

This section describes the actual locations in which health or social care is delivered. The government has widened the availability of the places where health and social care is delivered, and there is a move towards delivering more services locally in the communities where people live, so that people do not have to travel to hospital. The range of health and social care services is provided below.

GP surgeries

GP surgeries are based in a local area to serve a certain number of patients. Each general practitioner (GP) will be responsible for an average of 6,487 patients (King's Fund Briefing Paper, 2009). GPs are a key part of the primary care services as they are the first contact with the health services for most people. They have responsibility for providing advice on promoting health, preventing illness, managing pre-existing conditions, diagnosing disease, prescribing treatment and medicines and referring to a specialist if necessary for confirmation of diagnosis and treatment. GPs can work alone in a single-handed practice, or be part of a group of GPs – group practice.

Health centres

Health centres are specially built premises housing GP practices and other services, such as pharmacies and special clinics (e.g. family planning clinics where sexual health services can be delivered). Community nursing staff, such as community midwives, district nurses and health visitors, are often based in health centres and will provide services to the population served by the GP practices – for example, well-baby, well-woman and well-man clinics. Most health centres also have one or more practice nurses who work with GPs to provide treatments and in some cases consultations that previously may have been given by the GP, so freeing them up to see more patients.

Typical activities carried out by the practice nurse include wound dressing, removal of stitches, immunisations and injections, as well as taking blood, monitoring blood pressure and a range of other nursing tasks, which enable GPs to manage and monitor the condition and treatments of many patients.

Polyclinics

Polyclinics are a new model of providing services. They are currently located mainly in London and other big cities where there is a high concentration of people and a correspondingly high demand for services. Polyclinics are 'super-practices' in which GPs work alongside a range of other health professionals, such as nurses, hospital doctors and consultants, dentists and social workers, to offer patients *integrated care.* They are open for longer hours than health centres and can be accessed by anyone, which means that the person does not need to be registered with a specific practice GP. It is intended that polyclinics will be equipped with the technology to offer a range of services that were traditionally provided by hospitals (e.g. diagnostic scans, minor surgery, dermatology, diabetes care), as well as other services, such as speech therapy, audiology, physiotherapy and stroke rehabilitation. In other words, primary, secondary and tertiary care. This will allow hospitals to provide more specialised treatments and take full advantage of advances in medical technology and treatment and also means that patients do not need to keep travelling between the GP and hospital.

Key term

Integrated care – when organisations and practitioners work closely with each other and the patient to deliver exactly what the patient needs, when they need it. With integrated care, it does not matter which practitioner provides or delivers the care, as long as they have been properly trained and it meets the patient's needs.

Heart of Hounslow

The polyclinic in west London provides the following services:
Outpatient care – podiatry and chiropody (foot care), tissue viability (wound care), diabetes screening and a leg ulcer clinic. All these services would previously have been provided in hospital.
GPs – there are three GP practices employing 18 family doctors based in the polyclinic.
Dental care – specialist dental care for people with phobias or requiring complex dental surgery (e.g. wisdom teeth extraction and root canal fillings).
Independent living service – this is a multi-disciplinary service of district nurses, community matrons, physiotherapists and rehabilitation specialists.
Clinics – offering mental health services, sexual health services, children's health services and speech therapy.

Hospitals

There are different types of hospitals, offering different services.

- Teaching hospitals: these are usually foundation trusts. They provide specialist care and may be the regional centre for the treatment of certain conditions, such as cancer services. They often deal with complex cases and may be linked to a university, supporting research and medical training.
- District general hospitals, usually called NHS trusts: these provide general hospital care, such as diagnostic procedures, general surgery and medicine, maternity services (delivery) and services for women. They may or may not provide children's services; there are also specialist children's hospitals that are teaching hospitals (see above).
- Community hospitals are often situated in a local community and do not usually have an accident and emergency department, although they may have restricted opening hours. They provide services such as minor injuries units for dealing with less severe trauma, services for older people and screening services such as breast screening.

Hospices

Hospices provide full-time care for terminally ill people and those with life-limiting conditions. They are usually charitable organisations.

Day centres

Day centres for older people are often provided by social services or voluntary organisations. They give personal support, supervision and advice on adaptations to living accommodation, as well as meals and some health services, such as chiropody or psychiatric support.

Residential care homes

Residential care homes provide a 'home from home' for older people who are no longer able to care for themselves. They provide accommodation, meals, leisure activities, medicines and general care. They are usually privately owned and run; any health services needed by residents are provided by the GP and primary care services (e.g. district nursing service).

Nursing homes

Nursing homes provide the same facilities as residential homes but also provide nursing care. They are for people with long-term medical conditions who are unable to manage independently and who require regular medical attention.

Special schools

Special schools are often provided for children and young people who are unable to attend mainstream schools – for example, for sensory impaired or disabled children or for those suffering from eating disorders. Health services may be provided within these schools and some provision may be funded by either health or social services, or jointly.

Domiciliary care

Domiciliary care services are provided in the person's own home by care organisations on behalf of LA social services. They help people remain independent by providing help with everyday tasks, such as getting up and dressed, or getting ready for bed.

Foster care services

Foster care services are provided for children assessed by social workers as being at risk, and who are unable to live with their family. Both short-term and long-term fostering services are available and foster care can provide respite for parents who have children with long-term or life-limiting conditions.

School premises/drop-in centres

Health services are increasingly being provided at school premises and drop-in centres, particularly health promotion advice and issues specific to young people.

Children's centres

Children's centres are the location of integrated services, bringing together services for children and families, such as health visiting, day nurseries, parenting advice, information and guidance on a range of issues affecting families.

Pharmacies

Pharmacies provide health advice as well as advice on medicines. Their premises also often host screening services, such as cholesterol testing and allergy testing. Pharmacists can also prescribe certain medicines, such as emergency contraception.

Dentists

Dentists and orthodontist surgeries provide advice on dental health and treatment for dental problems. They may employ a dental hygienist and dental nurses.

Opticians

Opticians provide eye tests and prescriptions for lenses to correct vision. They can also diagnose potential ill health from the condition of the eyes and refer to consultant ophthalmologists (specialist eye surgeons) based in hospital. They also take referrals from the same consultants.

Activity 4

P1

Read the following case studies of people requiring services and try to identify what services should be available to them. Remember, one person might need access to several services.

 ### Case Study

Mrs Maxwell is an 82-year-old widow who lives alone in a first-floor flat, which she owns. She is registered as partially sighted. Recently she had a fall and has a wound on her shin, which is not healing well.

- What services might help Mrs Maxwell now and in the future?
- Are they health or social services?
- How can she access these services?

Case Study

Maureen Billington is the single parent of Suzie, aged five. Suzie has a degenerative condition (one which gets progressively worse until the person dies) and is severely disabled. Maureen is the full-time carer for Suzie and has two other children, Oliver, aged ten, and Simon, aged eight.

- What services might be available to the family?
- Are they health or social services?
- How are they funded?

Activity 5

P2

When you have completed Activity 4, investigate your local area and see if you can identify where these services can be accessed and how to access them.

2 Know barriers to accessing health and social care

Although there are a wide range of health and social care services available, it is not always possible for people to access and use them. The difficulties people face are called *barriers to access*. There are different reasons for people facing barriers to care and different ways of accessing health and social care.

How services are accessed

When you feel unwell and you think you need to see your GP, you ring up to make an appointment. Because you are able to take this decision yourself without consulting anyone, it is called *self-referral*. Referral is the term used – it means recommending for a medical appointment. You access your GP through self-referral and you go to the surgery for your appointment.

If your GP thinks you may have something more serious, or a condition that needs specialist treatment, he may refer you to a hospital consultant for further investigation or treatment. This is called *professional referral*. This type of access to specialist services can be done only by health professionals, such as doctors, nurses and physiotherapists. Not all health professionals can refer, and there may be limited circumstances under which they can refer.

One other type of referral is called *third-party referral*. This is where someone other than the person concerned or a healthcare professional refers an individual to a service. An example of this would be where a domiciliary care worker became concerned about an older person (e.g. if they were beginning to neglect themselves or were suspected of drinking too much) and contacted the social worker or health visitor. Similarly, if a childcare worker suspected a child was being abused, they may refer to social services, who have a duty to investigate.

Activity 6   P2

What other examples of third-party referral can you think of? Try brainstorming in groups and share your thoughts or experiences.

Types of barriers

Difficulties in accessing services can be due to a number of factors, some of which will be outside the individual person's control. Examples of barriers that some people face when they need services are given below.

Physical barriers

People who have a disability may experience physical barriers. Although the Disability Discrimination Act 1995 (amended 2005) requires that all public buildings are accessible, and that information be provided in an accessible format, actually getting to the health centre may still pose difficulties for some groups. For example, in the case of Mrs Maxwell in Activity 4, her poor sight may mean she has difficulty in phoning for an appointment if she cannot see to read the number. Getting to the doctor's surgery without assistance may also pose a problem; perhaps she needs to get a bus and is frightened of getting on the wrong one because she cannot read the destination on the front. She may not be able to afford a taxi, so she is likely to need some assistance.

Psychological barriers

Psychological barriers are much more common. You may know of people who are frightened of the dentist, or scared of injections, but fear of finding that their symptoms may be those of a serious or life-threatening illness keeps many people away from the doctor, despite the fact that most people recognise that the earlier you deal with illness, the easier it is to treat and the better the outcomes. Similarly, people with mental health problems may not be aware that they need to seek medical help or they may be too frightened.

Financial barriers

Financial barriers can prevent access to health care in several ways. For example, if you live in a rural area, you may have to travel a considerable distance to your local hospital, even if your GP is nearby. If you are on a low income, you may not be able to afford both the fares and your prescription.

Similarly, if you have a personal preference for a particular type of treatment, you may find it is not available through the NHS and you would be required to pay. An example of this would be where a mother wanted her baby to have three single vaccinations for measles, mumps and rubella instead of the normal single injection combining all three vaccinations. (All babies are routinely immunised against these diseases as part of the Child Health programme.)

These are individual barriers; however, there can also be structural financial barriers to accessing health care. Primary care trusts are allocated a budget for health care in their local area. Because the budget is fixed, they will be obliged to make decisions about how the money is spent. They will want to spend it so that it benefits the greatest number of people and they will look closely at the health issues in the local community.

For example, if the local area has a high number of people with heart disease, the PCT may decide to put money into preventive programmes for people at risk of heart disease so that the need for expensive heart surgery is reduced. This means there will not be as much money available for less common or very expensive treatments (e.g. weight loss surgery).

In order to make the system fair, the National Institute for Clinical Excellence (NICE) carries out research into the effectiveness of medicines and treatments and provides guidelines for doctors and PCTs. If a particular treatment will only be effective for a small number of people, and is very expensive, NICE may recommend that it is not funded through the NHS so that the funds benefit the maximum number of people. These are, however, only guidelines and a PCT can decide what treatments and services to offer to meet local needs.

Geographical barriers

Geographical location can affect access because services have not historically been distributed evenly across the country. For example, in London there are many large hospitals, which developed to meet the demands of the rapidly expanding population, and because it is where the medical professions were taught. The Royal Colleges – headquarters of the medical and nursing professions – are all located in London. In contrast, Cumbria in the Lake District has only two main hospitals, supported by a number of community hospitals and other provision. Similarly, some areas have many more GPs than others. For example, Oxford has almost twice as many GPs as Salford in Lancashire.

Cultural barriers

Cultural barriers may occur where the person does not speak good English, for example, or where the culture requires that individuals be treated by the same sex. Resources may be available to translate health information into only the most common languages spoken in the local community, and signs in hospitals and health and social care premises are likely to be in English. This is a significant problem in very ethnically diverse areas. For example, in 2006, primary school children in one London borough spoke 133 different languages at home as well as English (London Borough of Barnet, 2008). For individual people, it could mean that they are unable to understand the instructions on their medicines, for example.

Activity 7   P2   M1

In small groups, look at the barriers people face in accessing services.

If you were in charge, what actions would you take to help people overcome these barriers?

3 Understand principles of partnership in health and social care

People become vulnerable for many reasons, often through no fault of their own. Because people's circumstances are complex, they often need both health and social services.

Purpose of partnerships

The purpose of partnerships is to share information, skills and sometimes resources for the benefit of the service user, their family and carers. This is particularly important when planning care and monitoring and reviewing the effectiveness of *interventions* – for example, whether the adaptations to a person's home are helping them to remain independent or whether they need additional help. ('Interventions' is the term used to describe actions taken on behalf of a patient or services put in place to help.) Health and social care services are increasingly working together and the way services are organised is encouraging the delivery of *integrated services* (see section on polyclinics above).

> **Key terms**
>
> Multi-disciplinary – practitioners from different specialisms (e.g. nurses and physiotherapists).
> Multi-agency – different health, social care or related organisations (e.g. local authority services, such as housing, and voluntary agencies, such as Age Concern).

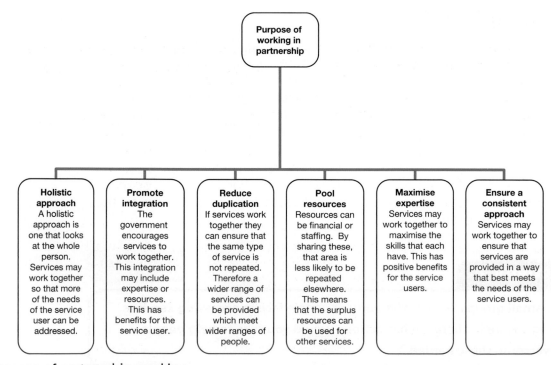

Purpose of partnership working

How partnerships work

There are huge advantages in people working together in multi-agency and multi-professional teams; they get to understand each other's job roles better, they share information and pass on skills. It is much better for patients and service users because they will usually be allocated a *key worker* who they get to know and who knows their story and understands their needs. The person only has to tell their story once; the role of the key worker is to work with the rest of the multi-disciplinary team and arrange services and support.

However, it is not enough for services and people to be based in the same location; if partnership working is to take place, it has to be planned and there have to be clear working arrangements in place so that everyone involved knows their role and the role of the other practitioners. This is best achieved when the managers of services sit down together and develop *policies* and *protocols* for integrated working, then make sure all the staff involved follow them. Shared budgets have to be agreed by the wider organisations. Care trusts and children's trusts are examples of partnership working.

PCTs and local authorities are required to consult with local people about the services they want and involve them in decisions about the development of services. The NHS constitution outlines people's rights to health care and local authorities are also required to consult their local populations about the organisation of local services.

Key terms

Key worker – this is one individual practitioner from one of the partner agencies who acts as the first point of contact for the patient. The partner agencies agree who will be the key worker and they then become responsible for passing information between the patient and the different agencies and helping to organise the agreed care plan.

Policies – these describe the correct course of action as agreed by the organisation, often to comply with the law, or with good professional practice, or with the stated ethical approach of the organisation. Policies are usually written and must be available to all workers within the organisation.

Protocols – a formal statement or written rules (e.g. a code of conduct).

4 Understand requirements for job roles in health and social care

There are a huge number of jobs in the health and social care sector, all of which make some contribution to the health and well-being of people using services. However, when we think of jobs in health and social care, we tend to think only of the professional roles, such as doctors, nurses and social workers. However, there are more than 300 careers within the NHS alone! Because of the wide variety of work, it is helpful to group jobs together. A brief overview of some of the job roles is given below. For more information, go to www.nhscareers.nhs.uk.

Nursing and midwifery

There are many types of nurses working in the health and social care sectors, not all of whom are based in a hospital. To be a nurse, you will need to have a degree or diploma to be qualified (from 2013, you will need a degree; the diploma will be phased out) and you also need to be registered with the Nursing and Midwifery Council (NMC). It is possible to start working as a healthcare assistant and obtain qualifications while working in the first instance, until eventually you can apply to study for a degree. Alternatively, you can be accepted onto a place with A-level qualifications.

Nurses train to work with particular groups of people (e.g. adult nursing, children's nursing, mental health nursing, learning disabilities nursing). Some nurses then take additional specialist qualifications to become health visitors, district nurses or midwives. It is also possible to train to be a midwife without doing nurse training first but you cannot be a district nurse or health visitor without doing adult nurse training (general training) first. Midwives work with expectant mothers, families and newborns in both hospital and community settings, including home visiting. Nurses work in many health and social care settings – for example, prisons, schools, GP practices and sometimes within local authorities (e.g. in child protection teams).

To be a nurse, you will need to be able to work as part of a team and you will need to have a range of personal skills. For example, you have to be good with people and able to be sympathetic to everyone, irrespective of their age, sex or background. You need to be a good listener and be able to answer questions and give advice, and you need to be observant so you can quickly spot changes in people's behaviour or condition. You need to be able to deal with emotionally charged situations, which requires self-control and self-discipline. All these qualities are aspects of professional practice.

Medicine

Medicine is concerned with diagnosing and treating illness, providing advice and guidance, respecting and understanding the health needs of individuals and improving the health of both individuals and populations. Medical training takes many years of study, starting with a degree at medical school lasting four years. This is followed by further study and additional qualifications, depending on the chosen specialism. The General Medical Council (GMC) regulates all doctors.

There are over 60 different specialties. A few of these are described below.

- Medical specialisms – concerned with different aspects of bodily functions such as cardiology (heart), rheumatology, oncology (cancers) and neurology (nerves and muscles).
- Surgical specialisms – carry out surgical interventions on different parts of the body – for example, orthopaedics is concerned with bones, and deals with injuries and diseases or lessens the problems caused by degenerative (progressive, incurable) diseases.

- General practice – doctors who decide to become GPs must undergo additional training. They are experts at diagnosis and either prescribe treatment for common conditions or refer to specialist colleagues for further investigation and treatment.
- Paediatrics and child health – doctors diagnose and provide treatment for babies, infants, children and adolescents. They are experts in child health and development.
- Obstetrics and gynaecology – a specialism that is concerned with female reproduction, pregnancy, childbirth and newborns.
- Pathology – an area of medicine that is concerned with the scientific investigation and detection of disease. Pathologists work closely with other doctors and advise on treatment options. They also help prevent the spread of disease in the wider community, working with public health-qualified doctors.
- Radiology – a branch of medicine that uses a range of technology (e.g. MRI and CT scanning) to investigate and detect abnormal body function and diagnose disease.
- Anaesthetics – this is about controlling consciousness and unconsciousness, allowing surgery to take place without pain. Anaesthetists are, therefore, skilled in pain relief and can help relieve chronic pain. They also manage patients in intensive care following major surgery or trauma.
- Ophthalmology – this is the medical specialism concerned with the health of the eyes. Doctors diagnose and treat diseases and conditions of the eye, including surgery for conditions such as cataracts. They work closely with opticians, who are responsible for providing visual aids (glasses, lenses, etc.).

To be a doctor, you need to be open minded, have an interest in people and an enquiring, rational mind. You also need to be imaginative but determined with an ability to work hard. You will need to be good at making decisions and able to cope under pressure, as well as working with others, all of which require patience and understanding.

Allied health professions

These professionals are either concerned with different aspects of the body or have technical expertise in a particular area. They work alongside doctors, nurses and others as part of the healthcare team. The training and qualifications vary but the Health Professions Council regulates them all in the same way as the NMC regulates nurses and the GMC regulates doctors to ensure they are fit to practice.

- Chiropody and podiatry is concerned with the health and care of the feet. Professionals deal with all types of foot conditions in all age groups.
- Dieticians are concerned with nutrition, particularly important when people are ill. They make sure that patients who have dietary problems

as a result of illness are able to maximise their recovery through effective nutrition. They also deal with obesity.

- Psychologists help people who are mentally distressed but not mentally ill. They can help with things like phobias.
- Speech and language therapists help children and adults who have speech problems – for example, following a stroke in adults or cleft palate or stammering in children.
- Audiologists deal with hearing problems and hearing aid technology. They carry out tests to assess hearing loss in adults and children and often work with speech therapists to deal with communication problems.
- Radiographers carry out diagnostic X-rays and undertake radiation treatment and imaging technology. They are scientifically trained.
- Occupational therapists help people overcome physical, psychological or social problems associated with illness and ageing. For example, they would be instrumental in helping a person following amputation, providing mobility aids, etc.
- Physiotherapists help with rehabilitation through exercise and are concerned with the effective functioning of the heart and respiratory systems, as well as bones, muscles and joints.
- Prosthetics and orthotics professionals are responsible for making and fitting artificial aids, such as limbs, eyes, breasts, etc., following amputation or surgery. Prosthesis means an artificial body part.
- Orthoptists assess and manage eye problems that are caused by faulty movement, such as squint.
- Operating department practitioners are an integral part of the surgical team. They help with equipment and assist the surgeon and anaesthetist to ensure that operations are efficiently performed.

Ambulance service

There are two main aspects of the ambulance service: emergency response and routine transport. Consequently, there are a range of different roles requiring different levels of technical expertise, as well as roles dealing with 999 calls and ambulance dispatch.

- Call handlers take the incoming 999 calls and log necessary information, asking relevant questions.
- Emergency medical dispatchers assess the information received and decide on the level of emergency, dispatching the appropriate vehicle (e.g. ambulance, motorcycle, rapid response car or helicopter). It is sometimes necessary to get medical help to an accident scene quicker than would be possible by traditional ambulance. Sometimes the roles of call handler and medical dispatcher are combined.
- Paramedics are the senior healthcare professional at the scene of an accident or emergency. They are responsible for assessing the patient's condition and administering treatment. They are specially trained in emergency medical techniques, such as inserting drips, giving injections and defibrillation.

- Emergency care assistants attend emergencies as part of the ambulance crew and give emergency treatment under the direction of the paramedic.
- Patient transport services controllers manage the transport arrangements for patients needing to attend routine appointments at the hospital's outpatients department or on discharge.
- Ambulance care assistants drive and accompany patients on routine journeys from home to hospital, etc. They are trained in lifesaving skills so they can respond in case of an emergency because the patients they are transporting are sometimes ill or frail.

Healthcare science

Healthcare scientists use their scientific skills to help prevent, diagnose and treat illness and disease. There are over 50 different job roles within healthcare sciences, which can be grouped as follows:

- Life sciences and pathology is concerned with microscopic examination of body tissue and blood to establish the cause of disease (e.g. bacterial infection and its likely progression). Practitioners may work in hospital laboratories or in public health, perhaps based in the community. Life science covers genetics (inherited causes of disease) and embryology (the scientific study of development from conception to birth).
- Physiological science uses specialist technical equipment to investigate the functioning of body systems and organs, aiming to maximise the functions and reduce any disabling consequences of long-term conditions.
- Physical sciences and clinical engineering is concerned with devising methods of measuring what is happening in the body and maintaining technical equipment.
- Pharmacists are trained to make the most effective use of medicines, advising doctors on things like drug interactions and dosage. They dispense medicines prescribed by doctors and manage and maintain stocks of medicines.

Wider workforce

These are the people that look after the buildings, information technology, administration, finance and human resources (staff recruitment and retention).

Workers in clinical support services help healthcare professionals and often work alongside them under supervision. For example, they may work as laboratory assistants or healthcare assistants.

Support services workers help move people and equipment around the hospitals or between hospitals and the community and look after security. They ensure there are sufficient supplies to maintain the services.

Domestic services take care of all the 'hotel services', such as cleaning, catering and laundry facilities. Many organisations do not directly employ these workers but contract with outside agencies.

Social care and social work

Social work is an internationally recognised profession with a set of distinct values based on 'respect for the equality, worth and dignity of all people' (International Federation of Social Workers).

The International Federation of Social Workers defines social work as follows:

> 'The social work profession promotes social change, problem solving in human relationships and the empowerment and liberation of people to enhance well-being. Utilising theories of human behaviour and social systems, social work intervenes at the points where people interact with their environments. Principles of human rights and social justice are fundamental to social work.'

Source: International Federation of Social Workers

Social workers

Social workers help people to improve their lives and personal situations by helping them to understand and claim their rights, and access services. They carry out assessments into people's circumstances, provide advice and information, make recommendations and provide advocacy to enable individuals to exercise their right to choices in how they live their lives. They have a key role to play in the safeguarding of vulnerable adults and children, and are required by law to act where abuse is suspected or proved.

In practice, this means that social workers increasingly work as part of multi-disciplinary teams. They often work with complex situations and, together with individuals, help them find solutions to their problems.

Social workers must undertake a degree in social work, during which they learn about general social work theory and practice, followed by post-qualifying practice in specialist areas during the first year. They are expected to meet agreed standards of practice during this time and have their work assessed. Social workers may choose to specialise in work with older people, mental health, learning disabilities or children and families. Social work is a *protected title*, which means it can only be used by people who have had the relevant training and who are registered with the General Social Care Council (GSCC) in England.

Social care workers

Social care workers work alongside social workers and their work must be supervised. They support individuals and families by monitoring and feeding back information to the social worker.

Social care workers may also work in residential care for adults or children, or for domiciliary care agencies. They can also work in multi-disciplinary teams. Training for social care workers usually takes place on the job as they work towards their National Vocational Qualification (NVQ), which will be a requirement for registration in England with the GSCC.

Management

Managers in the health and social care services can be from any background and do not necessarily need to be health or social care professionals. In practice, however, a large proportion tend to have moved into management as a career pathway. Managers have degree-level qualifications at a minimum of Bachelor's level and many also have Masters degrees.

Managers are responsible for planning the efficient organisation and delivery of health and social care in a particular area or locality, for a specific group of service users (e.g. older people), or for running an organisation and managing the finances. They have to make sure there are sufficient numbers of qualified and unqualified staff, including the wider workforce, and that all staff are performing effectively. There are managers at all levels within health and social care organisations.

The NHS has a graduate training scheme for new, highly qualified graduates aiming to become managers. Social services have leadership and management programmes for social services managers.

Activity 8

In pairs, investigate two job roles from those listed. You will need to find out what qualifications are needed, how training is organised, what standards are in place for that role and who is responsible for regulating workers if they do something wrong. Put this information together in a presentation (e.g. PowerPoint) and, using visual and other aids, present it to the rest of your class.

Core skills

Having the right skills means being able to apply your knowledge and abilities to your job. When you can do this well, it is called being *competent*. In order to become competent, you need to be trained and also to learn while you are doing your job. Depending on your job, you will need some or all of the following skills.

- Communication and interpersonal skills – these are essential to most job roles as you will need to be a skilled and effective communicator with a wide range of people, including other professionals, patients and service users. You need an understanding of human nature and human behaviour to be a good communicator.

- Scientific skills and the ability to think rationally – these skills are especially important if you are required to carry out assessments or diagnostics, or if you work in a laboratory. Doctors require scientific skills to understand how treatments and medicines work.
- Management and leadership skills – the ability to motivate people and be able to criticise constructively, organise and manage finances.
- Practical skills – you have to be technically competent in those aspects of your job role (e.g. if you are a nurse, you will need to be able to give injections).
- Supportive skills – you need to be able to understand things from the other person's point of view and *empathise* with them, which means you need to try and imagine how they feel, and be able to ask them and respond in a way that encourages them and makes them feel better.

Personal attributes

There are certain personal qualities or *attributes* you must have to be able to cope with work in health and social care, particularly if you are working directly with patients or service users. These are outlined below.

- Patience and understanding – the people you come into contact with are usually having some kind of crisis in their lives, and as a result they may feel frightened and uncertain. They may be ill and in pain. In such situations, people do not behave as they would normally; they can be rude and occasionally aggressive but mostly they need to be reassured in a firm and calm manner.
- Organising skills – you will be busy and may be trying to manage several tasks at once, or you may be managing or supervising the work of others so you need to be able to prioritise, memorise and organise!
- Observation skills – you will need to be able to pay attention to details and observe changes in situations or people's conditions or behaviour so you can take appropriate action. After a while, you will be able to predict changes.
- A non-judgmental approach – this means you must remain open minded and be prepared to deal calmly and professionally with any person requiring services, irrespective of your own views – for example, on their lifestyle, behaviour or attitude towards you.

Workforce development

For each work sector in the UK, there is an organisation to represent employer needs, called a Sector Skills Council (SSC). SSCs have responsibility for workforce development across their particular sector. The health services, which include the NHS and other organisations and agencies providing health care, are represented by Skills for Health across all the countries of the UK.

Skills for Health work closely with Skills for Care and Development, an alliance of five organisations across four countries acting as a Sector Skills Council for health and social care. This is because health and social care services across the different countries of the UK are organised and regulated slightly differently.

Skills for Care and Development's priority is to ensure the workforce meets the wide-ranging needs of those who use social care, children's, early years and young people's services. The organisations within Skills for Care and Development are:

- Care Council for Wales – sponsored by the Assembly government, they have legal responsibility for registration and regulation of individuals working within social care services (children and adults services) and for the development and regulation of education and training for this workforce to ensure fitness to practice on the part of all workers.
- Children's Workforce Development Council (CWDC) – sponsored by the Department for Children, Schools and Families, the full Children's Workforce in England includes sectors covered by other Sector Skills Councils; for example, children's nurses (Skills for Health) and play workers (SkillsActive). But CWDC has the remit for reform and development of the children and young people's workforce in England.
- Northern Ireland Social Care Council (NISCC) – sponsored by the Social Services Office of the Department for Health, Social Services and Public Safety NI, who have responsibility for registration and regulation of individuals working within personal social services and for the development and regulation of education and training for social workers and social care staff to ensure fitness to practice.
- Scottish Social Services Council – sponsored by the Scottish government and is responsible for registration and regulation of the social services, including the early years and childcare workforce, as well as delivery of workforce development and the SSC remit in Scotland.
- Skills for Care – a private company and charity funded primarily by the Department of Health. It is responsible for the strategic development of the adult social care workforce in England.

These organisations consult with employing organisations and agencies to decide on how the workforce should be developed, including what job roles are available and how services will change to meet the needs of their respective populations. The SSCs develop National Occupational Standards, which give details of the skills and competencies required by workers in particular roles. The professional bodies decide on standards of practice for registered professionals and work with SSCs on career pathways.

Non-professional workers in assistant practitioner roles, such as healthcare assistants, are required to undertake work-based qualifications such as National Vocational Qualifications, which are based on the National Occupational Standards. SSCs have also developed Induction Standards for new entrants to the workforce, to provide initial guidance on what is required of them.

Summary

Practitioners working in the health and social care sectors need to know how health and social care services are organised in the UK, including any particular differences within their home country. It is important to understand the health and social care services as an aspect of the wider welfare provision in the UK and the principles underpinning such provision, namely that it should be available to everyone and free at the point of use.

A necessary requirement for this unit is an understanding of the role of national government in setting the policy for delivering health and social care services, to meet the changing needs of the population. For example, making sure there are enough maternity services – obstetricians, midwives, hospital maternity beds – to meet the predicted birth rate, or enough social workers to ensure all older people can access services to enable them to live independently. This responsibility is one aspect of the role of Sector Skills Councils who, together with the various professional bodies, make sure that the workforce is planned, trained and developed to meet these needs.

Similarly, you need to understand the different types of organisations and agencies who provide health and social care and, in particular, understand the difference between statutory and non-statutory provision and the range of services provided. This includes where organisations and agencies may work in partnership to provide services that meet the specific needs of particular people, and the role of the emerging polyclinics.

Not everyone is able to access health and social care services equally and as a care worker you will need to have some understanding of the main barriers that people can face in accessing health and social care services. These range from psychological barriers, such as fear of being diagnosed with a life-threatening illness, to geographical barriers, such as the treatment you require only being provided in a regional centre to which you have to travel, putting a strain on family finances. It is important that you know how these barriers can be minimised so that people have access to services they need, when they need them.

If you wish to work in health and social care, you will need to know what types of jobs and careers are available and the qualifications and personal qualities you need to do such work. If you are successful, you will be meeting other health and social care practitioners and possibly working in partnership with them so you will also need to know what they do.

Grading grid

In order to pass this unit, the evidence that the learner presents for assessment needs to demonstrate that they can meet all the learning outcomes for the unit. The assessment criteria for a pass grade describe the level of achievement required to pass this unit.

Assessment and grading criteria		
To achieve a pass grade the evidence must show that the learner is able to:	To achieve a merit grade the evidence must show that, in addition to the pass criteria, the learner is able to:	To achieve a distinction grade the evidence must show that, in addition to the pass and merit criteria, the learner is able to:
P1 identify the key elements of health and social care services (see Activities 1, 2, 3 and 4) [IE2, RL5, TW1, SM2, EP2]		
P2 identify the main barriers to accessing health and social care (see Activities 5, 6 and 7) [IE1, CT1, RL5, SM2, EP2]	**M1** describe how barriers to accessing health and social care may be overcome (see Activity 7)	
P3 explain the benefits of interagency partnerships [CT1, CT3, CT4, CT5, RL5, SM2, EP2]	**M2** discuss the ways in which agencies work together to benefit individuals	**D1** assess factors that could prevent these organisations working together
P4 explain the skills required for two different job roles in health and social care (see Activity 8) [CT3, CT4, CT5, RL5, SM2, EP2]	**M3** compare the skill requirements of the two different job roles in health and social care (see Activity 8)	**D2** assess potential workforce development activities for the two job roles (see Activity 8)

Further Reading

Community Care Magazine (Reed Business Information)
King's Fund Briefing Paper (2009) *General Practice in England: An overview.*
London Borough of Barnet (2008) *Interpreting and Translation Policy* (www.barnet.gov.uk)
The Nursing Times (Emap)

Weblinks

www.ageconcern.org.uk – Age Concern
www.dh.gov.uk – Department of Health
www.kingsfund.org.uk – the King's Fund
www.macmillan.org.uk – Macmillan Nurses
www.mencap.org.uk – Learning Disability voluntary group
www.scie.org.uk – Social Care Institute for Excellence
www.scie-socialcareonline.org.uk – Adult social care
http://ssia.wlga.gov.uk – Social Services Improvement Agency

Unit 11
The Impact of Diet on Health

This unit explores the key principles of nutrition and how it is linked with good health. It highlights the dietary needs of individuals and looks at different requirements – for example, life stages, culture or specific health needs. This unit also considers health problems that are linked to unbalanced diets and how they can be avoided. It provides information about safe preparation of food and hygiene practices.

In this unit you can also work towards Functional Skills, ICT, English and at Maths Level 2 and towards Personal, Learning and Thinking Skills.

Learning outcomes:

In this unit you will learn about:

- the dietary needs of individuals at different life stages
- the effects of unbalanced diets on the health of individuals
- the dietary needs of specific service users
- the principles of food safety and hygiene.

1 Know the dietary needs of individuals at different life stages

A person's dietary needs depend on many factors. One of the main factors is life stage. A balanced diet is one that contains a variety of foods or nutrients, so that the individual eats the correct amounts according to their needs. Factors that affect our diets are discussed later in this unit.

Activity 1

Consider your diet over a day, and then compare it with a toddler's diet and with an older person's diet. What differences do you notice?

Life stages

Infancy 0–3 years

Newborn babies are unique in that they can rely on a single food, milk, in order to meet all their nutritional needs. Breast milk is ideal for many reasons:

- It contains all nutrients in correct amounts.
- It contains antibodies that protect the newborn baby against diseases in the first few months of life.
- It is clean.
- It is in correct proportions and readily available.
- It does not cause allergies.

A mother is encouraged to breastfeed for at least the first few weeks of her newborn baby's life. However, some mothers are unable to breastfeed or prefer not to, so formula milk (modified cow's milk) is given. As the infant's kidneys and digestive system are immature, it is important for mothers to follow instructions on how to prepare formula feeds – this prevents the risk of infection.

6 months

When the baby is introduced to solid foods the process is called 'weaning'. This can be started around six months of age so that damage to the young kidneys, as well as obesity and allergies, are avoided.

Key term

Weaning – this is the gradual introduction of solid foods from a milk diet; it should normally start around 16 weeks after birth.

8 months

At this age, more solid foods such as cereals, pureed fruit and vegetables can be introduced. As the baby continues to grow, lumpier food can be introduced, although some babies take longer than others to learn how to chew and swallow lumps.

12–18 months

The toddler can now be given cow's milk (full-fat milk) and they should be eating quite a varied diet. They will be drinking less milk as they start to eat more solid foods with the rest of the family. Skimmed milk should be given only after the age of five. Up to the age of three the diet should include iron-rich foods. Children who are weaning are also starting to move around and use more energy, so their diet should contain enough carbohydrates, which provide a good source of energy for crawling and toddling youngsters.

Activity 2

In small groups, research which foods are rich in iron. Plan a menu that would be appropriate for a toddler (2–3 years).

Childhood 4–10 years

At this age children are actively exploring and also beginning their education, so their diet should reflect their growing needs. Their energy requirements will be high, but only in relation to their body size (clearly they have smaller stomachs than adults). This is a very important time for children's nutrition. By encouraging healthy meals, snacks and drinks we can help children establish good eating habits for the future. Sweets, fizzy drinks, fatty and sugary foods should generally be avoided, as they can cause a range of health problems including obesity, but they can be given occasionally, as treats. They are best given at the end of mealtimes as this will help to avoid tooth decay. We should encourage social skills, such as eating with a knife and fork and drinking from a cup at a table. We should also encourage them to get into the habit of regularly brushing their teeth.

Key term

Obesity – excess body fat having a BMI of over 30. Obesity will cause health problems.

Adolescence 11–18 years

Adolescents grow rapidly in weight and height, and many physical changes are taking place, both internally and externally. These changes all require energy so an adolescent's appetite can be large – but their diet should still be well balanced. A diet high in sugar, salt and fat could lead to health problems such as obesity, heart disease or diabetes in later life. Adolescents should also participate in regular physical exercise to help avoid these health problems. They should be informed about the risks of severe dieting that some teenagers are susceptible to.

Adults 19–65 years

Adults need to maintain a healthy, well-balanced diet. This age group should limit their intake of carbohydrates and fats to avoid heart disease, obesity and diabetes. Adults' nutritional requirements reduce with age as they become less physically active. They should still be advised to take regular physical exercise. Adults should also be advised about the safe intake of alcohol per week:

- Women – 14 units
- Men – 21 units.

Pregnancy and breastfeeding

In teenage pregnancy girls are more likely to suffer with nutrient deficiencies as their bodies are still growing and developing, so they should eat extra nutrients to help the foetus grow and provide breast milk. During adult pregnancy and breastfeeding a woman's nutritional needs increase slightly, for the development of the foetus and the placenta and the production of breast milk. The saying 'eating for two' is well known, but is not entirely accurate. Rather than eating a lot more food, women should ensure that their diet is nutritious and well balanced. When planning to get pregnant and during early pregnancy, women are advised to take extra folic acid in the diet or in tablet form. Folic acid has been proven to lower the risk of spina bifida in the foetus. Generally, if the mother and family have good dietary habits they will be able to pass them on to their growing children.

Older people 65+ years

As we age we become less mobile, so our energy requirements decrease slightly. Although they do not need a lot of food, older people still need good sources of protein, vitamins and minerals. Some older people may not eat enough or they may not have the correct balance of nutrients. This could be because they are living alone, or they lose their partner and do not feel like cooking meals for one person, or they may just lose their appetite.

In order to maintain their appetite, older people should be encouraged to cook tasty, easy, nutritious meals. Clearly, this will help them to avoid illness. Gentle exercise should also be promoted to help with their physical, mental and social wellbeing.

Concept of balanced diet

Intake and needs

Apart from the mother's milk for her newborn infant, there is no one single food that provides enough nutrients for a healthy, balanced diet, so we depend on a variety of foods to keep us healthy. Generally there are no unhealthy foods as such – it is unbalanced amounts of foods that can lead to health problems. These will be discussed later in this unit.

Energy balance

The term energy balance refers to a person's intake and output of energy being equal. Energy intake is mainly from carbohydrate and fat in the diet, and output is the energy used during everyday processes like breathing, moving and metabolism. If the input exceeds the output then the excess is stored as fat and over a long period of time will result in chronic conditions like obesity.

Children may need a higher intake of energy foods as they are growing rapidly. Since the mid-twentieth century, people living in developed countries have generally become less active due to changes in types of work, transport and technology, so are more at risk of developing obesity.

Dietary Reference Values

Dietary Reference Values (DRVs) were developed by the Department of Health in 1991 to replace Recommended Daily Amounts (RDAs). DRVs are benchmark intakes of energy and nutrients – they can be used for guidance but should not be seen as exact recommendations. They show the amount of energy or an individual nutrient that a group of people of a certain age range (and sometimes sex) needs for good health.
Although DRVs are given as daily intakes, people often eat quite different foods from one day to the next and their appetite can change, so, in practice, the intakes of energy and nutrients need to be averaged over several days. Also, DRVs apply only to healthy people.

DRV is a general term used to cover the following:

- **Estimated average requirement (EAR)**: the average amount of energy or a nutrient needed by a group of people.
- **Reference nutrient intake (RNI)**: the amount of a nutrient that is enough to meet the dietary needs of about 97 per cent of a group of people.
- **Lower reference nutrient intake (LRNI)**: the amount of a nutrient that is enough for a small number of people in a group with the smallest needs. Most people will need more than this.
- **Safe intake**: this is used when there is not enough evidence to set an EAR, RNI or LRNI. The safe intake is the amount judged to be enough for almost everyone, but below a level that could have undesirable effects.

Malnutrition and nutrient deficiencies

The term malnutrition means unbalanced eating habits, which in time can lead to poor health. It can also relate to under-nutrition or over-nutrition. Under-nutrition is mainly linked to the less developed countries where there is not enough food for the whole population. A long-term lack of protein, carbohydrates and other nutrients can cause disorders such as *marasmus* (caused by lack of overall calories) or *kwashiorkor* (caused by lack of protein) both of which cause wasting of the body. Young children and old people are most at risk from starvation. Under-nutrition in a developed country such as the UK is relatively rare, since there is usually plenty of food to go round. Iron deficiency is an example of under-nutrition and can lead to anaemia. Over-nutrition is mainly linked to developed countries where there is excessive consumption of food. This can cause disorders such as obesity, heart disease, tooth decay and liver damage. (These are discussed later in the unit.)

'The Balance of Good Health'

The Food Standards Agency (FSA) produced 'Eight Guidelines for a Healthy Diet' (source: www.food.gov.uk), from which is derived 'The Balance of Good Health'. This aims to convey a practical message about healthy eating and to reduce the confusion about what healthy eating really means. The distribution of 'The Balance of Good Health' in a number of public settings, such as health centres, supermarkets, schools and workplaces aims to help to maintain a consistent message.

'The Balance of Good Health' gives the following guidelines:

● Enjoy your food.
● Eat a variety of different foods.
● Eat the right amount to be a healthy weight.
● Eat plenty of foods rich in starch and fibre.
● Eat plenty of fruit and vegetables.
● Don't eat too many foods that contain a lot of fat.
● Don't have sugary foods and drinks too often.
● If you drink alcohol, drink sensibly.

It is based on five food groups:

● Fruit and vegetables – to provide a variety of nutrients such as carbohydrates for energy, vitamin C to help heal wounds, and fibre. The aim is to eat a variety of five a day.
● Bread, other cereals and potatoes – to provide energy from carbohydrates and fibre. The aim is to eat this in good amounts at every meal.
● Milk and dairy – to provide calcium, protein necessary for growth and repair, and vitamin D, which helps calcium and phosphate absorption and healthy teeth and bones. These should be eaten in moderate amounts and where possible lower-fat alternatives should be used (except for babies and young children).

- Meat, fish and alternatives such as soya – this group provides iron, protein and zinc necessary for the growth of tissues. These should be eaten in moderate amounts and lower-fat alternatives should be used where necessary.
- Foods containing fat and sugar – this group of foods provides fats and carbohydrates. It is recommended to eat these in small amounts.

The '5-a-day' campaign aims to encourage people to eat a variety of fruit and vegetables every day. Different amounts of fruit or vegetables count as one portion. (See www.5aday.nhs.uk.) Eating a healthy diet that includes enough fruit and vegetables provides a range of vitamins, minerals and nutrients, and can reduce the risk of illnesses and disease, such as heart disease and strokes.

Components of a balanced diet

A balanced diet contains five main groups of nutrients:

- protein
- fat
- carbohydrates
- vitamins
- minerals.

Fluid is also needed in the diet – without fluid we could not survive.

Nutrients can be split into two groups:

1 Macro nutrients (macro means large/big). These are needed in our body in large amounts. They are proteins, fats and carbohydrates.
2 Micro nutrients (micro means small). These are needed in small amounts in our body. Micro nutrients are vitamins and minerals.

Carbohydrates

There are two main types of carbohydrates: sugar and starch.

Sugar

Sugar is found in foods like jams, sweets, honey and soft drinks. It is also added to desserts, cakes and biscuits. Sugar contains monosaccharide (simple sugars) and disaccharides (complex or double sugars).

Foods containing sugar and starch

Some names of monosaccharides are:

- fructose
- galactose
- glucose.

Some names of disaccharides are:

- sucrose
- lactose
- maltose.

Starch

This is found in foods like bread, potatoes, rice and pasta. Starches are called polysaccharides (poly means many), which means starch is made up of many units of monosaccharide (single sugars). Non-starch polysaccharides are more commonly known as cellulose or dietary fibre. This is found in foods like vegetables, fruit and cereals (it used to be called roughage). It is fibrous and we cannot digest it, but it has many health benefits. It encourages us to chew our food thoroughly and adds bulk to the diet, so encourages our digestive tract to work effectively. It also helps to avoid constipation and may prevent some bowel disorders and diseases.

Sugar and starch carbohydrates both provide equal amounts of energy, but starch carbohydrates are the healthier option. Sugar carbohydrates are strongly linked with tooth decay. Carbohydrates are needed in our diet to provide our main source of energy. Experts have estimated that over half the energy in our diets should come from carbohydrates.

Proteins

Proteins are essential in our diet and are used in the body for repair and growth of new cells in the body. The immune system, which fights infection, is also made up of protein. Therefore, it is really important that groups of people like babies, children, older people and people who are ill in particular have a good supply of protein in their diets. Protein is found in a range of foods, the main sources being red meat, poultry, fish, eggs, milk and yoghurt. Obviously, vegetarians (who do not eat meat or fish) need their supply from other foods, such as nuts, pulses (peas, beans and lentils), soya protein and some vegetables. Vegans also need to be very careful about including good sources of protein in their diet.

Protein foods

Proteins are made up of building blocks called amino acids. Some of these amino acids are called 'essential amino acids'. These have to be supplied by diet. There are eight essential amino acids:

- Isoleucine
- Phenylalanine
- Leucine
- Threonine
- Lysine
- Tryptophan
- Methionine
- Valine.

Fats

Fat is required in the diet to help to build cells in the body. It provides energy and helps with the absorption of Vitamins A, D, E and K into the body. It also provides taste and texture to food.

- Saturated fats are found in foods such as milk, cream, full-fat cheese, lard and butter. They are sometimes called animal fats. If eaten in excess they can cause heart disease.
- Polyunsaturated fats are found in foods such as soya oil, corn and fish.
- Monosaturated fats are found in olive oil and are said to benefit the heart. Many unsaturated fats come from plant oils.
- Essential fatty acids are polyunsaturated fats that cannot be made by the body so have to be provided by the diet. They help to build cells. Omega 3 fats can help prevent heart disease and are helpful in joint diseases – they can be found in oily fish. Omega 6 fats can help prevent heart disease as they reduce cholesterol levels. They can be found in sunflower oil, corn oil, soya oil, cereal, eggs and poultry.

Vitamins

Vitamins are essential in a healthy diet – they help with metabolic functions in the body.

Vitamin comes from the word 'vital'. They are needed in the body in very small amounts. We need varying amounts to stay healthy, according to factors such as age and gender.

There are two types of vitamins: fat-soluble and water-soluble vitamins.

Fat-soluble vitamins are stored in the liver and do not have to be taken in every day. They are vitamins A, D, E and K. Water-soluble vitamins cannot be stored in the body so should be taken in daily. They are the vitamin B group and vitamin C. The chart below shows the sources, function and requirement for vitamin intake (fat-soluble in red, water-soluble in blue.

Table 11.01 Source, function and requirement for vitamin intake

Vitamin	Sources	Role in the body and effect of shortage
A (Retinol)	Animal foods, milk, cheese, eggs, oily fish, fruit and vegetables. In animal products it is known as retinols and plant carotenes (which the body converts to retinol).	Essential for vision in dim light. A prolonged lack can lead to night blindness. It helps with the maintenance of healthy skin and keeps mucous membranes (such as eyes and throat) free from infection, supple and smooth. It also assists in the growth of bones and teeth and helps the body fight infection. Too much Vitamin A can lead to a toxic effect as the liver cannot process it. There is also a link between too much Vitamin A and birth defects. As a consequence pregnant women are advised not to take nutritional substances which contain Vitamin A.
D (Cholecalciferol)	Found in fish liver oils, oily fish, eggs, dairy products, and is added to margarine by law. It is also found in the UV rays in sunlight. Vitamin D is stored in the liver and can be used as required.	Required for bones and teeth – these contain large amount of calcium and phosphorus. Vitamin D helps the absorption of calcium. People are unlikely to be deficient in Vitamin D unless they have limited exposure to the sun. Lack of Vitamin D can cause weak bones and teeth. Bones may then bend, which can cause rickets in children or osteomalacia in adults. Too much, though, can lead to deposits of calcium in the joints, which can damage organs.
C (Ascorbic acid)	Fresh fruit and vegetables Fruit juices	Aids absorption of iron and helps build bones and teeth. It aids Vitamin E as an antioxidant and is necessary to build and maintain skin and digestive system. Helps fight infection by protecting immune systems. Shortage can lead to scurvy and poor healing of damaged cells.
B1 – Thiamin	Milk, eggs, vegetables, fruit	Helps release energy from carbohydrates. Shortage causes beri beri (linked with alcoholism), depression, pins and needles.
B2 – Riboflavin	Milk and milk products	Helps utilise energy from foods. Shortage causes sore mouth and tongue.
B3 – Niacin	Cheese, meat (especially chicken)	Helps utilise food energy. Shortage causes skin peeling, diarrhoea, memory loss, insomnia.

B6 – Pyridoxine	Meat, fish, eggs	Metabolism of amino acids and helps form haemoglobin. Shortage causes nerve problems and fatigue.
B12 – Cyanocobal- amin	Meat (especially liver) milk, eggs, cheese. Does not occur in vegetables.	Needed by cells that divide rapidly. One example is bone marrow, which helps make red blood cells. Shortage causes pernicious anaemia and degeneration of nerve cells.
Folate (Folic acid)	Leafy green vegetables, potatoes and oranges	Helps Vitamin B12 with rapidly dividing cells. Important in pregnancy. Shortage may cause anaemia.
E (Tocopherol)	Vegetable oils, nuts and egg yolk	Major role as an antioxidant. Stored in the body to protect body cells from free radicals (unstable compounds that damage healthy body cells). It also maintains a healthy reproductive system, nerves and muscles. Shortage causes muscle and cell disfunction.
K	Widespread in many foods including leafy vegetables such as spinach, cauliflower. It can be produced in the body by bacteria.	Essential for blood clotting. Babies tend to be given an injection of Vitamin K at birth. Shortage is rare, and is usually in babies, called Vitamin K deficiency bleeding.

Minerals

Minerals are split into essential minerals and trace minerals. Below is a chart showing the sources and roles of essential minerals in the body.

Table 11.02 Sources and roles of essential minerals

Mineral	Sources	Role in the body and effect of shortage
Calcium	Milk, cheese, eggs, bones of canned fish and is added to white flour by law.	Calcium combined with phosphorous gives strength to teeth and bones; it helps with blood clotting and nerve functioning. Shortage causes poor teeth development, rickets in children and osteomalacia in adults. Tetany may result if muscles and nerves do not function properly.

Iron	Red meat, offal, fish, dark leafy green vegetables, pulses, cereal, nuts, dried herbs and spices	Iron carries oxygen in the blood to all cells. Vitamin C helps the body absorb more iron. Shortage causes anaemia, particularly infants 6–12 months, teenage girls who are menstruating and older people.
Sodium	Found in many additives, snacks and preservatives, naturally found in eggs, meat and vegetables	Helps to maintain fluid balance with potassium and sodium chloride. Important for nerve and muscle impulses. Shortage causes muscle cramps; excessive amounts can lead to high blood pressure.

Diet variation during life stage development

Activity 3

Visit www.food4life.org/key-stage-three/games/ and click on the section 'Introducing Ages and Stages'. Suggest a suitable menu for each person, making sure you have considered their life stage and the balance of good health.

The table below has some tips to help you.

Table 11.03 Dietary needs during life stage development

Life stage	Dietary suggestions
Preconception and pregnancy	Before pregnancy, the couple should both be in the best health possible and should consider their diet and alcohol intake. High levels of alcohol can affect sperm production and in pregnancy can affect the child intellectually and physically. The woman should include folic acid in her balanced diet, which will help with the development of the spinal cord in the baby. During pregnancy, protein is essential for new growth. Foods that may contain bacteria should be avoided, for example unpasteurised milk and cheese and uncooked eggs.
Baby	Up until around 6 months old the baby should be totally breastfed or given formula feed, depending on the choice of the parents. Weaning onto solid foods is not recommended until after six months. The food should have a variety of tastes and be introduced in a smooth consistency, gradually getting lumpier so the baby can learn to chew.

Child	At this stage, the diet should be high in protein as the child is growing rapidly. Carbohydrates are required for energy, as the child is becoming more mobile and learning new skills. Calcium and vitamin D are required for bone and teeth development.
Adolescent	Girls reaching puberty need a diet high in iron. All adolescents require enough protein in their diets as growth spurts are common at this life stage. Peer pressure may lead to eating 'junk' foods, which can lead to obesity and tooth decay. Education is required about the benefits of a balanced diet and the dangers of excessive alcohol intakes.
Adult	Adults should have good knowledge about a balanced diet. Later in adulthood the metabolism slows down so portion sizes should be adjusted. Diets should contain enough iron.
Older person	In this life stage, activity often slows down so the diet should be lower in fats and contain more protein to help with repair of cells, particularly in times of illness. The diet should contain calcium to help maintain bone density. Portion sizes should also be reduced as the person is less active.

Factors influencing the diet of individuals

Religion/culture

Culture and religion play a large part in food choices. Also, certain foods may be accepted by one member of the family and not by another, even if they share the same background, culture and religion. In other words, people have different tastes. People may make different choices for ethical or religious reasons, and we all have personal likes and dislikes.

Activity 4

Investigate the following groups and identify their dietary rules:

- Hindus
- Jews
- Muslims
- Sikhs
- Buddhists
- vegetarians
- vegans.

Social class

There is some evidence that different social classes may also make different dietary choices. You may want to talk about this in your group. For example, people from higher social classes may eat a healthier diet because they have been well educated and can afford better food, whereas people from a lower social class with less money may have a poorer diet because of a lower income. However, people who have highly paid jobs involving travel and stress may eat an unbalanced diet as it is hard to find time to buy and cook fresh food. They may eat too many foods that are high in fat and sugar.

What makes you choose your food?

What do you think? Discuss these points as a class. You may also want to consider the following questions. Is fresh food more expensive? What about so-called 'fast food' – is it really cheaper than fresh?

Key term

Social class – a method of looking at people by what occupation they do in society.

Personal preferences

Clearly, personal preference influences dietary choices. This is not just about taste, likes and dislikes but can also be linked to habits. For example, you may be in the habit of not having breakfast – if so, it is not a good start to your day. It may be difficult to change long-term habits. As we have seen, food choices may also be linked to religion or culture. For example, it may be your personal preference not to eat meat, or it may be part of your religion.

Peer pressure

People around you may influence you in your dietary choices. Children and young people are particularly influenced by their peers. The influence may be towards making choices that are healthy or unhealthy.

The media

Information in the media such as television adverts, magazine articles, leaflets, posters and soap operas on television, published research articles and news events all have an influence on our food choices, although we sometimes don't realise it.

Activity 5

Using the internet, research some food-related items in the media and discuss how they may have influenced people's food choices. Here are a few ideas to get you started:

- **Find out about the salt content in food. Are you aware that some foods are very high in salt?**
- **Find out about the debates concerning food advertising during children's television. Are unhealthy foods targeted at children?**
- **Could healthier foods be made more attractive to children and young people? How would you do this?**

Position in family

The position in the family may determine your dietary choices for various reasons. The person who is doing the shopping is likely to make food choices for the rest of the family. When we are very young, our food is chosen for us. As we get older we begin to make our own choices.

Geographic location

This may relate to how close you live to shops or supermarkets. For example, if you live in a rural area your choice of shopping may be limited to a small local store, but you may also have a plentiful supply of fresh produce. If you live in an urban area your choice of food may be much wider. Some urban areas have shops selling a wide range of healthy and organic produce, while others may have mainly fast-food outlets or small convenience stores.

Geographic location also relates to the country where you live. A developed country will have a wide variety of food and can import wider choices, for example, seasonal foods may be available all year round. A poor country may suffer from extremes of weather, so crops may be destroyed, or food may be of low quality or limited supply. In extreme cases in less developed countries, starvation may result when a crop fails or when families simply cannot afford to buy enough food.

Availability of food

This can be linked to geographical location but is also to do with access and transport. Large supermarkets are usually on out-of-town sites and transport is needed to access them. Sometimes older or disabled people may be unable to get to them. Even if public transport is available, carrying and storage may still be a problem.

Financial resources

This is a major factor that affects our dietary choices. Groups of people who have a very limited budget may have less choice in their diet. High earners may be able to afford rich diets and expensive meals out in restaurants (but as discussed earlier, this can be either an advantage or disadvantage according to how much rich food they eat and how often).

2 Understand the effects of unbalanced diets on the health of individuals

Medical conditions related to unbalanced diets

Malnutrition

Unbalanced diets have a detrimental effect on our health. They can cause malnutrition, which means unbalanced or disordered eating. Malnutrition can occur as a result of under- or over-eating over a long period of time, which can lead to illness or disease. Types of malnutrition include:

- over-nutrition, e.g. coronary heart disease (CHD), obesity, type 2 diabetes
- under-nutrition, e.g. *marasmus* and *kwashiorkor*
- nutrient deficiency, e.g. anaemia, rickets, tooth decay, night blindness, beri beri, scurvy.

Over-nutrition

This is more likely to happen in developed countries where there is over-consumption of fatty foods. Over-nutrition can result in conditions such as the following.

Coronary heart disease

Coronary heart disease is the term that describes what happens when the heart's blood supply is blocked, or interrupted, by a build-up of fatty substances in the coronary arteries. Over time, the walls of the arteries can become furred up with fatty deposits. This process is known as athero-sclerosis and the fatty deposits are called atheroma. If the coronary arteries become narrow, due to a build-up of atheroma, the blood supply to the heart will be restricted. This can cause angina (chest pains).

Obesity

Obesity means more than just a few extra pounds gained in weight. It is the heavy accumulation of fat in the body, to such a degree that it greatly increases the risk of various diseases. It can damage health and cause death from conditions such as heart disease and diabetes.

For medical purposes, the body mass index (BMI) is used to determine whether your weight is in the healthy range. Go to www.eatwell.gov.uk/healthissues/obesity/ to discover information about BMI and how to calculate it using a special formula and web calculator.

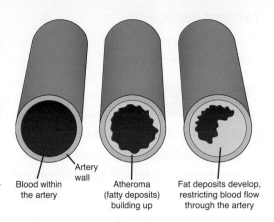

Blood within the artery — Artery wall

Atheroma (fatty deposits) building up

Fat deposits develop, restricting blood flow through the artery

How atheroma builds up in the arteries

Type 2 diabetes

In this type of diabetes the receptors on cells in the body that normally respond to the action of insulin fail to be stimulated by it – this is known as insulin resistance. In response to this, more insulin may be produced, and this overproduction exhausts the insulin-manufacturing cells in the pancreas. There is simply insufficient insulin available and the insulin that is available may be abnormal and so doesn't work properly.

Activity 6

Research coronary heart disease, obesity and type 2 diabetes. Produce a poster highlighting the signs and symptoms of these conditions and what could happen if the condition is not recognised or treated.

Under-nutrition

This occurs mainly in underdeveloped countries where problems such as *marasmus* and *kwashiorkor* are seen. It results from too little dietary energy and proteins.

Marasmus: inadequate energy and protein intake; associated with severe wasting.

Kwashiorkor: fair-to-normal energy intake, but inadequate protein.

Activity 7

Investigate both conditions and highlight the differences and similarities between the two. Use a table to highlight your information.

Nutrient deficiency

Continued long-term shortage of some important nutrients can cause diseases and disorders.

Activity 8

In small groups, choose one of the disorders listed below and find out what nutrient causes the deficiency and what the characteristics of the disorder are. You could produce your findings in a poster for your classroom or an information leaflet for your colleagues.

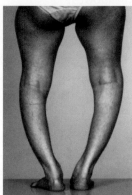

Rickets

Beri beri

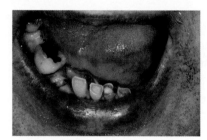

Tooth decay

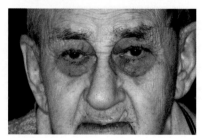

Anaemia

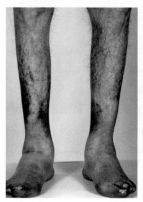

Scurvy

Night blindness

Activity 9

P1   P2   P3   M1

P1 – In a table, identify the components of a balanced diet, with examples of where the food can be found.

P2 – Design a poster that identifies all the life stages and their dietary requirements.

P3 – In a report, explain two medical conditions that are related to unbalanced diets. For example, you could discuss how coronary heart disease is related to a diet high in saturated fats and cholesterol.

For **M1**, your report should discuss how a balanced diet is important at each life stage. Use your poster in P2 for help and refer again to the Tweedie family, who we have already discussed at www.food4life.org.uk/dietary_advice

3 Know specific dietary needs of service users

Some service users have a particular need that means they have to eat a special diet. This could be for a number of reasons.

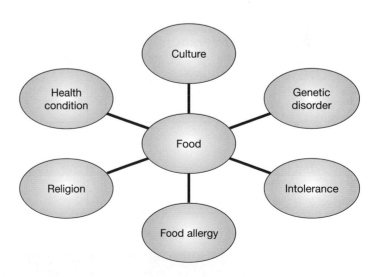

Reasons for specific dietary needs

Table 11.04 Medical conditions requiring a special diet

Medical condition	Diet required
Coronary heart disease The blood supply to the heart is reduced by a build-up of fatty deposits.	Avoid fatty red meat, cheese, egg yolks and limit intake of cakes and biscuits. Diet should contain grilled food, oily fish and fresh fruit and vegetables.
Obesity The person's energy balance is incorrect.	Regular meals with reduced portion sizes. High fat and sugar snacks should be avoided and regular exercise should be included. '5-a-day' of fruit and vegetables. Reduce alcohol.
Type 2 diabetes Constant high sugar levels cause the production of insulin to be affected.	Low-glucose intake. The diet should contain carbohydrate foods that are low-glycaemic, which means glucose is realised from the foods gradually to maintain a constant energy level.
Lactose intolerance Lactose is a sugar that is present in dairy products. Intolerance means some people are unable to accept this sugar in their diet. It causes stomach cramps and diarrhoea.	Dairy products should be replaced with soya-based foods, e.g. soya milk.
Gluten/wheat allergy (coeliac disease) Gluten is present in wheat, barley and oats. An allergy to gluten affects the digestive system and correct absorption of nutrients does not take place.	Foods that contain wheat, barley and oats should be replaced with gluten-free products.
Food allergies and intolerances An allergy is a reaction of the body to an allergen. These can include insect bites, drugs and some foods, such as nuts, fruits, dairy products and wheat.	Avoid the known allergen. Always check labels on packaging.
Phenylketonuria Phenylalanine is a amino acid needed for growth. This condition causes a build up of phenylalanine as the body is unable to use it properly. It causes brain damage.	People with this condition should have a special low-protein diet and also make sure that they check food and drink labels.

Table 11.05 Religious and cultural reasons for special diets

Religion or culture	Diet
Hindu	Diet should not include meat or fish. In some cases Hindus do not eat eggs. Some foods are seen to be sacred, especially the cow (beef). Consumption of alcohol is forbidden.

Judaism	Jews should eat kosher food. So a devout Jew can only eat certain types of meat and fish. Meat must be prepared in a ritually acceptable manner. Meat and dairy products must not be eaten in the same meal and pork is forbidden.
Muslim	Meat that is eaten should be 'halal', which means that the animal's throat is cut and the blood is drained out, then a prayer is offered to Allah. Animals that have died from natural causes should not be eaten. No alcohol.
Buddhist	Many Buddhists are vegetarian but it is not mandatory.
Vegetarian	Vegetarians do not eat meat or fish.
Vegan	Vegans do not eat any food that comes from animals, for example eggs and dairy products.

Activity 10

- **As a class, discuss the dietary needs outlined in the tables shown above.**
- **In small groups, choose one of the tables and list some food examples that would be appropriate for each dietary need.**
- **Choose two service users, each with a specific dietary requirement, then make a two-day diet plan for each service user. Use some ideas from your work experience to help you. Your two-day plan should include the following:**
  - **breakfast and a drink**
  - **mid-morning snack and a drink**
  - **mid-day meal and a drink**
  - **mid-afternoon snack and a drink**
  - **evening meal and a drink.**
- **When planning your menu, remember your service user's personal needs and preferences, their life stage, energy needs and ability to follow the plan. Make sure that your menu is appropriate.**
- **In a short report, explain why you have chosen the menus for each of the service user and why it meets their individual dietary needs. (For example, if you chose a service user who has coronary heart disease, you would explain why you have included grilled foods rather than fried foods.)**

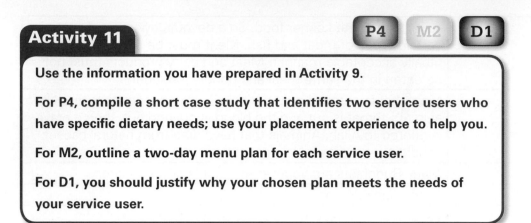

Activity 11 P4 M2 D1

Use the information you have prepared in Activity 9.

For P4, compile a short case study that identifies two service users who have specific dietary needs; use your placement experience to help you.

For M2, outline a two-day menu plan for each service user.

For D1, you should justify why your chosen plan meets the needs of your service user.

4 Understand principles of food safety and hygiene

Food hygiene is the action taken to ensure food is handled, stored and cooked in a way and under such conditions that as far as possible food contamination is prevented.

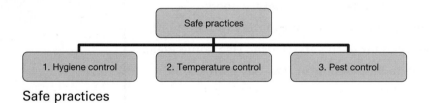

Safe practices

Safe practices of food preparation, cooking and service

Hygiene control

This means to use practices that reduce the risk of food contamination. The aim is to prevent the spread of bacteria. Contamination may occur by direct or indirect contact. Direct contact is close or actual contact with the source of contamination. Indirect contact is more common and can occur when something transfers the bacteria to the food, for example, via the hands, clothes, utensils or equipment.

Methods of food contamination
- Food-to-food contamination – raw meat to cooked meat.
- Equipment-to-food contamination – unclean surfaces where equipment stands, equipment not cleaned between uses, cloths for wiping surfaces are moved from area to area.
- Food handler-to-food contamination – use of fingers to test food, improper hand washing and personal hygiene routines.
- Others – food left to stand, not stored correctly, or contaminated by pests.

Activity 12

Choose one of the areas shown in the spider diagram below and create an information leaflet or poster that will give service users visual and written information about personal hygiene.

Temperature control

Bacteria will grow if they are given ideal conditions – food, warmth, moisture and time. Correct temperature control is an extremely powerful weapon against the infection of food by food poisoning bacteria. Remember, temperature danger zone is between 5°C and 63°C. Bacteria do not generally grow below 5°C or above 63°C. So follow these simple rules:

- Keep hot food hot.
- Keep cold food cold.
- Keep prepared foods out of the temperature danger zone.

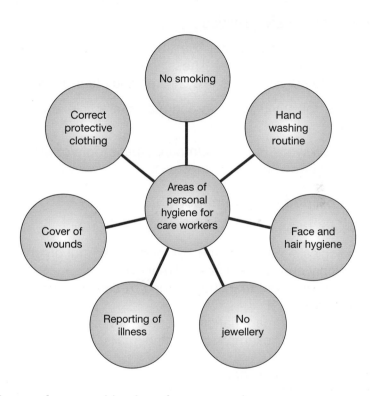

Areas of personal hygiene for care workers

Pest control

Pests eat and spoil food and are responsible for the transfer of bacteria to food.

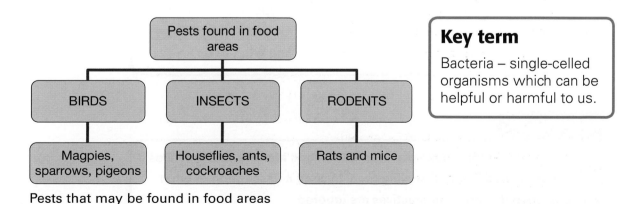

Pests that may be found in food areas

Key term

Bacteria – single-celled organisms which can be helpful or harmful to us.

Activity 13

Discuss in small groups how best to control or prevent contamination of food by pests in your working environment. You may have seen some methods enforced in your work placement.

Effects of unsafe practice

If we ignore safe practices we are likely to suffer the effects. These can be dangerous and can cause illness and even death, particularly in the case of vulnerable service users like children and older people.

Visit the following website and read the article about E.coli at a farm for children.

http://newsvote.bbc.co.uk/mpapps/pagetools/print/news.bbc.co.uk/1/hi/england/surrey/8252989.stm?ad=1

Types of food contamination

There are three types:

- biological – contamination of food by harmful organisms that can multiply and cause illness and disease
- chemical – contamination of food by cleaning products left near food or spilt over food
- physical – contamination of food by objects being accidentally dropped into food, for example glass, fingernails, hair, dirt or insect droppings.

Bacterial food poisoning

Activity 14

Using the web link to The Food Standards Agency (www.eatwell.gov.uk/healthissues/foodpoisoning/abugslife), find out the types of bacterial food poisoning that are common, how they grow and how they affect service users. Under 'Food poisoning', click on 'food bugs and what to do'.

Activity 15

Prepare an article for a newspaper or journal and identify safe practices for preparing, cooking and serving food. Include a description of what could happen if these safe practices are ignored.

Legislation, regulations and codes of practice

Food Safety Act 1990

This Act covers anyone who deals with food, from farmers through to the catering and restaurant trade. The Act protects the person buying the food (consumer) from poor hygiene standards and poor grades of food, and also from food that has not been labelled correctly. The Act allows local authorities to enforce laws and give out penalties if the laws are broken.

Food Safety (General Food Hygiene) Regulations 1995

These regulations specify standards for the structural requirements for the premises, equipment, personal safety and wholesomeness of the food. These regulations apply to food businesses, not to farms or abattoirs.

Food Safety (Temperature Control) Regulation 1995

These regulations require foods that are likely to allow the growth of pathogenic micro-organisms or bacteria to be held at or below 8° Celsius or above 63° Celsius. The regulations allow certain tolerances from the requirements (consistent with the need to ensure food safety), to take into account practical considerations relating, for example, to processing or handling.

Hazard Analysis Critical Control Point (HACCP)

HACCP is a system used by the food industry to ensure that all food consumed is safe to eat. HACCP is a systematic approach to hazard identification and assessment of risk and control. When implemented correctly, it ensures that every step in the process to grow, harvest, prepare and market foods for export results in food that is safe to eat. So, whether the produce comes from a smallholder or a commercial farm, it will be safe to eat if it has been routed through an HACCP-controlled process.

Activity 16

Find out how these regulations apply to care workers and service users in your work placement. If you can, ask staff who deal with food preparation and serving. Do they have any policies that relate just to that specific setting? What other policies and procedures do they follow? Do the regulations and policies differ from setting to setting? Share your information as a class.

Activity 17

P5 **P6** **M3** **D2**

Design a booklet that can be linked to your work placement, titled 'Food Safety in a Care Setting'. Use relevant pictures and diagrams.

Include the following;

- Section 1, P5 – Briefly outline the relevant legislation linked to safe food preparation, cooking and serving in your care setting.
- Section 2, P6 – Explain what safe practices are required when preparing, cooking and serving food in your care setting.
- Section 3, M3 – Discuss what may happen if safe practice is not followed in the care setting.
- Sections 4, D2 – Write a statement that assesses how useful the safe practices are in your care setting. Include how useful it is for staff and service users alike.

Summary

After working through this unit you should understand the differing dietary needs of individuals through the life stages and understand the importance of how beneficial a balanced and varied diet is to all service users and what effect a poor diet would have on an individual.

This unit will help you to understand the need to plan for diverse dietary needs of our service users according to medical conditions, culture and religion.

It is also important you understand the regulations around food safety and hygiene if you are responsible for food delivery or preparation in your care setting.

Assessment and grading criteria

To achieve a pass grade the evidence must show that the learner is able to:	To achieve a merit grade the evidence must show that, in addition to the pass criteria, the learner is able to:	To achieve a distinction grade the evidence must show that, in addition to the pass and merit criteria, the learner is able to:
P1 identify the components of a balanced diet (see Activity 9) [IE4, IE5, CT1, CT2, RL1, TW1, SM2, SM3]	**M1** discuss how the components of a balanced diet contribute to an individual's health at different life stages (see Activity 9)	
P2 identify different dietary needs at each life stage (see Activity 9) [IE3, CT2]		
P3 explain two medical conditions related to unbalanced diets (see Activity 9) [RL1, TW1, SM2, SM3, EP2]		
P4 identify two service users with specific dietary needs (see Activity 11) [RL1, TW1, SM2, SM3, EP4]	**M2** outline a two-day diet plan for two service users with specific dietary needs (see Activity 11)	**D1** justify how the two-day diet plan meets the dietary needs of the two service users (see Activity 11)
P5 outline relevant legislation relating to preparing, cooking and serving food (see Activity 17) [IE4]	**M3** discuss the effects of unsafe practices when preparing, cooking and serving food in a health or social care setting (see Activity 17)	**D2** assess the effectiveness of safe practices when preparing, cooking and serving food in a health or social care setting (see Activity 17)

P6	explain safe practices necessary in preparing, cooking and serving food in a health or social care setting (see Activity 17) [RL1, RL2, TW1, SM2, SM3, EP2, EP3]		

Further Reading

Learning and Skills Council, *Standards for Health and Safety*

Aldworth, C., 2008, *Nutrition and Well Being*, (knowledge sets), London: Heinemann

Blades, M., 2008, *Intermediate Nutrition and Health: An Introduction to the Subject of Food, Nutrition and Health*, 3rd edn., Doncaster: Highfield Publications

Weblinks

www.5aday.nhs.uk
www.eatwell.gov.uk
www.food.gov.uk
http://tinyurl.com/y8oc7el

Glossary

Active listening being involved, really listening and asking questions UNIT 1

Assessment a judgement or estimate (e.g. of the level of risk) UNIT 4

Bacteria single-celled organisms which can be helpful or harmful to us UNIT 11

Binge drinking drinking an excessive amount of alcohol in a short amount of time, leading to serious health and social consequences UNIT 3

Body language this term is used to describe how we unconsciously use our faces and bodies when communicating UNIT 1

Charter sets out what people would like UNIT 6

Code of practice outlines how people should behave UNIT 6

Criticism feedback. It can be helpful (positive) or unhelpful (negative) UNIT 5

Cross infection the passing on or transmission of harmful bacteria and viruses (germs) from one person to another UNIT 4

Cultural diversity different traditions that people follow UNIT 6

Culture this refers to a way of life and does not include just religious beliefs. Service users may be from a travelling culture or vegetarian culture UNIT 3

CV curriculum vitae a brief summary of your life UNIT 5

Deoxygenated blood blood which has no oxygen in it and is combined with carbon dioxide UNIT 7

Development acquiring skills and knowledge to perform tasks UNIT 8

Disclosure another way of saying 'telling someone' UNIT 2

Discriminatory selective

Discriminatory practice when people are not given the same chance. Discriminatory practice selects who will get a chance UNIT 2

Diversity difference or variety UNIT 2, 6

Empowerment a process whereby service users who have previously been dependent on care and support are enabled to make decisions and choices to take control of their own lives UNIT 9

Equality of opportunity giving people the same chances UNIT 2

Ethics what is right or wrong UNIT 2

Formal communication that which follows the proper conventional grammatical and cultural rules, usually used in communication with strangers or in an official situation UNIT 1

Genes our individual patterns in DNA, which make up our different characteristics, development and appearance UNIT 3

Growth this can refer to an increase in size, weight or height UNIT 8

Holistic care we should be aware that all parts of the individual are important and we should treat them as a whole; we should not just focus on one area of an individual UNIT 3

Hormones these are chemical messages released into the blood stream to affect organs and their functions UNIT 7

Informal communication the use of familiar terms, such as nicknames, slang and jargon, used with friends and people we know well UNIT 1

Inherited genetic characteristics passed down to the next generation UNIT 7

Integrated care when organisations and practitioners work closely with each other and the patient to deliver exactly what the patient needs, when they need it. With integrated care, it does not matter which practitioner provides or delivers the care, as long as they have been properly trained and it meets the patient's needs UNIT 10

Interpersonal skills the ability to get on with people and form relationships with them UNIT 1

Interrelationship how systems work together to perform required functions UNIT 7

Key worker one individual practitioner from one of the partner agencies who acts as the first point of contact for the patient. The partner agencies agree who will be the key worker responsible for passing information between the patient and the different agencies and helping to organise the agreed care plan UNIT 10

Legislation laws passed by Parliament. Some laws are called 'conventions' or 'regulations' UNIT 6, 9

Multi-agency different health, social care or related organisations (e.g. local authority services, such as housing, and voluntary agencies, such as Age Concern) UNIT 10

Multi-disciplinary practitioners from different specialisms (e.g. nurses and physiotherapists) UNIT 10

Obesity excess body fat having a BMI of over 30. Obesity will cause health problems UNIT 11

Objects of reference any objects that represent other things UNIT 1

Oxygenated blood blood which is combined with oxygen UNIT 7

Personal personal information relates just to you. It is private UNIT 5

Person-centred approach putting the person at the centre of care. This is the opposite of a service-led approach which puts the needs of the service first UNIT 2

Policies these describe the correct course of action as agreed by the organisation, often to comply with the law, or with good professional practice, or with the stated ethical approach of the organisation. Policies are usually written and must be available to all workers within the organisation. It may include instruction as to how to carry out actions to achieve the policy requirements UNIT 2, 9, 10

Private settings a care environment where people pay for the care and the owners make a profit UNIT 5

Professional approach the behaviour we would expect from a professional person such as a nurse, social worker, doctor UNIT 5

Protocols a formal statement or written rules (e.g. a code of conduct) UNIT 10

Reflexes actions which are not under our control. Babies have primitive reflexes which disappear UNIT 8

Regulation an enforceable guideline that must be followed in an organisation UNIT 9

Right an entitlement that someone ought to have UNIT 2

Services the organisations and people supplying a particular need UNIT 10

Setting the location in which health and social care activities take place UNIT 4

Sexually transmitted infection (STI) infections that are transmitted by unprotected sexual activity UNIT 3

Social class a method of looking at people by what occupation they do in society UNIT 11

Social interaction with people UNIT 2

Social justice laws that treat people equally UNIT 2

Statutory care care provided by the state or the government. It is not intended to make a profit UNIT 5

Stereotype making judgements or assumptions about a person or group of people without knowing the facts about them UNIT3

Therapeutic this refers to actions or activities that are particularly designed to provide benefits to an individual or group UNIT 9

Universal precautions precautions taken to protect staff and patients from contamination and cross infection (e.g. wearing gloves and personal protective clothing) UNIT 4

Vocational relates to work. Vocational experience is work experience UNIT 5

Voluntary care care provided by volunteers who work for charities. These charities have to raise funds themselves so they can offer the service. They do not aim to make a profit UNIT 5

Weaning this is the gradual introduction of solid foods from a milk diet; it should normally start around 16 weeks after birth UNIT 11

Index